The Sacralization of Politics in fascist Italy

The Sacralization of Politics in fascist Italy

Emilio Gentile

Translated by Keith Botsford

Harvard University Press
Cambridge, Massachusetts, and London, England   1996

DG
571
.G3913
1996

Originally published as *Il culto del littorio.*
La sacralizzazione della politica nell'Italia Fascista;
© 1993 Gius. Laterza & Figli Spa, Rome and Bari.

Library of Congress Cataloging-in-Publication Data

Gentile, Emilio, 1946–
  [Culto del littorio. English]
  The sacralization of politics in fascist Italy /
  Emilio Gentile ; translated by Keith Botsford.
      p.   cm.
  Includes bibliographical references and index.
  ISBN 0-674-78475-8 (alk. paper)
  1. Italy—Politics and government—1922–1945.
  2. Fascism and the Catholic Church—Italy.
  3. Fascism—Italy. I. Title.
DG571.G3913 1996
945.091—dc20   96-5074
CIP

Acknowledgments

While engaged in research on this volume, I incurred a number of debts to individuals and institutions that facilitated my work. In particular, I wish to thank the directors and staff of the Central State Archive, the Ministry of Foreign Affairs, the Library of the Department of Political Science of La Sapienza University, the Library of the Chamber of Deputies, the Library of Modern and Contemporary History of the Gentile Foundation, and the Gramsci Institute.

For their help, thanks are also due to several friends: Philip Cannistraro, Patrizia Ferrara, Marina Giannetto, Leonardo Lisanti, Franco Nuti, Cristina Mosillo, Amalia Rossi Merighi, Ettore Tanzarella. A special thanks to Colonel Franco Romano and Lieutenant Colonel Doctor Marco Ricotti, Director of the Historical Department of the Carabinieri.

The advice and suggestions of friends such as Giuseppe Conti and Niccolò Zapponi helped me fill gaps in my research. In archival research, the patient and expert assistance of Mario Missori was once again indispensable.

My greatest debt in completing this work is owed to Professor George L. Mosse, who, from the first sketch of this research, as set out in our essay *Il mito dello Stato nuovo* (Rome and Bari, 1982) and later developed in a 1990 article in the *Journal of Contemporary History* and *Storia contemporanea,* exhorted me—especially in moments of uncertainty—to finish it. His was the advice of a historian and the encouragement of a friend.

Contents

Preface

This reality that we seek in facts is made up of ways of thinking, and these too are positive facts.

—Jakob Burckhardt

It is impossible to understand the history of a people unless one also studies its sacred history. More than a few events that seem profane or even political or strictly economic in nature have—when carefully considered—deep religious connections.

—Raffaele Pettazzoni

f or two decades under Fascist government, the piazzas of Italy, whether in big cities or in tiny villages, were transformed into a huge stage on which millions celebrated—as one, to a single beat—the national holidays, the régime's anniversaries, the triumphs of the "revolution," the cult of the fallen, the glorification of heroes, the consecration of symbols, the appearances of the Duce. Countless other ceremonies, assemblies, parades, exhibitions, and special pilgrimages reproduced the annual cycle of the mass rites of the Fascist régime. People and nation were bound up in a thick web of symbols, which embraced town- and landscape, machines and monuments, art and costume, dress and gesture, and which stamped on every thing and in every place, from the weapons of the state to roadside milestones, the emblem of the lictor's fasces.

This book examines the interior of the symbolic universe of Fascism, the myths, rituals, and monuments of a popular movement whose ambition it was to imbue the consciences of millions of Italians with faith in the dogmas of a new, secular religion. This religion sacralized the state and assigned it the primary educational task of transforming the mentality, the character, and the customs of Italians. The aim was to create a "new man," a believer in and an observing member of the cult of Fascism, Fascism as a manifestation of the sacralization of politics. Through significant examples, I have sought to bring to light the links that conjoin

the various aspects of a "Fascist religion"—myth, faith, ritual, communion—to determine whether, and in what measure, they represent a coherent system of beliefs and rituals, these being the fundamental constit-
uents of any religion.

The primary focus of the following chapters is the formation and institutionalization of the "Fascist religion" as a collective cult seeking to
involve the whole Italian people in the myths and rituals of the régime.
My chief aim is to identify and analyze the origins, motivations, forms,
and scope of the "cult of the lictor" during its formation and full affirmation. In this effort I have sought to place the promoters and propa-
gators of this cult within the larger framework of the search for a "national religion," a constant in modern Italian history from the very dawn
of the Risorgimento. The period covered, which coincides with the apogee
of Fascist power, is that between the two world wars. The Second World
War brought no substantive innovations to the cult as institutionalized in
the prewar years; and the military defeat and the fall of the Fascist régime
both effected profound changes in the attitudes of the population as a
whole and the Fascists themselves toward the cult and violently shifted
the "Fascist religion" from its national context into an international
framework.

A few words concerning method and style seem necessary at the outset.
In dealing with the myths, rituals, and symbols of a political religion that
eventually demonstrated all too clearly its inherent fragility, one might be
tempted to present such material in caricature or in a moralizing style, to
scourge its retrospectively apparent excesses with derision and sarcasm.
But both such approaches are often the surrogates of an irony lacking
historical intelligence. Of all the deplorable attitudes toward history, this
seems to me the worst—perhaps because it is the easiest and most childish
line to take. My inquiry instead follows the guidelines established by the
anthropologist Clifford Geertz in *The Interpretation of Culture*:

> One of the main methodological problems in writing about religion scien-
> tifically is to put aside at once the tone of the village atheist and that of the
> village preacher, as well as their more sophisticated equivalents, so that the
> social and psychological implications of particular religious beliefs can
> emerge in a clear and neutral light. And when that is done, overall questions
> about whether religion is "good" or "bad," "functional" or "dysfunctional,"
> "ego strengthening" or "anxiety producing," disappear like the chimeras
> they are, and one is left with particular evaluations, assessments, and diag-
> noses in particular cases. There remains, of course, the hardly unimportant
> question of whether this or that religious assertion is true, this or that reli-
> gious experience genuine, or whether true religious assertions and genuine
> religious experiences are possible at all. But such questions cannot be asked,

much less answered, within the self-imposed limitations of the scientific per-spective.

This criterion seems equally valid for the historiographic study of a secular religion. It seeks to restore rationality to a phenomenon that, though not without its own historical rationality, was sited deliberately and ostentatiously in the camp of the irrational.

The Sacralization of Politics in Fascist Italy

Introduction: In Search of a Civil Religion

Were princes to revive illusions, breathe life, spirit, and a sense of their own worth into their peoples; were they in some substantial way to reanimate those errors and imaginings that are the fundamental building blocks of nations; were they to give us back a fatherland; were triumphs, public contests, honors rendered for merit and service to the nation once again common usage; then all nations would surely come back to, or spring into, life and become great and strong and formidable.
—Giacomo Leopardi

The state is like religion; it works if people believe in it.
—Errico Malatesta

When the nation-state of Italy was created in 1870, the highest aim of Risorgimento patriots was the civil and moral renewal of the Italian people. A population that had been politically divided since the fall of the Roman Empire, that differed radically in its histories, cultures, and social conditions, was to be transformed into a free people and educated in the faith and worship of the "national religion."[1] As with all the national movements in the heyday of romanticism, the Italian revolution wrapped the idea of the nation in a sacred aura, raising it to the status of the supreme collective entity to which a citizen owed dedication and obedience—to the point of sacrificing his own life on its behalf.

From the beginning of the eighteenth century, the "divinity" of the nation was the principle on which the conscience of modern nationalism had grounded itself. The fatherland, wrote the Abbé Coyer in 1755, was

a power as old as society itself, founded on nature and order; a power superior to all those powers it creates within itself . . . a power that submits to its own laws both those who command in its name and those who obey. It is a divinity that accepts gifts only to give them greater value, that requires love more than respect, affection rather than fear, that smiles when it does good, and sighs when it hurls its thunderbolts.[2]

From this idea of the nation, and especially with the French Revolution, grew the concept of the state as the people's mentor in the cult of the nation. For French patriots, disciples of Rousseau, a nation-state without religion was unthinkable, because the moral unity of the citizenry and the dedication of the individual to the common good could be based only on religious faith.

The nation-state, Rousseau wrote, must unite "the eagle's two heads"— political and religious power—and create a proper "civil religion" that would "lead everything back to political unity, without which there would never be a well-established government or state."[3] It was therefore one of the state's fundamental tasks to assume the role of guardian of morality and religion, and to be above all the *educating state,* whose mission it was to restore the unity of the body politic and form virtuous citizens, inculcating in them a sense of civic duty and obedience to the state. The educating state must

> give the life-force of the nation to all, and direct their opinions and tastes to the point where these are infused with patriotism by inclination, passion, and necessity. As a child opens his eyes he should see the fatherland, and he should see nothing else until the day he dies. Every true republican imbibes love of country, that is, of the laws and liberty, with his mother's milk. His whole being is in this love; he sees only his fatherland, he lives for it alone; no sooner alone than he is nothing; no sooner without his fatherland he is no longer, and if not dead, he is worse than dead.[4]

To that end, Rousseau sought to recreate Greek and Roman custom and devise collective festivals that would infuse in the people a feeling of moral unity and absolute love of the fatherland.

The sacralization of the nation, spread throughout Europe by the French Revolution, put the relationships between politics and religion into a new light; it made politics religious and gave an educational mission to the state. It thus initiated a new era of rivalry and conflict between "civic" and "traditional" religion. This rivalry particularly affected the national movement in Italy, where the presence of the Catholic church made the search for a "religion of the fatherland," on which the moral unity of the new, Third Italy could be based, more difficult and controversial.

From the very beginnings of the Risorgimento, the problem of how to construct a religion of the state figured dramatically in the political thinking of Italian patriots; it remained one of the central problems of the new nation-state even after Italy's unification, consistently—and sometimes decisively—influencing Italian history right up to the Second World War.

The Civil Religions of the Risorgimento

The search for a civic religion for the Third Italy continued throughout the Risorgimento. The many elements that emerged from this search became a part of the Italian cultural heritage, of its politico-religious mythology, and shaped later attempts to elaborate a national religion. Some of these elements—such as Carbonari sectarianism and especially Freemasonry—had a relevant part to play after unification. Characterized by militant anticlericalism, they helped create a secular religiosity based on the Risorgimento's democratic tradition. Others, derived directly from the new religion of the French Revolution, are to be found in the thinking of utopians and Jacobin reformers. Believing as they did in the revolution as moral regeneration,[5] Italian Jacobins considered inseparable the links between political and social revolution and religious transformation. The aim was to create a new secular religion with an appropriate apparatus of festivals and rituals to educate citizens about liberty and equality, respect for the law, and love of the common weal. For Filippo Buonarroti, this "political religion" was no *instrumentum regni*, but "the very substance of the new state to be established."[6]

The Jacobin religious-political movement met with no success, but the revolutionary myth of politics as moral regeneration, a regeneration to be entrusted to the teaching function of the state and to the cult of a patriotic religion,[7] put down roots in political culture. In the course of Italian history this idea reemerges several times, with different ideological connotations at other revolutionary moments—for instance, in the political mysticism of Giuseppe Mazzini and in Fascism itself, which took up the myth of moral regeneration while severing its connection with the idea of liberty and equality, effectively embedding it in the myth of the totalitarian state.

The search for a civic religion was not limited to revolutionary or secular milieux; similar attempts were made by a number of Catholic intellectuals and politicians. Vincenzo Gioberti's vision of a new Catholicism, one converted to modern progress and the idea of a nation, included the structure for a civic religion that would have its roots in the Catholic tradition and combine both Catholic universalism and national patriotism. Such a vision, Gioberti hoped, would afford the Third Italy a national conscience, one that would bring about a renewal of Italy's civil and moral preeminence among nations.[8]

However, attempts to reconcile a "patriotic religion" and Catholicism were soon shattered by the Church's intransigent opposition to the revolutionary movement and the new nation-state. This had a double effect: on the one hand it strengthened the alienation of Catholics from the new state, and on the other it radicalized the search for a new "patriotic religion" among the laity. In the secular culture of the Risorgimento, this found its highest and most fascinating expression in the political mysticism of Mazzini.

The notion of a "patriotic religion" was, for the Genoese revolutionary, the very essence of the national revolution. A religious revolution had to precede the political one because although politics "grasps all men, wherever and whatever they are, defines their tendencies and tempers their acts, only religious thinking can transform both."[9] "Young Italy" was a "new political religion"[10] that conceived of political life as the dedication of the whole being to the nation; it was an apostolate, revolutionary action devoted to the "religion of martyrdom" and leading to the resurrection of a "new Italy."

The nation-state should be the creation of a political and religious revolution; it should be made by Italians regenerated by the "new faith" of the fatherland. In Mazzini's ideal conception, the Third Italy, united as a republic, was a democratic theocracy based on a mystical and religious conception of the state and on the unified belief of the people. Indeed, for Mazzini, there could be no true political unity without moral unity, and there could be no moral unity without a common faith or consciousness of a mission. God and the people were the key elements in his political theology: the Mazzinian God was a "political God";[11] his idealized *people* was an association conceived as a mystical community of believers, united in the cult of the "patriotic religion." Mazzini assigned a mission to the Third Italy: to prepare the advent of a humanity of free nations, all brothers in a "universal harmony." This would have had its sacred center in Rome, the cradle of civilization and the city in which civilization was periodically renewed. Redeemed from papal absolutism, established as the capital of a united Italy, Rome would be the seat of a council of nations that would create a new religious unity in Europe.

The Soulless State

In the flush of his political mysticism, Mazzini dreamt of

> an Italy rescued from its grave by the sacrifice and virtue of its people, purified of its guilt by more than three centuries of expiation, splendid in its enthusiasm and faith, strong in the knowledge of battles fought and victories won by the shedding of its own life-blood, like an angel wearing on his crown the double baptism of glory past and glory future, bearer to the nation of good tidings of an era of Justice and Love: Dante's Italy, but with no empire but God's, no law but that enshrined in the Pact signed by its own people.

Hence, after unity had been achieved through the monarchy, Mazzini's condemnation of a new state that had not been created by a people regenerated by a renewed faith in the religion of the fatherland. "What we see today," he wrote in disappointment and defeat, "is an Italian lie." For the "inert organism of Italy" lacked the "fecundating spirit of God, the soul of the nation."[12]

The myth of the Risorgimento as an "incomplete national revolution" originated in this radical opposition to the liberal state on the grounds that the moral unity of a common faith was missing from political unity. Mazzini was defeated, but the heritage of his political mysticism was kept alive among his republican disciples. His influence persisted and spread through the most varied cultural and political milieux, in ways that were not always evident or even faithful to his message, but that continued to nourish calls for a civil religion. The myth of the "Italian revolution" as a spiritual and moral resurrection, realized by the people and consecrated by the regenerating sacrifice of its martyrs, became the unifying theme of that whole complex of movements, ideas, and myths that we call "radical nationalism." It was a movement that stood in constant opposition to the liberal and monarchical Third Italy, forever calling for the final, supreme trial of revolution or war from which the "new Italy" would arise, bearer of the message of a new civilization to the world.[13]

Mazzinianism made a notable contribution to the sacralization of politics. Its form of secular religion, especially in the particular interpretation offered by Giovanni Gentile, had an indirect influence on Fascist political theology, although it is only fair to recall that Mazzini was firmly committed to the principle of a free citizenry and individual dignity.

> [The] religion of the fatherland is most holy; but where it is not governed by a feeling for the dignity of the individual and a consciousness of the rights inherent in human nature, where the citizen is not convinced that he should add to rather than take lustre away from his country, then it is a religion that may make a country powerful, but not happy; it will be resplendent with glory to the foreigner, but not free.[14]

The principle is stated clearly and unequivocally. Nonetheless it remains difficult to see how, in a hypothetical Mazzinian theocracy, individual liberty could be reconciled with dedication to the nation, with the political mysticism of the national community, or with a unified faith. It is a problem that Mazzini's thought, prophetically vague, left unresolved; it resurfaces dramatically each time there is a demand for a civil religion in a democratic society.

How to Make "Italians"

Monarchical Italy was clearly something quite different from Mazzini's cherished Third Italy. Despite the decisive contribution that the conquest of national unity made to fulfilling Mazzini's ideas, the new state contained not a trace of his political mysticism. But although it was not animated by Mazzini's religious afflatus, the new governing class was not insensible to the question of a "patriotic religion." Indeed, faced with a population the majority of which had remained passive and alien, if not downright hostile, to the process of unification, the demand for a civil religion arose to the extent necessary: to create a collective, unitary consciousness; to strengthen the new Italy in its confrontation with the church; and to affirm its modern national identity before the great nations of Europe.

For Francesco De Sanctis, one of the most passionate and restless interpreters of this need, religion—understood as "the force by which one emerges from within oneself and feels one belongs to a whole"[15]—was fundamental to the task of "making Italians," to reforming the national character and liberating it from the "Guicciardini man," who thought only of "individuals." As De Sanctis wrote in 1869, "This Italian race of ours is not yet recovered from that form of moral weakness; it has not yet lost that Mark of Cain put on his brow by double-dealing and pretence. The Guicciardini man *vivit, imo in Senatum venit;* you find him everywhere. It is this fatal figure who blocks our way: unless we can bring ourselves to kill him in our souls."[16]

Because it had not undergone a religious reform of the sort that might have given it moral consciousness, Italy suffered from a want of civic virtue, of character and seriousness in life. As De Sanctis said in a lecture on Mazzini in 1874,

> The result is dispiriting: Italy is as it always was. Political unity has been achieved; wanting is any intellectual and moral unity based on a religious unity. And if we continue to treat religion as a political weapon without restoring religious feeling, which for me consists in a feeling of individual sacrifice, in the duty to get outside of ourselves and communicate with others for the general good, then Italy is condemned to oscillate between paganism and hypocrisy.[17]

Once political unity had been achieved, there remained a moral and ideal unity of the masses to be created, for "political unity is of no use without an intellectual and moral redemption, it is of no use, as d'Azeglio said, to have made Italy without making Italians. This task was not given to him, nor to our generation; it remains a task for the next generation."[18] For De Sanctis, too, a civil religion was indispensable to the moral consolidation of political unity. Italians should be taught "sincerity and conviction in their opinions,"[19] something religion alone could offer. He was not thinking of a dogmatic religion, but rather of "religious feeling, which is a vital base for education."[20] To this end he sought the help of an active science reunited to life: "Science must organize this national education; it must imitate Catholicism, whose power lies not in the catechism, but in man taken in his swaddling clothes and held tight until the hour of his death; it must mirror its granitelike organisms, against which science has thrashed for centuries, always in vain."[21]

In contrast to Mazzini, De Sanctis realistically took into account that "new religions and religious reform are not to be based on passing opinion, but are all the stronger when they are rooted in tradition."[22]

But what new religion should Italy adopt to "make Italians"? This was one of the first great obstacles facing the institution of a civil religion in the newly united Italy. Throughout the fraught history of liberal Italy various replies to this question arose, accumulating and contradicting one another. There were those who thought the principles of the new secular religion might be found in positivist science; some envisioned a secular reform of Catholicism; others reinvoked Roman principles of civic virtue; and finally there were those who thought any form of religion, secular or otherwise, was a matter of individual conscience, whereas an individual's public conscience should be concerned with a secular ethic derived from reason, freedom, and tolerance.

The main current in all this thinking, however, tended toward the founding of a "national religion" that could be reconciled with the principles of liberty on which the new régime was based: a civic religion that would create a national faith for the collective without sacrificing individual liberties. Beyond the problem of defining the content of a civic religion, there was that of finding the appropriate means by which to diffuse it among the masses and make it a common credo for all Italians. The means proposed were just as various and contradictory. Attention passed from one project to another, projects and initiatives were mounted, but each clashed with the other, and most of them bogged down or were simply dissipated, leaving no lasting traces.

The problem of a new religion coincided with that of national education for the masses. Liberal Italy's principal investment on behalf of the establishment and diffusion of a "national religion" was made in the schools and the army, the two pillars of national education on which rested all hopes for creating nationhood for the masses of the Third Italy. Liberal governments after 1870 extended the state's power over education and, while guaranteeing academic freedom, sought to make schools a means to reinforce unity.[23] The more rationalist and anticlerical liberals saw the school as the "modern church." The Casati Law of 1859 required that Catholic doctrine be taught in the schools, but after 1870 this requirement was progressively weakened, in effect abolished.[24] When in

1877 primary education from age six to nine became mandatory, "the first notions of the duties of man and citizen" were introduced into the curriculum.[25] The aim of elementary education, the minister Michele Coppino laid out in a circular, was, "to the degree possible, to instruct the citizenry, but in the main to make them honest, hard-working, useful to their families and loyal to the nation and the King."[26]

The outlines of a civic religion built around monarchical patriotism now emerged in the schools, and thence grew the image of a new kind of believer, the "good citizen" of the liberal state: trustworthy, virtuous, honest, rooted in his family, and devoted to king and country. Even physical education played its part, helping form "good citizens" by making them healthy, strong, and manly in defense of their country. De Sanctis had made physical education obligatory in the school system for, as he said in the Chamber of Deputies on May 13, 1878, "If we are to recover the status our nation, which has twice led the world, deserves, then we must make certain that these exercises, coordinated with the education of intellect and will, should become a part of our way of life, an integral part of our celebrations and our national institutions."[27]

The gymnastic societies, too, proposed to "substitute the patriotic ideal for religion" in the popular mind.[28] These clubs or societies addressed themselves not only to the bourgeoisie, but sought to include the proletariat, educating it, through gymnastics, in the values and ideals of the motherland.[29] The Florentine Gymnastic Society, for instance, founded in 1876, proposed to take the "sons of the poor from the streets and piazzas and make them capable of entering good society, educated, and useful to their country." By furthering their physical and moral development, it sought "to instill in them energy, bravery, and belief in themselves" and to train them "in all forms of exercise, especially military"—in short, in "everything that a man needs to become a good soldier and true citizen."[30]

But in the minds of the ruling class and of a fair part of liberal and monarchical public opinion, the most apt place in which to forge the national consciousness of the masses, uniting physical education with moral formation, the study and the practice of patriotism, was the army. By their very nature, the armies of the modern states had become the one institution dedicated to embodying and preserving the "national religion." The army celebrated its rituals and spread its beliefs among the masses of citizens called up for military service.[31] For these young men, most of them illiterate and with little civic sense, the army should be a "haven for generous feeling," a place in which to learn "love of country, affection and devotion for the King, and respect for laws and authority." Parallel with military training, the army performed a civic function, that of "spreading a feeling of national unity among the masses." When they reverted to civilian life, the recruits would have become apostles of "national virtues" and preach the cult of the nation and institutions among their own families. Thus the army would have made its contribution to cementing national unity.[32]

So far as we know, this pedagogical activity on behalf of a mass civic religion seems not to have produced the expected results, among other reasons because the ruling class itself showed little consistent and coherent conviction or zeal for the task. Although the school system exalted the cult of national virtue and the glories of the Risorgimento, it failed to inculcate a national religion or belief in liberty and democracy among the masses.[33] The gymnastic clubs, often riddled with rivalries, had few members and lacked the active support of the state. They were thus unable to pursue their teaching functions for the masses. Too few and inadequate to realize their ambitions, it was ultimately the state that had to employ the means necessary to obtain results in spreading physical education through the school system.[34]

Nor was the army able to create an orderly and systematic plan to increase national awareness among the recruits or, for that matter, to apply such a plan with any success.[35] Even the attempt to create a soldier's handbook "aimed at the formation of the national character" failed. This was a sort of breviary, containing military information, notes on the history of the nation, and a few guides to civic and moral education, and was supposed to become the bible of the "national religion." The War Ministry sponsored a competition to produce such a handbook in 1885, but nothing came of it for want of any suitable submissions.[36]

The Liturgies of Condolence

Attempts to create a "patriotic religion" were not confined to school and army. There were moves made to popularize the new cult through ritual, feast days, and symbols. The monarchical state had its own symbols, the rituals, holidays, and parades through which it celebrated the nation and its institutions, the heroes of independence, and the monarchical version of the epic Risorgimento.[37] The civil liturgical calendar, however, was a thin affair. Until 1922 the single national holiday was that honoring the Statute and the Unification of Italy, established on May 3, 1861, and celebrated on the first Sunday in June with military parades in all garrison cities and the illumination of all public buildings. In Rome the day was marked by a parade, the traditional *girandola,* or sunburst fireworks, and a solemn public session of the Lincean Academy at which royal prizes were presented. On July 19, 1895, September 20, the anniversary of the capture of Rome in 1870, was declared a public holiday. Its celebration, however, became the pretext for anticlerical demonstrations by Freemasons for clerical counterdemonstrations against the usurping state, as well as for clashes and polemics between monarchists and republicans, liberals and democrats, over the heritage of the Risorgimento.[38]

Attempts to establish a national liturgy naturally began with the cult of the monarchy—presented as the main protagonist of the Risorgimento—and the figure of Vittorio Emanuele II, "the father of his country." The high points of this cult were his grandiose funeral in 1878 and the national pilgrimage to the Pantheon in 1884 to pay homage at his tomb.[39] Similar ceremonies were organized on the death of Umberto I in 1900. A year later there was a pilgrimage to the tomb of the "Martyr King." In the minds of their promoters, these ceremonies were more than just acts of commemoration; they were intended to exalt the monarchy's role in forging unity, to legitimize its authority, and by so doing to create a national consensus, using symbols of considerable emotional force. As the promoters of the pilgrimage to the tomb of Umberto I wrote, by this ceremony "Italy desires to demonstrate its religious devotion to the memory of a good and generous King as well as to tighten the bonds of affection that bind it to the glorious dynasty of the house of Savoy." The ceremony was to celebrate the monarchy's institutions: "with faith in the Statute, the cultivation of liberty, zeal for the good, and constant devotion to Italy."[40]

During the first decades after Unification, many ceremonies commemorated the Risorgimento. Monuments and burial places—some forty of these were built between 1861 and the turn of the century[41]—were dedicated to the wars of independence. Many of these were erected on the battlefields themselves by veterans, local administrations, or citizens' groups. The priestly functions at these memorials to the Risorgimento were exercised primarily by veterans, the most active of patriotic-religious groups.[42] The busiest of these was the Solferino and San Martino Society, founded in 1869. Under the energetic leadership of Senator Luigi Torelli, it undertook a number of important initiatives toward founding a cult of the fatherland and the building of monuments, such as the Ossuary of San Martino della Battaglia, inaugurated in 1870, and the Tower dedicated to Vittorio Emanuele II, erected on the same spot in 1893.[43] These monuments were conceived as proper "sacred spaces" in which to celebrate the cult of the fatherland, places of pilgrimage to sustain and promote faith in the "patriotic religion." The Tower, Torelli said, should become the "solemn center" of patriotism, and the October feast day of San Martino della Battaglia should be "the patriotic holiday par excellence."[44]

Although many took part, it is doubtful that this memorial liturgy was really a successful means of spreading patriotism among the masses. These were funereal occasions, and the ultimate effect was a sort of hybrid liturgy. At its most solemn, it was a *ritual of regret,* with funerals and pilgrimages to tombs; sorrow dominated, and nostalgia, and rue for the loss of the "father of the nation," the "good and generous King," or the other avatars of the new state, Cavour or Garibaldi. It was not the sort of liturgy calculated to make people enthusiastic for a "patriotic religion." What was missing in these memorial rituals was the necessary vital and exalting spirit, a communal myth of regeneration and rebirth through the sacrifice of life—that cult of martyrdom, of the fallen, which took such a strong hold after the Great War and especially under Fascism. Rather than affirmations of faith in life and the future of the fatherland, these occasions seemed like tormenting manifestations of sorrow by a collectivity that in ever more uncertain and troubled times felt abandoned by its patron saints. They were shows of weakness rather than strength.

Antagonism and Fragility of National Cults

Despite all the efforts made to create and popularize devotion to the fatherland, there are reasons to believe that civic religion did not make great progress during the period of Italian liberalism (1870–1915). Nor were the results any more consistent in the area of rituals. Rituals were not wanting, but more often than not these were circumscribed and occasional, discontinuous, uncoordinated, and organized, as the promoters admitted, against a background of countless difficulties, including skepticism and indifference on the part of those who should have supported and encouraged them.[45] Indeed, the promoters often had to fight "against a cowardly crowd of the skeptical and the slothful."[46] Participation in such rituals, even of the most imposing sort, with tens of thousands of people present, did not represent true collective worship: they were an occasional crowd rather than a liturgical mass.

But there were other and deeper reasons why these rituals failed to take root as an institutional form of civil religion. Such a secular church called for unity of faith and of beliefs in the divinity of the nation. As it happened, rather than summoning up feelings of unity, the myth of the nation was a source of division and conflict. The Third Italy had inherited from the Risorgimento many differing and contradictory versions of what the true civic religion of Italy should be. The "patriotic religion" professed by the liberal ruling class was always opposed by faithful Mazzinians and democrats, who sought a cult in direct opposition to the monarchical liturgy. Then, with the coming of the "socialist religion," the old patriotic church had a new and dynamic opponent competing for mass support.

Still, the most likely reasons for the liberal failure were the lack of organizational support, of any real, collective enthusiasm, of a *democratic sensibility* in regard to mass action, and the liberal culture's failure to conceive and set in motion a mobilization of the masses through the systematic use of ritual and symbol. Here, a fundamental diffidence toward the masses, seen as dangerous, even explosive, human material, full of seditious energy, kept the country's liberal, rationalist leaders from any steady and convinced commitment to mass politics. Francesco Crispi, who was probably the most active promoter of such a religion among the statesmen of the Third Italy, was an exception. For most, the idea of a piazza overflowing with a fervent crowd raised fearful visions of revolt and anguishing problems of public order. This fearful view hardly favored the creation of periodic mass rituals to celebrate the cult of the fatherland; nor did it contribute to the growth, let alone the invention, of a "new politics" to mobilize a national mass movement.[47]

The degree of success of a "patriotic religion" as a basis for the national state is epitomized by the monument to Vittorio Emanuele II, the most ambitious and grandiose architectonic project ever conceived by Italian liberalism. It was meant to consecrate, in marble and bronze, the cult of the monarchy and the "patriotic religion." The idea was discussed immediately after the king's death in 1878, and the project was adopted in 1885. Realizing it, however, took another half-century, and it advanced amid continuous polemics as to how the "patriotic religion" ought to be interpreted, symbolized, and made tangible. Once again, the experience was marred by differing traditions deriving from the Risorgimento, only partly and marginally smoothed by the passing of time:

> The monument to the Father of the Nation in Rome is destined to repeat what happened with the great cathedrals . . . The works continue from one century to another . . . These huge constructions have reached our own time still incomplete, while we, the faithful, work on them—even though, alas! the old faith is weakened in our souls . . . This Roman monument has already exercised two generations of artists, and no one can say how many more will have to labor on it in the future . . . but the works continue, to the rhythm of a state function, whose measure is not our own time, but eternity . . . But we will never know what that monument will be when it is finished, and for those of our descendants in a remote future who will see the finished work, time will have done its work, which makes every ruin seem venerable and beautiful.

Thus, with resigned irony, *L'illustrazione italiana* on November 4, 1921.[48] On that same day, the anniversary of Italy's victory in the Great War, the still-unfinished monument was dedicated to the cult of the nation with the entombment of the Unknown Soldier beneath the Altar of the Fatherland.

The Religion of the Educated

As the century turned, the liberal bourgeoisie, while not altogether abandoning the patriotic celebrations held with much pomp on the fiftieth anniversary of Unification, shifted to a form of government that did not pursue religious ideals about regeneration. Nonetheless, among intellectuals and politicians with high national ideals, those who with a youthful and aggressive spirit proposed to mold the conscience of modern Italy, the search for such a religion remained a major preoccupation.

In fact the modernistic, avant-garde intelligentsia of the early 1900s thought that making a new lay religion was a necessary condition if Italy were to be culturally and morally regenerated.[49] The religious question was at the heart of Giuseppe Prezzolini's *La Voce*, that lay seminar for those concerned with spiritual matters, and Prezzolini himself theorized about "an irreligious religion"—or rather, as the educator Giuseppe Lombardo Radice put it, a "new religion,"[50] a religion of integral humanism, based on the idealism of Benedetto Croce and Giovanni Gentile, one designed to replace a Catholicism in decline in human consciences and institutions and to become the new faith of modern Italians.

The issue of a civic religion thus transcended the national question, to become a part of a more general spiritual crisis of "modern man," caught between the decline of traditional religions and the resulting fear of the void, and awaiting the rise of a new faith. "What concerns us, what we seek to remedy, is the present state of crisis in which the myths and transcendental elements of another time wane, while others seem to have not yet arisen. We feel an urgent social and ethical need (for ourselves, for the educated, so as not to deceive) not to use the old myth, and we suffer from the want of another."[51]

The search for a new secular religion found its most passionate converts among these intellectuals. They were susceptible to the torments of the "modern soul" in its craving for "a new, unitary concept with the power to move like that of religious faith."[52] Most of them, however, sought an intellectual religion, one that was culturally elitist; their vision of the intellectual and moral reform of Italians either ignored, or did not take into account, the creation of a national liturgy, complete with ritual and symbols. They would rather have built a library than erected a monument. For *La Voce*'s seekers after a new faith shared Croce's view that "a new civic religion could not come into being without a new departure in thought, both sign and instrument of an elevation of the soul."[53] Nonetheless, it was within this circle of men devoted to the spirit, of searchers after a new faith, that some of the future adepts of the Fascist religion, including its leader, were formed.

At that time, Benito Mussolini regarded himself as a militant atheist.

He practiced a kind of rough-and-ready anticlericalism but also had a certain interest in religious problems; he studied the heretical doctrines of the Reformation, meditated on Marie-Jean Guyau's "irreligious religion"; was inspired, like Nietzsche, by the prospect of a transmutation of values with the coming of "new men"; and did not hesitate to describe his conception of revolutionary socialism as "religious." For Mussolini, socialism was not just a scientific concept, but a whole culture, and should mold the conscience of the "new man" through faith: "We want to believe, we have to believe; mankind needs a credo. Faith moves mountains because it gives us the illusion that mountains do move. This illusion is perhaps the only real thing in life."[54] At the time, the future Duce attached little importance to ritual. He considered it a secondary aspect of religion, but often used metaphors derived from the Christian tradition to define his concept of a revolutionary party as an *ecclesia* of the faithful and the militant.[55]

Light from the East

At the beginning of this century, the search for a secular religion that would convert the masses to nationalism and actively involve the cult of the fatherland made new strides within the nationalist movement. The motivation—to defy the political mobilization of socialists and Catholics—was strong. It was a project, however, that definitively abandoned the humanitarian and liberal aspects of the Risorgimento tradition of the "patriotic religion." Instead it moved, open-eyed and decisively, toward a *political religion,* an absolutist cult in which the fatherland became a *living divinity.*

The impetus for this new faith came from the Far East. Enrico Corradini, the founder of the movement, greatly admired the "religion of heroes and nature" he found in Japan. Worshipping nature, heroes, and the Emperor, the Japanese had devised a rite of self-adoration. It integrated the individual into the collective and consolidated a national consciousness capable of defying and defeating the great Russian empire in war. "Japan is the God of Japan. The strength this people draws from religion is a strength drawn from its own bowels; its heroes are great men from the past, nature and the fatherland. It becomes auto-adoration."[56] Corradini proposed to create a national religion with a strong paganizing element, imitating the traditions of the patriotic cults of the French Revolution:

> A religion of heroes and Nature is a magnificent thing. The French Revolution honored two great things: martial valor and the cult of the fatherland and Nature. In this respect we should revive these revolutionary traditions

. . . We offer a religion that encompasses a feeling for Nature as it exists in the salutation to Mithra, joined to a cult of heroes—that is, that element in humanity that existed on earth to exalt the eternal human ideal.[57]

The cult of heroes was fundamental to this religion, not as some generic remembrance and regret, but as an active celebration of the divinity of the nation and a spur to life: "Thanks to heroes, the nation becomes a fatherland, action becomes religion. Heroes are the living soul of the motherland." These live "in the depths of the people's heart as in the highest thoughts of poets . . . Every great people has a heaven over its land, the home of its heroes; greater is the people with the greater and most numerous heroes . . . Heroes are those who struggle ferociously with fate and who extend the limits of human power for all men. For all men, they overcome time and death."[58]

The new religion should be one that fused the individual and the nation into a collective unit; from generation to generation, it would make itself eternal in the becoming of time; it would draw its life-force from heroes and from the blood of those who, in the wars that marked the rhythm of an ascension toward greatness, sacrificed themselves to this ideal: "War is the greatest possible manifestation of life that humans can offer. Indeed, war can, and should, be worshipped: the worship of heroes, the cult of traditions. No nation can aspire to greatness that does not venerate the past and exalt its own power."[59]

The Consecration in Blood

To assume its sacred nature, the Italian nation had to pass through trial by sacrifice and be sanctified with the blood of its children. The symbol of blood, life-giving, purifying, and sanctifying, and the myth of violence as regeneration now become part of the rhetoric of nationalism. This was a nationalism with an inferiority complex. Its national tradition lacked major wars or great victories; in compensation, it had a revolutionary myth and could not conceive of revolution without a purifying violence. The relationship between violence and the sacred occurs when politics is made sacred in the form of war and revolution.[60] Both are catastrophic events through which man is regenerated. Through struggle and sacrifice, a "new man" is born. On the eve of the European war, the myth of the "Italian revolution" had already managed to compact war and revolution into a single idea, into the "great palingenetic event" from which the "new Italy" would arise. This required but one further step within the national myth: the sacralization of politics.

The "Generation of 1914" aspired to give politics a secular religious basis, and thus achieve a "revolution of the spirit." Such a state of mind was widespread throughout Europe on the eve of war. "To the profane eye, contemporary religious despair seemed very like a religious revival." It is typical of transitional periods that "unbelievers seek to create a religion at all costs."[61] Many restless young people, worried about their loss of faith and in search of myths, motivated by a desire to act and dedicate themselves to a cause, expected a new surge of idealism from war or revolution. A new religious spirit would arise that would regenerate— with violence if necessary—a society that they considered materialistic and decadent: "The spiritual content of Europe is, or at least was, weak. There seem to be no great moral forces to garrison the cause of arms and raise the tone of struggle. The old religion, which brought forth so many ideals in its millennial history, has vanished from our souls without a new one, or at least a fresh spirit, having yet taken its place or reviving it."[62]

On the eve of war, the dominant perception among those closely linked to the myth of war-as-regeneration was that of a "crisis of the times," of a society on the threshold of the determining moment, of one of those catastrophic events that precede and underlie great shifts in values, and the rise of a new form of spirituality, religion, and civilization.

Many young people took part in the Great War animated by the desire, as Carlo Rosselli wrote, to "immolate themselves, body and soul, for a cause, any cause, that would transcend the pettiness of everyday life."[63] The war brought about a "state of social effervescence" that was the prelude to religiosity.[64] It was seen as a tragic hierophany: "Everyone acts as though seized by a holy terror. On the battlefield, he feels close to God," Scipio Slataper noted in his diary on November 23, 1915.[65]

The tragedy of war, of mass death as lived by millions in the trenches, prompted the revival of traditional religious feeling, all the while contributing to the development of new kinds of secular religiosity that derived directly from the war. The national myth was invested with a new sacredness, and this in turn assisted the renewal and diffusion of new forms of "civic religion," encouraged by patriotic propaganda and the cult of the martyrs and heroes sacrificed for the fatherland.[66] "A renaissance of religious thinking and faith is highly probable in such times, and in fact there is no lack of signs that a powerful revival of the Catholic spirit and religious values is now taking place," Agostino Lanzillo wrote in 1922.[67] At the same time, Filippo Marinetti wrote in his diary: "Humanity needs a new religion *today*, one that synthesizes and organizes all superstitions, all the lesser religions, all secret cults."[68] Sergio Panunzio expressed a like sentiment: "There is a desperate need for *one* religion. There is a generalized feeling of religiosity . . . but the religion itself is missing."[69]

The mythical experience of war gave further impetus to the sacralization of politics; it brought new material for the construction of a national religion: the myths, rituals, and symbols born in the trenches. The Christian symbolism of death and resurrection, dedication to the nation, the mystical connotations of blood and sacrifice, the "communion" of comradeship—all these became ingredients for a new "patriotic religion."[70] Among the mass of combatants, these myths gave fresh life to the myth of revolution as regeneration. From these myths, veterans derived the idea of a new form of politics. Politics could be a saving mission and an integral experience destined to renew all forms of being. The war recovered and continued the Mazzinian revolution. Politics should not revert to the banalities of the traditional order, but perpetuate the heroic impetus of the war and the mystical sense of the national community; thus the "Italian revolution" would come to fruition.

During this period, the major force in the construction of a national religion through rhetoric and action was Gabriele D'Annunzio. For years the poet had assumed the mantle of prophet, bard, and high priest of a renewed "patriotic religion." He was an inexhaustible creator of religious metaphors, freely drawn from Christian tradition, from classical mythology, from the cult of the trenches. With these he elaborated a refined politico-religious rhetoric that filtered into the language and the mythology of the revolutionary nationalism produced by the war. His participation in the interventionist campaign contributed to transforming mass meetings into a new national ritual; he defined new "sacred spaces," such as the Piazza Campidoglio, where the poet donned the robes of the priest to celebrate his nationalist ritual and renew the cult of heroism "in the perennial novelty of myth."[71] D'Annunzio revitalized the myths of the civil religions of the Risorgimento and "Roman pride."[72] He syncretized these two concepts into a new political theology that celebrated the dogma of the nation. With an abundance of artistic imagination, he invented new symbols and rituals for the cult. Arts and politics were fused, especially during the Fiume adventure.[73] They created a "lyrical order," a new "reign of the spirit," exalting the cult of the war dead, the martyrs who had fecundated the resurrection of the fatherland with their blood, as an exaltation of the new life.[74]

The cult of the fallen, present in the ritual traditions of many nationalist movements, was the first universal, liturgical manifestation of the sacralization of politics in the twentieth century, and gave a fresh impetus to the sanctification of the nation. War graves, and the number of monuments raised to the memory of those who fell in the Great War, remain as visible witnesses to the universal nature of the cult of the national community.[75] In Italy, the spread of this cult to the fallen—whether as a manifestation of the sincere idealism of those who had personal knowledge of the war and had lived through it, or as an artful expedient by which a nationalistic mystification could conceal the horrors of war—for the first time gave a truly national dimension to the ritual and symbolic activity of the "patriotic religion."

A large part of this activity was concretized through the erection of monuments dedicated to the fallen, and many such arose, in disorderly fashion, in all parts of Italy: initiated by local authorities, patriotic and veterans' associations, or groups of citizens. The inauguration of a monument, a new "sacred space" in the community, was an occasion for celebrating patriotic rituals; the symbols of war and the nation were venerated on these occasions in ways that involved, in greater or lesser numbers, the local population.[76] The climax of this new patriotic cult, however, came with the ceremonies attendant on the choice of a tomb for the Unknown Soldier, the conveyance of his body to the capital, and his entombment under the Altar of the Fatherland on November 4, 1921.

The catafalque, displayed on a special railway car and followed by seventeen carriages filled with wreaths and flags, arrived in Rome from Udine via Treviso, Venice, Padua, Ferrara, Bologna, and Florence. All along the way it was greeted by a huge, greatly moved crowd, which rendered its homage kneeling beside the train tracks. The ceremonies in the capital were probably the most solemn patriotic rite ever celebrated in the Third Italy.[77] Not without reason it was written that this was the first patriotic celebration generally felt by the whole people.[78] "The apotheosis of the Unknown Soldier marks a return to the religion of the fatherland," affirmed *L'illustrazione italiana*.[79] To celebrate the end of their convention, which had approved the transformation of its movement into a political party, a large procession of Fascists paid homage at the Tomb of the Unknown Soldier on November 10. The Fascists considered themselves the main authors of this return to a "patriotic religion."

Notwithstanding the numerous polemics about the artistic worth of many monuments—by and large, these merits were considered very modest—and the arguments as to their symbolic value—between those who sought to glorify virile heroism and those who chose to recall the tragedy of the war and the piety of sacrifice—these monuments played a notable part in preparing the foundations for the official institution of a national liturgy built around the myth of the Great War and the "resurrection" of the fatherland.

A new altar to the nation had been raised. Fascism appropriated it: in the name of the nation it placed upon that altar the idols of its own religion.

1

The Holy Militia

The Fascist Militiaman serves Italy in purity; his spirit is pervaded by a profound mysticism, subject to an immutable faith, controlled by an inflexible will; he scorns opportunity and prudence, as he does baseness; sacrifice is the ultimate aim of his faith; he is convinced of the weight of his terrible apostleship, to save our great common mother and give her force and purity . . . Leader or follower, he obeys with humility and commands with force. In this voluntary militia, obedience is *blind, absolute, and respectful* to the peak of the hierarchy, to the Supreme Leader and the Leadership of the Party. The Fascist Militiaman has a morality all his own. Common morality, morality with a familiar face, political, social morality, prismatic, many-faceted, loosely linked, is of no use to the Fascist Militiaman. For him honor is, as it was for the knights of old, a law that seeks, without ever reaching its goal, the peak of a limitless perfection, even if he falls into error; it is all-powerful, absolutely just, even outside, and always superior to, written and formal law. Absolute honor is the law of discipline for the militiaman and is defended not only by the political organs but by the leaders of the hierarchy. The Fascist Militiaman refuses the impure, the unworthy, and the treacherous.
—Regulations of the Fascist Militia, October 3, 1922

When the Fascist movement began, the prevailing attitude toward a national religion was entirely favorable. This was especially true among the veterans, for whom the memory of the war was sacred, as well as among intellectuals in search of a faith, among the young thirsting for myths, delirious with dedication and action, and among the patriotic bourgeoisie, which considered itself the natural guardian of the Risorgimento tradition. Those who were to found the Fascist religion flourished at the very beginning of the movement, when it consisted of no more than a few veterans and the very young who made common cause in the myths of interventionism, war, and the "Italian revolution."[1]

The Origins of the Fascist Cult
A Fascist "religion" was already emerging in the early days of the movement. The terms used here to describe it are those used by Albert Mathiez

to define the religious nature of the cults of the French Revolution and the structure of a new civic religion. They seem equally valid in this context.

All religions, as Emile Durkheim wrote, are social phenomena; they originate in a collective enthusiasm and are based on a system of beliefs and external practices, both obligatory to the cult. These obligations confer a sacred character to the symbols that represent the object of belief. In addition, according to Mathiez,

> The phenomenon of religion is always accompanied, in its formative period, by a state of superexcitation and a longing for happiness. Almost immediately, religious beliefs are made concrete by material objects, by symbols. These are the signs that bring them together; they are like talismans in which the adepts deposit their most intimate hopes. As such, the adepts do not permit them to be despised or ignored. Even more often, believers, especially neophytes, are moved by a destructive rage against the symbols of other cults. Often, too, when they can, they interdict those who do not share their faith, do not worship their symbols. For this crime alone, they devise special punishments, banishing sinners from the community of which they form a part.[2]

The origins of the Fascist religion fit Mathiez's model perfectly. Like many other more or less ephemeral movements—*combattentismo,* the *Arditi,* political futurism, *fiumanesimo*[3]—born of the Great War's state of "social effervescence," the Fascist movement sprang up to affirm the right to victory and to pursue the "Italian revolution," to fight against "internal enemies" and the old ruling class, to bring about the moral and spiritual unity of the new Italy.

As is true of the early stages of new religions, the uniting factor for early Fascism was a common *experience of faith*—interventionism and war—lived through in a state of exhilaration and vitalism. The Fascists transformed that experience into a conviction that they had a mission to regenerate the nation in defense and affirmation of their patriotic idealism, which was absolute and sacralized.

Fascism, as Giuseppe Bottai wrote in 1932, "was, for my comrades or myself, nothing more than a way of continuing the war, of transforming its values into a civic religion."[4] Adhering meant dedicating one's life to the nation: "In a moment of sublime agitation, I consecrated my youth and my future to the good and the greatness of my country." So wrote a young man at the beginning of 1920 in seeking membership from the local Fascist secretary: "The youth of the new Italy has picked up . . . the torch of justice and social equality (a true equality, not that of the *pussisti*) . . . the blood of socialist rebels will extinguish the fires that threaten our flowering, happy gardens."[5]

The political experiences of its militants, who came from a wide assortment of movements but were joined together in the cult of the nation and the myth of war, created a Fascist mythology. The principal myths of Italian political culture, which had emerged during the long search—from the dawn of the Risorgimento to the Great War—for a civic religion for the new Italy, readily accommodated themselves. Fascism was able to present itself as the heir and successor to national radicalism, as a protagonist of the struggle for intervention, as the spokesman for war veterans, defender of the Italian victory in the war, and the avant-garde of the new Italy born of the trenches. For the Fascists, an "Italian revolution" meant not social subversion and the overthrow of the pillars of bourgeois society, but a reconsecration of the cult of the nation and a regeneration of the Italian people. The aim was to transform Italians into a strong and united community, capable of facing the challenge of the modern world, of conquering new heights and fulfilling a civilizing mission that would renew in modern times the spirit and greatness of Rome. As Benito Mussolini wrote at the end of 1920: "We worked with alacrity, to translate into reality Giuseppe Mazzini's aspiration: to give Italians a 'religious concept of the nation' . . . to lay the foundations of Italian greatness. The religious notion of Italianism . . . should become the impulse and fundamental direction of our lives."[6]

From this original nucleus grew the Fascist religion, whose essential character lay in codifying these myths and syncretizing them into a coherent set of beliefs, a secular religion centered on the sacred nature of the nation. At first Fascism did not differ substantially from all previous forms of national religion. As it grew into a mass movement, however, it created a new version in which the myths that emerged from the experience of Fascism as an armed militia became determinant. By its very nature as a party and a militia, Fascism brought something new to the search for a national religion: for the first time this religion became the *credo* of a mass movement, one determined to impose its religion on all Italians, and to deal with opponents unwilling to convert as reprobates, as the damned, as enemies who should be persecuted, punished, and exiled from the national community.

From the first, Fascism accompanied its sacralization of the idea of the nation with a broad use of ritual and symbolism. Of course such use was not unknown among the other political parties—from republicans to socialists, from nationalists to the *popolari*[7]—but none of them had developed their political liturgies so methodically or given them a mass dimension, a presence and a territorial extension, as great as Fascism. The Fascists further differed from other parties by giving political symbolism a dominant place in their organization and activity. They attributed to that symbolism, in both language and gesture, explicitly religious expression and significance. In its liturgy as in its mythology, Fascism acted like a syncretic religion, assimilating such material as it found useful for its own stock of rituals and symbols, openly incorporating ritual traditions from other movements and integrating them with its own. The Fascists were not in the least concerned with originality; they sought efficacy from their rituals and symbols, demanding that they represent their myths and reinforce the identity of the movement. They were to be valid instruments in the struggle against the "enemies of the nation," a form of propaganda to impress onlookers and gain converts.

In the *squadristi* years,[8] before the movement became a party, a great number of these rituals and symbols came into being as much by invention as by imitation. Their arrival was more or less spontaneous, in the sense that their adoption and diffusion was not preordained, ordered and directed by the movement's leaders, but born of individual or group initiatives. These were then imitated and adopted by other groups and, in time, became the common patrimony of the whole composite and heterogeneous Fascist agglomerate. The fundamental rituals distinguishing the particular life-style of the party militia were already well established in 1921 and 1922: the Roman salute, the swearing in of the squads, the veneration of symbols of war and the nation, the blessing of pennants, the worship of the fatherland and the war dead, the glorification of the Fascist "martyrs," the mass meetings.

The National Crusades

From the very beginning the Fascists used religious metaphors as an expression of their lives and activities. Fascist religion manifested itself by its sacralizing rhetoric and by a liturgy that in both language and form echoed Christian ritual as transmuted through D'Annunzio. There was a powerful tendency for Fascists to transfigure the events of their own political lives into epic-religious terms; they felt themselves to be the emulators and heirs of the early patriots of the Risorgimento. Fascists, Camillo Pellizzi wrote in his diary in 1921, "are the overt *carbonari* of sacrifice."[9] Fascists considered themselves the prophets, apostles, and soldiers of a new "patriotic religion" born in "the huge conflagration of war,"[10] rendered sacred by the blood of heroes and of martyrs who gave their lives to bring about the "Italian revolution." As the organ of the combat Fascists, the paramilitary successors to the *squadristi*, affirmed in 1921: "We are those who have overcome . . . [We are] the heirs of a generation that has long outlived its historical reality and now marches ineluctably towards the future . . . We are the perfection of perfection . . .

The Holy Eucharist of war molded us of the same generous, sacrificial metal."[11]

The blood of the fallen had renewed the sacralization of the nation; the Fascists elected themselves the defenders of that sacred nation against the "internal enemy": first and foremost the Socialists, who were desecrators of the nation, perverters of the masses by showing their materialist scorn for spiritual values; then Catholic neutralists and the militants of the Populist party; and finally those "enemies of the nation," the Republicans—despite the fact that for more than a half century the latter had been fervent supporters of the "patriotic religion." But the Fascists were also at war against the governing class and the liberal bourgeoisie: to Fascist eyes, their cowardice and impotence had insulted and denigrated the symbols of nationhood, of the war, of Italy's victory.

While the Fascists were still a tiny band compared to the huge Socialist organization, they made themselves out to be like "Christian missionaries, scattered in the unexplored regions of the world among savage and idolatrous tribes."[12] They were armed with courage and a fanatical determination to spread their gospel, and ready to defend it to the death: "The truth is one. He who possesses it must defend it with his life."[13] The Fascists set out to propagandize their faith by practicing violence, mythologized and sublimated as a manifestation of virility and courage, and the instrument needed to rid the nation of its desecrators. The *squadristi* offensive against the proletariat was, in Fascist eyes, a holy crusade. The true believers set forth to annihilate those who profaned their country. They sought to redeem the proletariat from idolatry, from the false gods of internationalism, to reconsecrate the symbols and holy places of the motherland, to bring the country back to the altar of civic devotion. They took on the role of defenders of traditional religion against those who denied it; they were the paladins of the right to private property and freedom to work against the violators of these rights among the proletarian organizations.

The early *squadristi* sorties were not limited to aggression and destruction; they were also symbolic in nature. The first were *defiant* expeditions. Little groups of Fascists would go into the areas dominated by their adversaries. Their aim was to prove their audacity and bravery; these were a sign of their faith and their will to sacrifice. The Fascist offensive can be seen as a *war of symbols*. On their adversaries they sought to impose veneration for the flag and the celebration of the national cult. Thus was founded the image of Fascism as the bold defender and restorer of the "patriotic religion."

When their numbers increased along with their organization and strength, the *squadristi* switched to expeditions of *conquest;* they destroyed their enemies' headquarters, they "liberated" villages and cities their enemies administered and brought them under Fascist domination. The *manganello* (truncheon) and arson were the terroristic symbols of the *squadristi*'s purifying violence. The truncheon was a talisman, and a kind of goliardic cult was devoted to it. They sang a hymn to "Saint Manganello," their protective amulet, exterminator of their enemies, and liberator of the fatherland's sacred soil:

> O holy Manganello,
> Wise and austere,
> Better than bomb or knife,
> With the foe be severe;
>
> Son of knotty oak,
> The miracles you perform,
> If in the hour of peril,
> You beat those who won't conform.
>
> Manganello, Manganello,
> You brighten every brain,
> You, always you alone,
> Our Fascist hearts inflame.
>
> From the Brenner to Suello,
> From the Quarnaro to the Ticino,
> You, my healing Manganello,
> More than Dante are divine . . .
>
> Where Garibaldi was born,
> Where Corridoni died,
> Neither deserter nor fool
> Shall ever rule;
>
> Five hundred thousand dead
> Tell us our duty:
> Tolerate no alien wrong
> To our fatherland.
>
> Manganello, Manganello,
> Who brightens every brain,
> Every hero from his grave
> Will bless your holy work.[14]

Fire was the symbol of the destructive and purifying force of *squadristi* violence. Every raid ended with the public burning of the symbols and cult centers of the enemy: furniture, papers, portraits of Marx and Lenin were heaped up and burned in the piazza. In his diary Italo Balbo described the "tower of fire" that accompanied a raid, "destroying and setting fire to the houses of the reds, the headquarters of Socialist and Communist organizations. It was a terrible night. Our passage was marked by a high pillar of fire and smoke."[15]

Once the destruction and purification were over, the next step was to consecrate the local people and the place to the cult of the nation. The flag would be raised and saluted, a pilgrimage made to the local monument, or a Fascist rite held dedicating the squad's pennant. Once a new zone had been taken over, the blessing of the pennant was often offered as a symbolic ritual, marking the reconsecration of the local people to national ideals. By this ritual, wrote the organ of the Fascist movement in 1921, the people "restores its conscience and returns to the path of its history, its destiny from time immemorial."[16] Anyone refusing to take part in this ceremony, showing scorn or indifference to its symbols, or refusing to salute the militia's new flag, was punished with all sorts of humiliating harangues and violence. Where the Fascists dominated, enemies who did not yield were interdicted and banished.

The Ritual of the Militia Communion

Fascist "religious feeling" developed principally within the militia organization. The *squadra* was not only an armed body, but a group linked together by a common faith, by comradeship, by a sense of *communion*.

The glorification of this communion was the dominant purpose of all the early Fascist liturgical rites. For a new adherent, participation in a raid was a rite of passage in which he had to show himself to possess the necessary qualities to join the militia. His enlistment was solemnized with an oath that represented his total dedication, the consecration of his loyalty to his fellow *squadristi*. The ritual of swearing-in, already used in D'Annunzio's Fiume, was one of the first elements of the Fascist liturgy, and was celebrated with a solemn, martial ceremony. It took place in public, in a piazza decorated with flags and Fascist symbols, and in the presence of the squads, formed up in a square with their banners. On a few occasions, Mussolini himself was present, although as he was not yet himself an object of worship, he was not included in the ritual.

The words of the oath, not yet standardized, were read by the squadron commander or another officer. It was, in effect, a declaration of dedication to the fatherland:

> I swear by my faith as an Italian that I shall execute whatever orders I may receive from my colleagues, even if these orders should, for the good of Italy, call for the gravest responsibility and sacrifice; I swear to maintain absolute secrecy about orders given me, or about any disposition of which I may

come to have knowledge; I swear that in every place and at all times I shall be ready to defend our holy cause, which is that of Italy.[17]

By the time of the March on Rome, in October 1922, the official form had become more concise: "In the name of God and Italy, in the name of all those who have fallen for the greatness of Italy, I swear to devote myself now and forever to the good of Italy."[18] The swearing-in ceremony was often accompanied by the blessing and presentation of banners. The squadron flag was always an object of special veneration, even during the years of Fascist power, for it was the main symbol of a common faith and of the bonds that held a squadron together, of the moral unity that linked its living and its dead.

"A flag is always a symbol of faith, and above all of sacred duty," wrote Aldo Finzi to the Fascists of Rovigo, after he had joined the Mussolini government. "When with indomitable ardor I blessed it, I felt a religious sense that the mission of Italianhood contained in that symbol would be pursued by all of you with purity."[19] The blessing of the pennant was usually performed by a priest, but in his absence the rite was celebrated by a militia commander. Often, too, the swearing-in and the blessing of the insignia took place during memorial services for the "Fascist martyrs."

Death was already a dominant image in the formative years of Fascism. This constant evocation of death did not reflect any predilection for a decadent, nihilistic view of life or any form of pleasurable, voluptuous pessimism devoted to dissolution; it was, on the contrary, understood as a defiant act of a "tragic and vigorous optimism."[20] The consideration of death was an affirmation of faith in life and immortality. Fascism's attitude to death is the most valid evidence of its religious base. So affirmed a pamphlet called *Fascism and Religion* issued by the party in 1923:

> Religion is the feeling of mystery that appears in determined forms. Any human work to which one applies a moral concept is religion. Dogma, which can be reduced to a single fundamental truth, and ritual, which can become but one single ritual, are the basic expression of religion.
>
> A people, or a militia, which faces death on command, which accepts life as a mission in its purest sense, offering it as a sacrifice, has a true sense of that mystery which is the basic theme of religion, affirming truths that do not derive from human reasoning but are the dogmas of a faith.
>
> The silent meetings of the black-shirts with companions who have abandoned the earthly struggle are religion. Fascist public prayer before a priest in church, when particularly meaningful circumstances call for the public celebration of sacrifice and the invocation of God, are the rituals of *one* religion.[21]

The cult of the fallen was immediately a central feature of Fascist liturgy; it probably best expressed Fascism's secular religiousness and its heroic conception of life. "We must approach martyrdom with attentive and suffering devotion, as the believer who genuflects before a god," wrote Mussolini in 1917. "Commemoration means entering into the community of souls that binds the living and the dead, the generations that were and those that shall be, the bitter sorrow of yesterday and the yet more bitter duty of the morrow."[22] This "profession of faith," with its potential sacrifice of life, was the supreme value in Fascist religion. Within the cult of the dead, and again with recourse to metaphors drawn from Christianity, there developed a whole symbology referring to the regenerating and fecundating blood of martyrs. An eloquent example is given in the oration for three dead Fascists in 1921 by Carlo Scorza, leader of the Lucca *squadristi:* "O Holy Trinity, born of blood: your blood, our blood. The veins are emptied of their most vital flow to create a new baptismal font: the chalice full of its scarlet gift. Let our hearts, my brothers, rise to the highest heaven, to rescue the future from the past."[23]

The funerals accorded Fascists killed in action were, for both the participants and the crowd, the most intense and involving rituals. The funeral cortège was made up of all the Fascist organizations with their banners and flags; the pace of the march was slow, to the beating of the drum and a funeral march; all the shops along the way would be closed in sign of mourning. If the procession occurred at night, the atmosphere, with its torches, was even more emotional. The culminating moment of the ceremony was the roll call: one of the leaders of the squad would call out the dead man's name, and the crowd, on its knees, bellowed "Present!" Raised as saints and heroes in the symbolic universe of the Fascists, the dead charismatically watched over the communion of Fascists, living on in their memory. The roll call gave life to the sacred bond between the dead and the living, joined together in the faith: "Life, perennial child of death; the memory of every individual is transmitted forever in the immortal soul of the nation."[24]

For Fascists, the roll call became the supreme rite of Fascism, the principal testimony to their religiousness. Throughout the Fascist régime it was celebrated for all those who had distinguished themselves in the revolution or national life. Its importance may be judged by the fact that the Fascist roll-call has its own entry in the party's 1940 *Dictionary of Politics,* which Mussolini considered a sort of *summa theologica* of Fascist doctrine: "The rite of the roll call is part of our recognition that there are spiritual forces beyond the physical. In religion we express these by venerating saints; throughout civilization, the people has venerated heroes."[25]

Even in celebrating the rites of death, Fascism sought to emphasize life and faith in the future. Melancholy and regret did not dominate in the cult of the fallen. The austere and martial form of the ceremony made it possible for pain felt for the dead to be submerged in an act of devotion to the fatherland; sorrow was mitigated by faith in the immortality of the fallen who were in communion with the living. The blood of the martyr regenerated; it gave life to the nation and fed its rebirth. By transforming the rites of the dead into a rite of life, Fascism sought to give prominence to the mystical sense of communion that was at the heart of the Fascist concept of a political movement or party. From the party, that communion was projected onto the concept of the nation, a nation organized into a totalitarian state.

The Consecration of Rebirth

The mass meetings of Fascism had various meanings and symbolic functions. In part they were a show of strength to terrorize the enemy, to stimulate and reinforce the sense of identity and power of the Fascists themselves; but they were also spectacular propaganda demonstrations, and their choreography was designed to fascinate their audience, with a view to instilling in them the faith of fresh proselytes. "Religions," Bottai observed, "often subdue minds and souls, not with the preachings of their priests, but with the solemnity of their ceremonials; it is through these ceremonies that the divine afflatus finds its way to the hearts of men."[26] The symbolic purpose that linked all these rituals, from parades to funerals, was to make Fascism a visible community of belief and a force for renewal in the life of the nation. "The Fascist marches," *Il popolo d'Italia* noted in 1922, "are like a rite of spring, the awakening of the will, of a song, of a spiritual unity."[27]

The date chosen to symbolize this reawakening of the nation, and to replace the First of May, was April 21, the day of Rome's founding. The myth of Rome, which took off sharply in the 1930s, was present in Fascism from its beginnings; it was already at the heart of its mythological cosmos. "Rome, which is Italy, the World, which is the History and Civilization of the World; Rome which is Strength, Light, Youth, Beauty!"[28] This exaltation of Rome was meant as an act of faith in the continuing vitality and great destiny of the Italian race. All Fascist rites, in their early stages, were symbols of a "new birth" for the nation. Tied to the Roman tradition and led by "love of the common faith" to a spiritual unity that transcended party, class, and gender, they marked the beginning of the palingenesis of the nation, the coming of the "kingdom of the spirit."[29] It is as such that these rituals were fitted into a different political and institutional context during the régime; they became the legitimation and consecration of the new communion of the nation, embodied in the cult of the lictor.

Fascism's self-portrayal as a religion was not confined to its symbolism, to ritual and mythology; it was also useful as a means by which its institutions and its totalitarian ambitions could be made real. It was the fundamental principle around which Fascism formed its esprit de corps, its sense of identity; it enabled Fascism to transform itself from a *situational* movement, as it was in its beginnings, into a new kind of party, with all the characteristics proper to a national militia, preserving the organization, culture, and life-style of the *squadristi,* together with the whole complex of myths, rituals, and symbols that had originated in their experience and remained basically unaltered until the fall of the régime.

The Fascists managed to monopolize patriotism, to represent themselves to the bourgeoisie and the middle class as those who would save the country from the "triumphant beast" of Bolshevism. By 1922, the whole scene in many Italian cities had changed radically. The great processions with red or white banners had been taken over—after a victorious war of symbols, by the conquest of public spaces—by marchers waving the Italian flag or the black banners of Fascism. These processions brought together thousands, and presentations of the flag, militia swearings-in, solemn funerals and celebrations in memory of Fascist "martyrs," became a near-daily spectacle. On the eve of the March on Rome, Fascism could claim to have begun the moral regeneration of the Italian people, to have helped transform them into a compact, disciplined, united people, without partisan bitterness, without class, gender, or generational antagonisms:

> For the first time, that human entity which we call "the people" appeared in all its fullness, in the Roman meaning of the word "people." People: that is, the sons of a common earth, all united and quivering with love for the common motherland. People: all sons of that Great Mother, whatever class they belonged to, whatever their origin, whatever their tasks in life. People: all men who make up a working society, who produce, who give life its daily ration of will, sacrifice, and inventiveness.
>
> The precepts of the Word according to Fascism finally reunited in a common passion this marvelous Italian people; it taught them to march together in serried ranks, by battalions, by legions. Here is the bronzed, rude, sturdy peasant who has rediscovered his individuality in the collective of his brothers, who now walks head high, filled with a new pride. Here is the office worker, strong, open-hearted, serene in a new faith, with a fresh conscience. Side by side with them, close not just physically, are all those other men who once were considered enemies: those who work not with their hands but with their invention, with their intelligence. All, from the most modest em-

ployee to the hard-working professional man, the thinking intellectual, united in brotherhood, as not so long ago in the trenches; all led by a discipline spontaneously recognized and obeyed; all fitted into a steadfast and fraternal hierarchy.

And with them, their women, those superb, modest, hard-working, wise Italian women; and the young, who quickly acquire the iron laws of discipline, a sense of duty, of sacrifice, and love for the land of their fathers blessed and sanctified by the sacrifices of our martyrs. And all ages: the young who bravely bear the standards of war, parents who temper their austere dignity with the irrepressible enthusiasm of their children, the old who relive their finest hours while marching sturdily to the joyous rhythms of the songs of the young.

It is Italy, in fact, the whole people of Italy, finding itself for the first time truly united under the flag of the Fatherland, in a spiritual unity that makes it finally worthy of its victory and its highest aims![30]

This text is particularly significant because it sets out the essential characteristics of that "harmonious collective," as defined by Mussolini in 1941, a collective that was the matrix for his project to transform the character of the Italian people, a transformation to which the policy of the totalitarian state was to dedicate itself with fanatical determination.

A Political Religion in Power

With the triumph of Fascism, the cult of the fatherland was restored, and no one openly dared to dissent from it. The change of climate that Fascism brought to Italy was also noticeable in the rhetoric of war monuments. This shift, as *L'illustrazione italiana* noted in 1922, "happened in some places under the influence of recent events. Words like 'Italy, Victory, Glory, Appreciation, Gratitude' take the place of 'Sacrifice, Holocaust, the Fallen, War,' without adjectives attached. Today there is less of the cemetery and more of the Pantheon."[31]

An armed militia now supervised the national religion. Piazzas and monuments now became permanently "sacred spaces" in which a liturgical mass periodically celebrated patriotic rites, accompanied by declarations of gratitude and devotion to the "savior of Italy." Many people, moved by conviction and self-interest, fueled this restoration of the patriotic cult, which was now imposed on a proletarian mass that had previously ignored or rejected it:

Look how the media exploits the patriotic theme; any occasion, from Dante to the Unknown Soldier, will suit. Look how intolerant our patriotic religion has become. Twenty years ago it was in the shadows; today it dominates. This isn't just a trick. For the industrial democracies it's a guarantee for the future: it means that a center of gravity has perhaps been found for the masses, an ideal discipline to propose to the people, and they seem not to find it repulsive.[32]

The bourgeoisie applauded the Fascist government because it had finally instituted a national, civic religion with a bloodless revolution that had brought discipline and unity back to the country.

But what many thought was a civic religion for a united Italy of free citizens, such as had been heralded by the prophets of the Risorgimento, was from the very beginnings of Fascist power really a new religion, one that, by ambiguously mixing together the symbols of the nation and those of the party, professed the totalitarian vocation of a nascent *political religion*, one readying itself to use the altars of the nation to celebrate, in a new, integralist state, the cult of the lictor.

2

The Fatherland Dons the Black Shirt

A party can covet control of public life, but it must never overstep the boundaries of private conscience, in which every human being is free to find his own refuge. Fascism, however, has not sought so much to govern Italy, as to monopolize control over the Italian conscience. To possess power is not enough: it wants to own the private conscience of every citizen, it wants the "conversion" of Italians.

Conversion to what? It has often been observed that Fascism lacked sufficient ideas with which to develop a program, and its fusion with Nationalism[1] came along to provide it with a political program. Yet Fascism has pretensions to being a religion . . . Fascism has the overweening ambition and the inhuman intransigence of a religious crusade. It does not promise happiness to those who convert; it allows no escape to those who refuse baptism.

The Good Shepherd, with the knotty club that now lords it over our Sundays, rudely goads Italians into his temple and threatens perdition to those who stubbornly remain without.

—*Il Mondo*, April 1, 1923

The patriotic bourgeoisie and the supporters of a restoration of the liberal régime raised hosannas to Fascism. It was the savior of a country resurrected from the ashes of war but dragged by its "internal enemies" to the edge of the abyss. It had restored the cult of the nation, complete with myths, rituals, and symbols. True, the Fascist restoration had a rhythm and style that bore little resemblance to the dusted-off patriotic religion as nostalgically envisioned in an earlier century, or to that yearned for—after the agnostic democracy of the Giolitti years and the desecrating chaos of the two "red" years—by those who supported a monarchical Italy above parties.

Still, few among the believers in the "patriotic religion" saw the difference; and when the difference became, through Fascism's propensity to abolish liberty, obvious, few protested and reacted in defense of the indissoluble link between freedom and the nation, a link that had inspired the search for a civil religion during the Risorgimento and then during the liberal régime. The seduction of nationalism was stronger than faith in liberty and allowed Fascism to become the paladin and restorer of the "resurrected nation."[1] The nation Fascists wanted to worship at the altar, the nation risen from the ashes of war, was one that they saw arrayed in black shirts. Only he who wore that shirt could love and venerate the fatherland. This early became evident in the way in which the Fascist government set about installing a liturgy of the fatherland, which was no more than the foundation on which to institutionalize the cult of the lictor.

This chapter presents a few examples of the elaboration of the Fascist liturgy, most of them taken from the first decade of the régime. They demonstrate the importance and prominence the Fascists gave to mass rituals in the context of a totalitarian policy.

There are two phases to the institutionalization of the Fascist liturgy: from 1923 to 1926, through a monopoly of power, the Fascists sought to gain full control over the symbolic universe of the state; and from 1926 to 1932 the Fascist liturgy was consolidated and absorbed the cult of the fatherland. In the following decade, even if expanded with fresh rituals, the cult of the lictor both preserved and built on the characteristics it had acquired in the previous period, in a process of crystallization and mechanical repetitiousness. During the first, key period in the institutionalization of the cult of the lictor, the Fascists followed two procedures, corresponding to the way in which, in the political arena, they sought to obtain and consolidate their monopoly on power. One procedure was direct: it reconsecrated the rites and symbols of national unity and of the "nation resurrected" (cult of the flag, celebration of the Statute, glorification of the Great War). The second was indirect: it introduced the symbols and rituals of Fascism into the symbolism and liturgy of the state, a procedure that eventually made the "patriotic religion" Fascist.

The Cult of the Flag

Among the many initiatives designed to create an official state liturgy, the Fascist government gave strong support to state and patriotic symbols, reinstituting uniforms for members of its government.[2] "The new state loves decorum and wishes to restore the dignity of formalities . . . Mussolini has an eye on something more concrete than sartorial reform: he wants a restoration of symbols," announced *L'illustrazione italiana*.[3] "Fascist passion," a Fascist journalist wrote a few weeks after the March on Rome, "has given all the reconsecrated symbols a fervent human and divine soul that beats as one within fifty million Italian breasts."[4] Rhetorical, but not completely unfounded.

The Mussolini government gave high priority to celebrating national holidays with due solemnity. The communes were ordered to provide the necessary budgets for secular holidays, "with all necessary outdoor cele-brations." Both government and commune were also ordered to fly the national flag.[5] Local administrations headed by antimonarchical parties had often flown party banners instead, or refused to fly the national flag on national anniversaries. Fascism took care of that omission: a decree on September 24, 1923, made the use of the Italian flag obligatory for all provincial and communal public offices, on holidays or at funerals and commemorations; it established its precedence over any other kind of flag at public functions, although formally the same obligation was imposed on associations.[6]

The cult of the flag was not confined to public offices, military cere-monies, or open-air demonstrations. On January 31, 1923, the Ministry of Public Instruction required that the flag be saluted in all schools. Every school had to have a flag, which was kept by the head of the institution and handed over during the ceremonies to a standard-bearer chosen from among the best students.[7] Every Saturday, at the conclusion of classes or on the eve of holidays, students were to pay homage to the flag with the Roman salute. The ritual was to be accompanied by choral singing of patriotic songs. Those mutilated or wounded in war, "the beloved sons of the race,"[8] were chosen as sponsors of the flag ceremony, thus estab-lishing a link between witnesses to the heroism of war and the new gen-erations.

During such a flag day in the Roman schools, in the presence of the king and queen, Dario Lupi, a Tuscan Fascist deputy and undersecretary of public instruction, the original moving force behind the ceremony, told the students that they should receive the flag as the "new eucharist." With the flag, he declared in high style, "You receive among yourselves and make forever yours the blessed and immense idea of the fatherland"; the flag should "penetrate your hearts, mingle with your souls, grace your grace; it becomes one with you and molds you."[9] To give the ceremony an "austere solemnity," Lupi decreed that it should be "elucidated with love and observed with true religiousness"; it should never be performed less than once a month, but in a "severe and suggestive manner."[10]

Saluting the flag was just one of many Lupi initiatives. He dusted off the requirement that portraits of Christ and the king should hang in the classroom; he encouraged schoolchildren to take part in national com-petitions for the singing of patriotic songs; he urged schools to make pilgrimages to the Tomb of the Unknown Soldier. Another initiative was to honor the memory of the fallen through "the living symbol of a plant." It was, he said, "a very ancient custom . . . returned to honorable usage after the carnage of the Great War to mark the survivors' desire to find the most eloquent way in which to show their gratitude."[11] On November 30, 1922, he decreed that every town and village should plant an avenue or park of remembrance, with a tree for every local soldier killed in the Great War. The planting should be done by schoolchildren.[12]

Living monuments in an urban environment, these "votive woods" symbolized the spiritual community of the living and of those who died for their country. They were the "sacred places" of the nation, in which the young were to be trained in "holy emulation" of heroes. These initiatives of Lupi's enjoyed a considerable success: by February 1924, the number of schools with flag ceremonies numbered 6,579 communities out of 8,893; 2,217 remembrance parks or avenues had been planted in 8,703 communes.[13] To make participation more active and attractive, the government also created a student honor guard to which the maintenance of monuments and "votive woods" was entrusted.[14]

Lupi certainly deserved the encomium given him by faithful of the "patriotic religion": "Initiator of original observances, of ensigns of remembrances, in the schools where a triumphant Italy was born and found its future."[15] Undertaken as part of the Gentile reform, such initiatives were part of a well-thought-out design for the politicization of education. In ways unknown in the past, these introduced fresh rites and symbols through which to educate children in love of country, promoting Fascism especially through the Great War. A circular issued on February 13, 1923, required that votive trees also be dedicated to the martyrs of Fascism, since "the faith that led these to the supreme sacrifice was the same as that which glorified the holy massacre of those who fell in war."[16] Creating a Guard of Honor was but a first step toward the militarization of the schools. By introducing the cult of the fatherland and of the fallen, the schools were, through successive reforms, transformed into institutions specially suited for educating the young in the cult of the lictor.

The cult of the flag became a near-daily affair. In 1923, the capital in particular saw a great number of flag dedications, sponsored by the armed forces, by veterans' associations, and by the Fascists. Piazza Venezia and the Altar of the Fatherland became a "sacred center," with frequent blessings and presentations of flags.[17] Opponents of Fascism found the proliferation of rituals a sort of rhetorical revel. But a Roman Fascist newspaper reacted sharply: "It is not rhetoric. There is no greatness in nations without ritual celebration of the religion of the Fatherland. Any people in history that has achieved greatness was also rich in symbols and public liturgies." The newspaper added that those who did not participate in celebrating the flag should be banished from the national community, for "whoever scorns that symbol fails in its 'human respect' for the spiritual patrimony of the Nation. Scorning the flag is a sign of baseness; in the

period of ignominious memory, decorations were hidden and flags carefully folded away." Flag days marked a "historic day, the bright dawning
of a new era."[18]

Such remarks from Fascist and philo-Fascist newspapers show that venerating the flag was more than just homage to the symbol of the fatherland: it marked the beginning of a radical change in the political climate
of the country, in which indifference, or, worse yet, hostility to the sacralization of the fatherland was no longer permitted. Fascism aimed to
affirm its privileged difference from all the other parties through the institution of a cult of the fatherland. This in turn was supposed to legitimate and consecrate the "Fascist régime"—an expression already current
in the immediate aftermath of the March on Rome—as the sole expression of will in the New Italy arising from the war, the only interpreter of
the national will.

Celebrations of National Unity

Right after gaining power, Fascism renewed and extended the calendar of
state holidays, likewise establishing how they were to be celebrated.[19] To
Statute Day, September 20, and November 4, it added holidays on May
24, the anniversary of Italy's declaration of war, and April 21, the day of
the founding of Rome, to take the place of Labor Day, previously celebrated on May Day. In the institutionalization of the cult of the lictor, the
latter holidays had different functions—or, in reality, didn't, as was the
case with the two traditional celebrations of Italian unity, the anniversary
of the Statute and September 20.

The anniversary of the Statute was a strictly monarchical and military
holiday. It had been ignored by many recent administrations and over-
shadowed even in the capital. According to a nationalist daily, postwar
governments had not dared permit the traditional military parade and
had confined the military ceremonies to barracks, where few could see
them. This arrangement was completely revised for the 1923 anniversary.[20] On June 3 the holiday was celebrated in Rome and other cities
with new pomp—public buildings decorated with flags, processions,
speeches, and military parades in garrison towns, all in the presence of
the civic and religious authorities. Fascist publicists, however, gave these
ceremonies a low profile: an account of the holiday appeared without
commentary in two half-columns on page 3 of *Il popolo d'Italia*.[21] Mussolini, who was visiting Venice, spoke there on the holiday after witness-
ing a "superb parade." In two speeches he made no reference to the commemoration.

In fact Fascism was never interested in Statute Day in the context of institutionalizing the cult of the lictor. The holiday was celebrated in various ways during the régime; it kept its monarchical and military character, but Fascist symbols were left out of the parade in the capital. The only anthem played was the "Royal March," although in other official events it was always paired with the Fascist anthem. The only Fascist element in the parade was the presence of the militia and of the Fascist youth movement.[22] The official press generally relegated accounts of the festivities to the inside pages, along with other celebrations and manifestations, while coverage of the cult of the lictor, in both the capital and the provinces, appeared on the front page, sometimes spilling over to inside pages.[23]

As a celebration of the old régime, Statute Day, unlike anniversaries marking the war, did not lend itself to incorporation into Fascist liturgy. Nonetheless, although the ceremony in the capital remained almost totally monarchical, it was steadily infiltrated by the Fascists, by party organizations and by the militia's presence in strength. In the official interpretation, this signified a rite of harmony between monarchy and régime, between army and militia.[24] In the provinces, although the army remained the chief actor in the celebrations, the monarchical holiday ended up being mixed in with the régime's other celebrations, to the point that in some of their reports the prefects spoke of "manifestations devoted to the régime and Il Duce,"[25] of "magnificent evidence of progress of the Fascist idea . . . and devotion to the National Government and Il Duce,"[26] avoiding any mention whatever of the monarchy.

The 1923 celebration of September 20 showed clearly that Fascism intended to suppress any trace of its democratic and anticlerical tradition and to transform the holiday into a conflation of the triumph of 1870 with the Fascist March on Rome. The ceremonies organized in the capital to celebrate "the key date in history of the creation of the nation and its unification" sought to provide them with "a united affirmation above and beyond parties," a manifestation of an "established solidarity among Italians." Italians had risen above that "single faith in the fatherland and that intransigence which religious devotion continued to keep alive in the minds of the faithful."[27] In the years that followed, the day was marked in a minor key until in 1930, after a series of punctilious debates between Mussolini and the Vatican, it was abolished on the altar of conciliation.[28]

Making the Cult of the Fatherland Fascist

The ceremonies on the anniversaries of intervention and of Italy's subsequent victory and, in general, glorification of the Great War, played a pivotal role. They served to legitimize Fascist power, to institutionalize the patriotic cult. Once it attained power, Fascism expended great energy in creating a myth of the war, transforming it into a veritable epic of heroism and martyrdom dedicated to the divinity of the nation. Italy had paid history the tribute of a copious sacrifice in blood, and the Great War had legitimated its aspirations to great-power status. As nationalists had sought, the Pantheon of its "sacred history" was now richly endowed with the dead, with heroes and martyrs.[29] A decree issued on November 3 elevated "our battlefields, bound to history by immortal feats of heroism and sacrifice, to the status of national monuments . . . the most sacred strongholds of an epic struggle." These "summed up in themselves and symbolized a true vision of war, epitomized its feats of heroism, and incarnated its torment, sacrifice, and apotheosis."[30]

In its very first cabinet meeting the Mussolini government, on the proposal of its president, decided to celebrate November 4 with special pageantry, the outlines of which were, without major changes, maintained for the future. On the morning of the fourth, after mass in Santa Maria degli Angeli with the king and all the major state officers present, the members of the cabinet and its president proceeded to Piazza Venezia, where they were greeted by a vast crowd. Mussolini and his government walked up the huge staircase to the Altar of the Fatherland and remained on bended knees for a full minute before the Tomb of the Unknown Soldier. Some foreign observers found the gesture theatrical, but its symbolic importance as an expression of Fascist mysticism was not lost on the crowd.[31]

Six months later, the anniversary of Italy's declaration of war was celebrated with equal pomp in the capital and other cities, with the participation of the armed forces, veterans' organizations, the disabled, widows, war orphans, and, of course, the Fascist party. Everywhere the holiday was celebrated with public buildings hung with flags and banners, with ceremonies, processions, and patriotic music. Often the celebrations ended with the dedication of a new monument or a memorial to the fallen, all accompanied by speeches proclaiming the fatherland resurrected and rendering homage to the national government. Mussolini undertook a "sacred pilgrimage" to the graveyard at Redipuglia, where, together with members of his government and high-ranking army officers, he took part in a mass meeting of veterans.[32] After mass the Duke of Aosta evoked "the glorious epic of the great Redemption" and the "first heroes" who had consecrated their lives "under the Habsburg yoke, and become for the Italian religion symbols of redeeming martyrdom, as the cross was in Christianity." He recalled the martyrdom of blood in battle, the "Golgotha" of Caporetto, the resurrection of "crucified Italy," and its eventual triumph. He concluded by calling on these "sublime martyrs," these "purest heroes," these "saints of the Carso," to watch over a nation "burning for the future and glory."[33]

The resurrection image was a commonplace in the cult of the Great War and its accompanying patriotic rhetoric, but it now acquired a special significance by giving a specific Fascist tinge to the myth of war. It became the founding myth of the Fascist symbolic universe, both in the ritual aspects of the cult of the lictor and in its epic aspects, developed during the creation of a "sacred history" for the Fascist religion. By using analogous Christian metaphors, Fascism extolled Italian intervention in the war, which it depicted as an act of will imposed on the nation by a "moral and spiritual aristocracy of the people." This aristocracy had arisen and "borne its own cross up the Mount Calvary of Redemption." Fascism claimed to be the main expression of this aristocracy, its only heir and legitimate representative. May 24, wrote *Il popolo d'Italia*, was a day that "no government to date has dared celebrate. It is the dazzling day that marks the threshold of a new life and clearly demarcates two periods, two epochs, two worlds . . . and there begins that deep, personal schism between the old Italy and the new." It was "the magnificent day on which Italy intervened, the epiphany of a new spirit,"[34] which Fascism had led to victory.

An analogous interpretation was given the anniversary of the Italian victory, celebrated in 1923 with the same splendor as the previous year, and in coincidence with the celebration of the March on Rome, marking the first year of Fascist government. The party newspaper claimed that increasing participation by the people in the ceremonies marking the Great War "testified to a recrudescence of patriotic feeling . . . annually celebrated and fed by the consolidation and colossal growth of the Fascist movement, which was the one and only moving force behind the recreated and recovered national consciousness of the people of Italy."[35]

The cult of the nation began with these war rituals; that they were converted into Fascist rituals is attributable in part to the very nature of Fascist religion. Its syncretic and totalitarian nature led it to absorb and put its own mark on other patriotic movements such as the veterans, the *Arditi,* and the veterans of the Fiume adventure. But there were also purely political reasons for this Fascistization. The cult of the fatherland was, for Fascism, a basic instrument in its conquest of consensus; but that consensus, on which the Mussolini government depended, was also under attack by anti-Fascist patriotic movements. The anti-Fascists, too, used the patriotic cult to challenge Fascism's claim to being the sole repository of the values of armed combat, the only interpreter of the nation. From

1923 through 1925, the anniversaries of the Great War were marked by tension and clashes between opposed concepts of the fatherland, just as happened after the Risorgimento.

For Fascism, gaining the monopoly of the cult of the fatherland meant battling for the celebrations against anti-Fascist veterans' movements, which could just as well, and with some right, claim to be the legitimate heirs to the myth of the war and of the "religion of the fatherland."[36] Once in power, the Fascists launched a new war of symbols and rituals against these other claimants, a war that reached its climax with the demonstrations on November 4, 1924.[37] In many cities the official ceremonies were challenged by counterdemonstrations led by anti-Fascist ex-combatants, as well as by rival ceremonies promoted by the association Free Italy (Italia Libera). These caused incidents, especially in the capital.[38]

Once the party régime had been installed and opposition parties eliminated, the risk of rival demonstrations disappeared. A rigorous security operation was mounted for Victory Day in 1925, aimed at "so-called dissident ex-combatants, the remains of dissolved opposition parties" and at "heading off and eventually preventing mass demonstrations competing with official ceremonies or with those organized by the national associations of veterans and the disabled."[39] Once the leadership of these associations had effectively been made Fascist, there was no further obstacle to the incorporation of the rites of the "fatherland resurrected" into the cult of the lictor, although the place of honor at the ceremonial, as well as a major share of the organizational work of such demonstrations, was left to the various associations representing veterans of the Great War. For May 24, 1927, the party took no initiative whatever, leaving the organization of the celebrations entirely in the hands of the ex-combatants' organizations.[40]

According to the orders of the Rome *questura* (police headquarters) for the maintenance of public order during the celebrations, "all the living forces in the country are united and in agreement; in line with the great work of renewal fostered by the national government, the fusion of spirit and intent between Fascist combatants and the ex-combatants' associations, the disabled and volunteers, is now perfect."[41] Ceremonies in the capital culminated in the homage paid to the secretary of the Fascist party by the veterans, the disabled, and the mutilated, followed by a declaration of loyalty and devotion to the Duce and the régime.

The rites had been made Fascist. It now remained for history to be definitively rewritten in Fascist form. The "radiant days" became "the origin and prime affirmation of that revolutionary will that will lead to the disempowering of the old régime and the coming to power of a new generation of Italians . . . the chief protagonists of which are the Fascist and national leaders, Benito Mussolini and his colleagues.”[42] In Fascist mythology, Mussolini assumed the role of protagonist and architect of intervention and victory, and hence the undisputed leader of the ex-combatants. The incorporation of Intervention Day, May 24, into the cult of the lictor in 1930 was ratified with a huge national assembly of veterans' associations in Milan. After Mussolini, with a priestly gesture, had lit the votive flame on the altar of the “Temple to the Fallen,” the president of the association of maimed veterans, Carlo Delcroix, presented him with the “baton of command” as “a sign of our gratitude to the Restorer of the Nation”; in so doing, he added, “we mean to recognize that it is for you to command, and for us to obey.”[43]

The same fate befell November 4, or Victory Day. Thanks to its proximity in time to the March on Rome it was easily assimilated to the anniversary of the latter, as another decisive day in the Fascist revolution. This was, the party newspaper explained in 1924, because “Fascism took power as delegated and empowered by those who fought the war, both living and dead.” Fascism “wants to continue to govern with that sublime investiture. Benito Mussolini is the man who . . . restored the temple of a profaned Italy.”[44] With the régime in power, the holiday retained its character as a veterans' day, but alongside victory, and steadily imposing itself on victory, there was now the ritual of a collective demonstration of surrender and obedience to the Duce and his government. To avoid strife between veterans and Fascists, however, the actual incorporation of this holiday into the cult of the lictor required a degree of caution in the early stages.[45]

In 1930, for the anniversaries of October 28 and November 4, all the veterans' associations issued a joint declaration that ratified the amalgamation of the two ceremonies: “United in love and faith, we annually salute two glorious dates: the one illuminates the other; both tell us of a generous present with its arduous struggles.”[46] In 1930 the ceremonies were dominated by the ritual swearing-in of young recruits to the recently established Fascist youth movement. On November 4, too, there was evidence of the incorporation of one ceremony in another. As the prefect of Modena reported in a telegram on November 4, 1930:

> This morning after celebration mass monumental temple this most sacred place in memory war dead civil military party authorities gathered party headquarters to lay wreath and stone in memory of Fascist victims and attend swearing-in Fascist youth stop afterward most imposing procession party and huge crowd laid another wreath and stone military academy then repaired monument to war dead for memorial speeches.[47]

With the passing years, Fascist symbolism continued to be superimposed on the rites of the “resurrected fatherland.” The ceremonies often combined into one the cult of the war dead and the cult of those who fell for the Fascist revolution. On Victory Day in 1932, at the inauguration of the monument to the fallen in Enna, Interior Undersecretary Ruggero Romano pointed out that "on the tenth anniversary of the Régime, the war dead and those dead for the Revolution were both wrapped in the same flag."[48]

The party further extended its control over the organization of such ceremonies and how they were carried out. A typical form for the rituals celebrated on anniversaries of the Great War, after their incorporation into the cult of the lictor, is described in the report of the prefect of Padua on November 4, 1932:

> Anniversary victory and intervention took place all communes in province with great enthusiasm and without incident. Here in capital after mass celebrated this morning in cathedral, in presence of civil and military authorities and party organizations, military detachments and representatives veterans and mutilees gather from whole province, huge procession to monument to fallen to lay wreaths and receive blessing H. E. the Archbishop.
>
> Procession reformed marched to patriotic songs to Remembrance Park where listened with much applause to bulletin victory and bulletin Navy and reasons award of War Cross this city. This afternoon in city theater, present authorities organizations and large audience ex-combatant federation effectively reinvoked victory to enthusiastic passionate demonstrations of common feeling devotion House of Savoy Duce and Regime.[49]

The Symbol of the New Era

The cult of the fatherland, centered upon the glorification of war, served to prepare the atmosphere for the establishment of the cult of the lictor as the state religion. Once in power, the Fascists accelerated the symbiosis between the national and the Fascist religions, which had originated in the *squadristi* militia. To make the irrevocable and revolutionary change of government that had come about with the March on Rome immediately perceptible symbolically, they began converting the symbols of the state into Fascist symbols.

A few weeks after the government, presided over by Mussolini, was formed, his colleagues conceived the idea of celebrating the event with a symbolic act. In the latter part of December it occurred to Giacomo Acerbo, the undersecretary in the Prime Minister's Office, to "interest Mussolini in the idea of immediately establishing a permanent seal to mark the coming to power of Fascism." His idea was that instead of the current ear of corn or flower-and-bee, "a new coin, of a denomination already in circulation, be specially designed and minted." On December 22 Acerbo sent his proposal to Alberto De Stefani, the minister of finance, with a request to "take the appropriate measures" because the prime minister had "been highly pleased" and had approved its "special meaning." Two days later Acerbo wrote directly to Mussolini, saying how "happy I am to be able to fulfill Your Excellency's wish." He had already, "a few days ago," he said, "ordered dies for new coins . . . to be inscribed with the lictorial fascio, the symbol of ancient Rome and the new Italy."[50] Announced on December 27 in *Il popolo d'Italia,* the proposal was submitted to Mussolini and approved at the cabinet meeting on January 1, 1923.[51] A royal decree on January 21 approved the issue of 100 million lire in pure nickel 1- and 2-lire coins bearing the picture of the king on one side and the lictorial fasces on the other. Margherita Sarfatti, an art critic with a notable understanding of the aesthetics of propaganda and the political importance of symbolism, made a public appeal to the prime minister, urging him to entrust the definition of the "design, the manner, and the form of the fasces on the new coins" to the undersecretary of fine arts, because such coins were "a powerful weapon in the diffusion of a sense of beauty" and "a humble agent of propaganda, which penetrates everywhere, passes from hand to hand, at home and abroad, and speaks to all, as it tells all, about Italy." The new symbol should carry "a worthy interpretation of authority and beauty" and proclaim "for all time, from under the upturned earth, the imperishable glory of Rome. Twenty centuries from now," she concluded, "the humble peasant, ploughing in his millennial way, will find a little coin in his brown soil and, wiping it clean, will find, impressed on a seal of beauty and sovereign nobility, the august name of our King and the Fascio, revived by, and to the honor of, Benito Mussolini."[52]

Future glory, as evoked by a writer familiar with the intimate ambitions of the Duce—who had confided to her that he was possessed by the desire "to impress his will on time"[53]—was unlikely to leave Mussolini indifferent. Responsibility for reconstructing the original Roman version of the lictorial fasces was given to an illustrious archaeologist, Senator Giacomo Boni, who had been excavating at the Forum and the Palatine Hill. The representation on the coin was given special care because of "the symbolic meaning of the fasces, which is not simply a token of force and power, but also possesses a deep religious significance."[54] Mussolini chose a model showing fasces of rods with a battle-ax at their side. This was considered more faithful to its Roman symbolism than the "arbitrary look" and the "deformations" to which the symbol had been subjected during the French Revolution and later in Risorgimento symbolism—that is, with a battle-ax or halberd with a Phrygian cap crowning the rods.[55]

Using the fasces on coins was no isolated episode prompted by a zealous colleague of Mussolini's. As noted by *Il popolo d'Italia* on November 14, 1922, Mussolini himself had wanted the symbol incorporated in the seal of the Ministry of Foreign Affairs. A few months later the newspapers announced the issue of a set of stamps with the fasces, to commemorate the "coming to power of the national government."[56] On October 21 the Official Gazette published the decree issuing 20- and 100-lire "gold coins commemorating the Fascist March that established the national government." The bills had a portrait of the king on one side and the lictor's fasces—"rendering the complete battle-ax, decorated with a ram's head, on the right"—on the other.

The lictor's fasces were thus officially introduced into Italian state iconography. The reference to Rome was hardly sufficient to conceal the strictly party nature of the Fascists' adopted symbol. Now the party itself, whose emblem was the fasces of the Risorgimento, began to adopt the Roman version, presumably to cleanse its emblem of a past that included a symbol of liberty, the Phrygian cap. For Fascism in power, the emblem of the lictor, symbol of unity, strength, discipline, and justice, had a religious meaning; alongside the "sacred vestal fire" it symbolized the sacred traditions of Rome; "the rods and ax are the elements necessary and sufficient to maintain the hearth and defend it in times of need."[57]

More important, the lictor's rods were the emblem of the Fascist revolution and of the Duce's resurrection of the fatherland, which had been prefigured by "the reincarnation of the lictorial fasces." "In the difficult, turbulent, and debased times that tormented our country in the wake of a terrible war for independence—to free Italy from spiritual more than political servitude—the lictorial fasces were heroically grasped by a leader," wrote an eminent archaeologist, "and with this symbol, and with this Duce, Italy was reborn."[58]

The emblem of the fasces as a symbol of the Fascist revolution spread quickly after 1923; it highlighted, according to an expression that quickly caught on, the "new era" that began with Fascism's coming to power. In their revolutionary form, the fasces were inscribed on the marble tablet that recorded the beginning of work on the autostrada linking Milan to the lakes, with the inscription: "In the rule of Vittorio Emanuele III, Duce of the government, Benito Mussolini."[59] In their Roman version, they can be found on the medal commemorating the "First Roman Exposition, 1923," with the inscription *Incipit vita nova* (A new life begins).[60] It was frequently used in both versions in advertising, associated with the ideas of innovation, modernity, and youth.

The Roman version became official when the fasces became a central part of the symbology of the state, developing simultaneously with the new régime. In a circular dated December 1, 1925, Mussolini required that the seal be displayed on all ministerial buildings; after a decree on December 12, 1926 had made the fasces the official emblem of the state, this requirement was extended to all government offices, even in the provinces. According to a deputy called Verdi, who had been the rapporteur for the committee converting the decree into law, the reason for this new official status was that the emblem of the fasces "sums up the traditions of the race and expresses its determination to be worthy of those traditions in a new era of greatness."[61] Simultaneously, any trivialization of the emblem was forbidden; no badge or flag with the lictor's fasces could be manufactured, sold or used without special authorization from government authorities or the Fascist party.[62] On March 1, 1927, the Ministry of Aviation ordered that the fasces henceforth be used on all airplanes under its command.[63] On March 27 it was decreed that the fasces should be added to the left side of the state's coat of arms, which was the shield of the House of Savoy. Early in 1928, Mussolini ordered that all building cooperatives financed by the state should bear the fasces on their façades. On June 14 of the same year, a further impetus was given by extending "the general use [of the fasces], the emblem of the Fascist revolution," as an expression "of the nation's feeling of devotion to the symbol of the régime's ideal." This was set out in a circular from the Prime Minister's Office, together with a decree that authorized the use of the fasces as an adornment on seals and official documents, or on buildings or public works executed by communes, provinces, charitable organizations, and other quasi-governmental organizations.[64] To crown the emblem's rise to prominence, on April 11, 1929, the government designed a new coat of arms for the state that substituted the fasces for the two lions that had supported the 1890 shield of the House of Savoy.[65]

The Rites of the Revolution

The rise of the lictorial fasces to the status of national symbol went hand in hand with the rituals celebrating the advent of Fascism. The very term "Fascist régime," which entered the political language of both Fascists and anti-Fascists on the morrow of the March on Rome, was a clear sign that the government headed by the Duce was not a government like those that had preceded it. The totalitarian orientation of Fascist religion, implicit in its missionary and integralist dynamism, did not express itself solely through its monopoly on the rites of patriotism—thus effectively outlawing any liturgies antagonistic to Fascism[66]—but was above all determined by the establishment of specifically Fascist national rites, such as the anniversary of the founding of the movement and the anniversary of the March on Rome. Alongside the fatherland, what was celebrated on Fascist altars was Fascism itself, and its Duce. In time these rites acquired such force that they began, if not to replace, to be merged with the cult of the fatherland.

The March on Rome was almost immediately garnished with a number of initiatives seeking to point up its nature as a major, epic historical event. In addition to its use in coins and stamps, in February 1923 a committee, headed by the mayor of Rome, was established to promote the erection of a monument in homage to the event.[67]

Mussolini himself chose to celebrate the first anniversary of his government in solemn and spectacular form. Obviously nothing prevented the Fascists from celebrating the rise to power of their leader. The party conceived of a number of measures for the occasion, including the coining of a commemorative medal, with a certificate signed by Mussolini,[68] and the publication of an official manifesto, the work of the painter Galimberti, available to all members of the party and to be "displayed in home, office, school and barracks."[69] The organization of the demonstrations, entrusted to a committee of the Council of State on July 13,[70] was also run by the party. Unprecedentedly, the celebrations were a national holiday, with the participation of the government and the principal civil and military authorities.

According to the program proposed by the committee and approved by the Duce, there were to be four days of celebration, from October 28 through 31. These were to lead off with a speech by Mussolini addressed to all Fascists and the whole nation.[71] All public buildings, barracks and other military installations, as well as private homes (as citizens were urged), were to be hung with flags for the entire period. The event was recalled as a "grandiose ceremony" in which—in Milan, Bologna, Perugia and Rome—"the triumphant march of the black-shirts retraced its route on the same date a year ago." On the morning of October 28, all of Italy saw a commemoration of the "Fascist martyrs fallen in the revolution, from 1919 to the present." An open-air mass was celebrated in the presence of the civil and military authorities, Fascists, the militia, and a large crowd. The committee had envisioned a "possible march" to the Vatican "to forestall any obstinacy from parish priests." The veterans, the mutilated, and war widows' associations were all invited.

The same day in Milan, Mussolini passed in review the legions of the Voluntary Militia for National Security after they had taken their oath,[72] and immediately afterward a parade wound through the city to Piazza Belgioioso, where Mussolini had given his final speech during his unsuccessful electoral campaign in 1919. The place, Mussolini said, was "now sacred to the history of Fascism." While he emphasized loyalty to the monarchy and praised Fascism for having reestablished respect for the army and religion, his speech also contained a warning to his adversaries. "There is no turning back," he said, praising the armed militia for protecting the revolution, and urging it to maintain its readiness for a future "great alarm." In the afternoon Mussolini attended the inauguration of Fascist headquarters in Milan. Fascist offices, he said, "should be temples, not just buildings; they should have powerful, harmonious lines. When a Fascist goes into his headquarters, he should enter a house of beauty, so that his heart will be roused with strength, power, beauty, and love."[73]

On October 29 the celebrations moved to Bologna, where both Mussolini and Giacomo Acerbo, undersecretary in the Prime Minister's Office, recapitulated the legislative and administrative accomplishments of Fascism's first year. In the afternoon another new party headquarters was inaugurated. The next day, in Perugia, a tablet was unveiled in the Brufani Hotel, which had been the Quadrumvirate's headquarters during the March on Rome. The Duce and the Quadrumvirate were given the freedom of the city, and in another speech Mussolini repeated his threats to his adversaries and bellicose appeals to the militia. He extolled the cult of Rome and "our divine land protected by all the gods." Michele Bianchi, the party secretary, declared that Fascism was not just a sign of "national rebirth" but "a new civilization experimenting with history."[74]

For the concluding ceremonies on October 31, Mussolini had planned that government offices should be open reduced hours in the morning, the courts be closed, and a school holiday be given. All Italian embassies and consulates were to fly the flag, all public buildings to be illuminated, and the standard flown on all Italian ships, at home and abroad. The capital provided the backdrop for the climax of the celebration. In the morning, while four hundred planes flew overhead, an imposing procession—led by the Duce and the Quadrumvirate, followed by the commanders of the columns that had entered Rome, the pennants and banners of all Fascist units, representatives of the veterans, the mutilees, mothers and widows of the fallen, the Lazio Fascists, the militia, the gold medalists, and all Fascist political, union, and youth organizations—marched through the city center, from the Piazza del Popolo to the Quirinale, following the route taken by the *squadristi* the year before. Accompanied by bands and songs, the procession took five hours to march—under the flag-filled balconies and windows and through the dense crowd on the streets—to the Altar of the Fatherland, where it paid homage at the Tomb of the Unknown Soldier. The parade then proceeded to the great square before the Quirinale, where the king, watching from the royal balcony, was given the Roman salute by Mussolini and received the homage of the marchers. In the evening Mussolini gave a formal reception in honor of the king in the Palazzo Venezia. There were more than two thousand guests, including the royal princes, members of parliament and the government, the diplomatic corps, high dignitaries of the state, ranking officers of all the armed services, and representatives of the Fascist party.[75]

This "glorification of the Fascist revolution," as the party newspaper characterized it, was a sort of "festival of the Fascist federation": a spectacular review of its power, serving to glorify Fascism and reinforce unity around Mussolini at a time when the party had only just come through a deep internal crisis. The purpose of the ceremonies was to impress sympathizers and intimidate adversaries with the armed power of the party, to be evidence of the consensus on the part of institutions, veterans, and the population that supported Fascism and the government. The celebrations also served to validate in formal fashion the pretensions of the Fascist party to be above and different from the party system, as well as, by transforming a party celebration into a national holiday, setting a seal on the indissoluble union between Fascism and the state.

The extraordinary gravity of the occasion, mixing state and party, did not escape an acute observer like Giovanni Amendola, who considered the commemoration of the March on Rome a symptom of a nascent "party state"[76] and a confirmation of the "totalitarian spirit" of Fascism, determined to impose on all Italians the *credo* of its religion:

> To tell the truth, the most salient aspect of the Fascist demonstration will, for those who study it in the future, be its "totalitarian" spirit. That spirit will not allow future dawns without the Roman salute; it will not allow the present to feed minds that have not yielded to the "credo." This strange "religious war" that has been raging in Italy for a year does not offer a faith (if you want to call this "faith" in Italy, then we could reply that we've long had one, many years before some of its current propagandists discovered it), but on the other hand it denies us a conscience—our own and not someone else's—and takes a leaden grip on the future.[77]

In 1924, in the midst of the crisis caused by the murder of Giacomo Matteotti, the Fascist Grand Council considered celebrating the second anniversary of the march with a less strident program: special attention to the military aspects of the ceremonies, including the oath of loyalty to the king, in two big meetings planned for Milan and Rome on October 28; public demonstrations in party headquarters the next day, along with propaganda sessions; an extraordinary, commemorative sitting in all Fascist and provincial communes on October 30; and an aeronautical display in the capital on the final day.[78] The crisis, which at that time seemed as if it might sweep Fascism away, and which could have led the veterans' associations to dissociate themselves from the Fascist party and the government, induced the Fascist leaders prudently to suggest an essentially

"party function . . . without involving associations or representations from other parties."[79]

The veterans' and mutilees' leadership in fact decided not to participate. Although the ceremonies were less spectacular than the year before, Mussolini still wanted to give an official character to the celebrations; he ordered the same measures as applied to national holidays, including closing all government offices for the whole of October 28, suspending court hearings, and closing public schools.[80] Despite the loyalty oath to the constitution included in the new militia oath, the ceremonies were dominated by a "show of force" by the militia.[81] This was a deliberate act of defiance by an armed party in the name of the Fascist revolution against what remained of the parliamentary régime, against doubtful or repentant supporters, and indeed against any opposition at all.[82] Presiding over the swearing-in of the militia from the turret of an armored car, Mussolini absorbed the loyalty oath to the king by asking the militia to swear fealty also "to the cause of the Fascist revolution, for which we are all prepared to live, to fight, and to die." He chose them as heirs to "my fire, our sacred fire."[83]

With the construction of a totalitarian régime well under way and its triumph over the parliamentary régime, with the opposition routed and marginalized by an ever-increasing state Fascism, and with the definitive identification of the Fascist religion with the "religion of the fatherland," the institutionalization of the rituals of the revolution proceeded apace. "There is no sense," *Il popolo d'Italia* could write on the eve of October 28, 1925, "in reducing the celebration to just a party affair."[84]

For the 1925 anniversary, the party planned a "particularly cautionary and solemn" celebration, one that would keep its "now traditional predominantly military nature," with a militia assembly, marches and celebratory speeches, an aerial review in the capital, and the like. The novelties of the celebration included the ritual placement by the administration of the lictorial fasces on public works realized by the Fascist government. Fascists were also required to wear the black shirt throughout the celebrations. Mussolini further ordered that on October 28, instead of their regular lessons, government schools outside the country should "celebrate and portray the March on Rome, with which Fascism opened a new chapter in our national history."[85] The same had been decreed by the Ministry of Public Instruction for public schools in Italy.[86]

Celebrating the anniversary in Milan, Mussolini declared that October 1922 was "not a mere change of ministries, but the creation of a new political régime," based on the principle of "all to the state, nothing outside the state, nothing against the state."[87] The following year October 28 was included in the liturgy of the state as a full public holiday.[88]

March 23, the anniversary of the founding of the armed Fascist move-ment, remained a party ritual for a longer period. In 1923 the ceremonies were held on Sunday, March 25, and were limited to speeches and un-official marches. Although the speeches extolled the Fascist revolution and its determination not to yield to a restoration of the old régime, the celebration was in fact pretty traditional. Mussolini restricted himself to a pair of congratulatory telegrams, reminding Fascists to remain disci-plined. The party was in full crisis; quarrels, dissent, and rebellions were tearing it apart. The times were not propitious for a large-scale celebra-tion.[89]

In 1924 the anniversary again fell on a Sunday. This time an electoral campaign was in full swing, and the party had recovered its internal unity. The celebrations were given an official character, the program being put together between the party leadership and the Prime Minister's Office. There was to be a procession of Fascist mayors, carrying the standards of their various communes, to the Tomb of the Unknown Soldier and the Quirinale. The mayors would then be addressed by Mussolini, and later there would be a reception at the Campidoglio hosted by the royal com-missioner. At Mussolini's request, the usual flags would be hung and buildings lit.[90] The party organized marches and speeches in every city, centered around a commemoration of Fascist martyrs and the ritual roll call. In Milan, a monument to these martyrs was inaugurated and a tablet unveiled on the palace in the Piazza San Sepolcro to recall to posterity "the few brave sparks roused by Mussolini's desperate passion" who, "gathered here, fashioned the great Fascist movement that brought the Italian people back to its faith in the Fatherland, freedom, the discipline of labor, and the respect of the world."[91]

In 1925 the birth of Fascism was given a strong military stamp with a celebration designed to be "solemn, and a warning to both friend and foe."[92] In the years that followed, Mussolini had his ministers attend the ceremonies and gave Fascist functionaries the day off so they could at-tend.[93] Finally, in 1930, when the Fascist liturgical calendar was over-hauled, March 23 too became a civic celebration.[94]

The Regime's Calendar

The insertion of the symbols and rituals of Fascist religion in the liturgy of the state was paralleled by another symbolic act designed to highlight the revolutionary character of the Fascist régime. In 1923 Mussolini had already begun dating letters in his own hand with "Year One of the Fascist Era" in addition to the date on the Christian calendar,[95] and this usage quickly spread among Fascists. The anniversary of October 28 was hon-

ored as the foundation of the "Fascist era." At the end of 1925 the prefect of Reggio Emilia thought the time had come to recommend to all provincial offices that both the Fascist and the Christian dates be used, "by affixing a Roman numeral, as the Duce does." This practice would "pay homage to the principle that our national life, even in its external appearances, should become entirely Fascist," in the spirit of the "measures taken to affix the lictorial fasces to public buildings, and the use of the Roman salute in the administration."[96] A year later, the minister of public instruction asked the Duce if he could have the "honor" of adding the Fascist revolutionary dating to the scholastic calendar in all official documents of the ministry, "so that it should be ever-present in the minds and hearts of the young," for the schools "were deeply moved by the beauty of the Fascist ideal . . . and live a new life ever since the day on which Fascism willed and achieved their regeneration."[97] Mussolini gave his approval and immediately issued a circular in which he expressed the wish that all official state documents should also bear "the year, counted from the accession to power of the Fascist government."[98]

This decision caused some perplexity in numbering the years. For some, for instance, "Year I" was the period from October 28 to December 31, 1922. The matter drew the attention of the king, who recommended that the Fascist years should be counted from October 28 of one year to October 27 of the next, not merely because the sovereign thought it unsuitable "to the historical importance of the Fascist Revolution to consider two months a whole year," but also because of the analogy to the first French republic.[99] Mussolini concurred and on October 27, 1927, ruled that all state documents should carry the date from the advent of the Fascist government, and that the new Year VI should begin on October 29.[100]

Once the cult of the lictor had become an integral part of Fascist liturgy under the leadership of the party in 1926, it was institutionalized under rigid norms that defined the manner of its development. The first consequence of its institutionalization was a prohibition on spontaneous celebrations, rites, and mass demonstrations. These had frequently taken place in a disorderly fashion and in the most banal circumstances; often they lacked organization, and thus imperiled the seriousness of Fascist liturgical symbolism, as well as compromising the religious and teaching functions that the régime assigned to such celebrations. "It's time to put a stop to such ceremonies, assemblies, and festivals," warned Mussolini; their frequency "strips them of any seriousness . . . and people are wearying of such ceremonies. Here again the proper formula is: rare and solemn."[101] At the request of Emilio Bodrero, Mussolini decided to intervene to limit the number of public ceremonies and demonstrations.[102] He issued a directive to all prefects that they should "control public events and incorporate the important social activity these represent into the spirit of discipline and useful industry that animates the nation; head off such demonstrations which, by their aims, are in opposition to this new consciousness; and limit and coordinate all others in such a way that they are more successful, waste less energy, resources and money."[103]

The government now set out legislative provisions to control public events, convinced that "the choice and coordination of these, inspired by utility and a high sense of national feeling, should raise the social usefulness of these important activities, incorporating them in the nation's search for that ever-higher moral and spiritual level to which the government and the people, in a splendid unity of intent, bend their efforts."[104] And because these measures did not have the desired effect, Mussolini decided to ban, from November 7, 1927, to May 8, 1928, "any ceremony, demonstration, celebration, anniversary, centenary great or small, as well as speeches of any sort: because the authorities should not be distracted from their work; because even minor economies, especially of time, have to be made; and because the public should not become satiated."[105]

These provisions did not apply to lictorial rites, to which this restriction gave an increased display and solemnity; but even for these events measures were adopted that, in harmony with the institutionalization of the Fascist liturgy, now strictly controlled the way in which such rituals were performed. Federal secretaries should curb "too frequent, recurring, too Sundayish manifestations and celebrations," not to shackle or limit "the warlike spirit of Fascism," but because "in a period of painful toil and pressing struggle, festive dress will not do, and should be replaced with a more austere uniform." For these reasons, the federations should reserve "the magnificent spectacle of their combined forces" for great occasions, such as the March on Rome and the founding of the Fascist movement.[106]

The Fascist Grand Council of State fixed the "official calendar of the regime," carefully marking the rhythm of Fascist liturgy and decreeing that "only three days should be devoted to the historic events in the life of Régime and Party": March 23 "for celebrating and affirming the youth movements"; April 21 "to celebrate the forces of production and labor"; and October 28 "for the invocation and exaltation of the event that, with the victory of the Revolution, brought to an end many years of struggle and sacrifice."[107]

The passage of the coffin of the Unknown Soldier. *L'illustrazione italiana*, November 6, 1921.

Giansardi, a propaganda postcard, 1923. The text reads: "Tempered by the fire of the living blood of our martyrs, our force vibrates. Kissed by the hopeful fertility of the olive, the victorious Fascist shines in the blue of our beautiful sky. Eja, eja, eja . . . alala!"

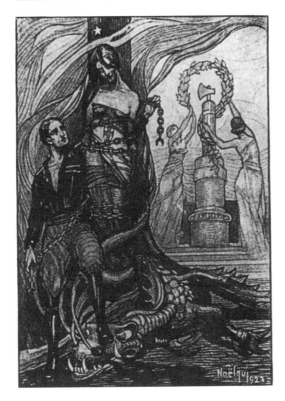

A Fascist postcard, 1923.

Mussolini at the Tomb of
the Unknown Soldier.

Mussolini, party leaders, and members of the government at the Tomb of the Unknown Soldier, November 4, 1937. *La rivista illustrata del popolo d'Italia*, November 1937.

The new Italian state coat-of-arms, adopted in 1929.

Lictorial prize-giving on the occasion of the fifth anniversary of Fascist Youth celebrated in Rome. *La rivista illustrata del popolo d'Italia*, October 1935.

Publio Morbiducci, preliminary model, "La storia de Roma attraverso le opere edilizie" (The history of Rome in its public works). Collection of A. M. Morbiducci, Rome.

Nighttime projections in Piazza del Duomo in Milan for the celebration of October 28, 1933. *La rivista illustrata del popolo d'Italia,* November 1933.

Mussolini speaking in Bologna, October 24, 1936. Central State Archives.

Mario Sironi, *Il Duce*.
Collezione Davide Cugini,
Bergamo.

Foreshortened view of the
façade of the Exhibition of
the Fascist Revolution at the
Exhibition Center. Central
State Archives.

Parade of *Avanguardisti* from the Campo Dux to the Exhibition of the Fascist Revolution, September 12, 1933. *L'illustrazione italiana*, September 17, 1933.

The reopening of the Exhibition of the Fascist Revolution in Valle Giulia in 1937. *La rivista illustrata del popolo d'Italia*, October 1937.

Mario Palanti's sketch of the Eternale Mole Littoria (1926).

Detail of the façade of
the Littoria Post Office.
Riccordo Mariani, ed.,
*Latina, storia di una
città* (Florence: Alinari,
1982), p. 185.

The *Casa del Fascio,* or party headquarters, in Predappio.

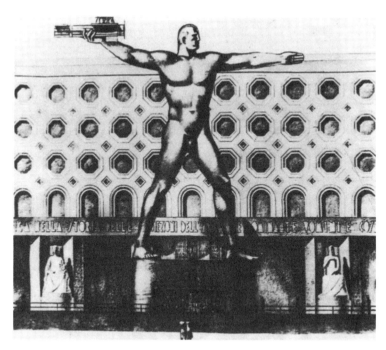

The G. Crescini proposal for the Lictorial Palace, 1934.

The Carminati-Lingeri-Saliva-Terrangi-Vietti-Sironi project (Project A) for the Lictorial Palace, 1934. Above, a model of the project; below, a foreshortened view of the façade.

Del Debbio-Foschini-Morpurgo project for the Lictorial Palace.

Model of the EUR, 1938, with the Arch of the Empire.

Mussolini rewards a colonist in Littoria, December 18, 1933. Riccordo Mariani, ed., *Latina, storia di una città* (Florence: Alinari, 1982), p. 237.

Mussolini among the colonists of the Pontine Marshes. Riccordo Mariani, ed., *Latina, storia di una città* (Florence: Alinari, 1982), p. 253.

3

The Archangel of This World

The true Educator State, which gives consciousness to the masses, which makes them a creating part of history, which directs them toward its own ends, in whose ambit are equally justified life and the work of greater and lesser, strides like a giant before all.

—Giuseppe Bottai

The Fascist State possesses the mystical and properly religious bond of a Church. It exalts principles of sacrifice and renunciation; it professes a philosophy of the heroic life, an antihedonistic way of life, an anti-intellectual and antimaterialistic idea of the world; it works toward the advent of a new, and essentially spiritual, person.

Like a Church, the State further attributes to itself the task of edification, education; it is apostolic and charitable. It consecrates itself to a constant apostolate among the lukewarm and the ignorant. Like Catholicism, with its different orders and congregations, the State multiplies good works: to help its members, to conquer those who still hesitate to believe in the benefits of the régime.

The party's fundamental role is to ensure this "ecclesiastical" role of the State by fulfilling a double function: that of dynamo and zealot of the State.

—Marcel Prélot

After the March on Rome, Fascism—in defining its ideology, in its way of life and the practice of its politics through myth, ritual, and symbolism—emphasized its character as a secular religion. It sought to use traditional religion as a way of smoothing its search for power, purporting to be a restorer of spiritual values and of the prestige of the Catholic religion after a period of agnosticism, atheism, and materialism. Apart from certain anticlerical, iconoclastic, and paganizing attitudes among the early Fascists, from 1921 onward Mussolini extolled the historical importance of Catholicism as "the only universal idea surviving in the Rome of today"[1] and a spiritual power of which Italians should be proud, a power that could "be used for national expansion."[2] Once he came to power, Mussolini cited among his accomplishments that of having neither touched nor diminished the church, "another pillar of Italian national society." Religion, he said, was "the sacred patrimony of peoples."[3]

This, however, was no reason for Fascists to stop referring to Fascism as a religion. They did not hesitate to make frequent comparisons between their movement and Christianity, their intent being to allow traditional religion to reverberate within Fascism, sublimating their own religious pretensions in order, by analogy, to lead a people, an enormous majority of whom were Catholic, to the cult of the lictor. Fascism, affirmed *Il popolo d'Italia,* "is a civil and political faith, but also a religion, a militia, a spiritual discipline that has, like Christianity, its saints, confessors and witnesses."[4] Faith in Fascism, said Mussolini, "my faith, is one that goes beyond a simple party or idea, beyond its necessary military structure, its syndicalism, its members. Fascism is a religious phenomenon of vast historical proportions; it is the product of a particular race."[5]

The Religion Is Revealed

The extraordinary speed of a movement that took power inside of three years readily lent itself to being seen as a miracle, one predicted by Mussolini and his tiny band of early followers. With their sacrifices and struggle, these had spread the word in an Italy devastated by the "triumphant beast" of Bolshevism; had then multiplied into legions of virtuous and manly crusaders, dedicated body and soul to their country; and by their Fascist faith, their readiness for a fresh struggle and new sacrifices, had defeated and slain the "Red Dragon," thus not only saving Italy from Bolshevism but also offering salvation for all mankind.

This transformation of the founding of Fascism into something sacred was already accomplished by 1925, and its main arguments were laid out in an article in the organ of Italian Fascists abroad:

> The mystical element in Fascism is the chrism anointing its triumph. Reason is uncommunicable, so is feeling. Reasoning does not attract; it convinces. Blood is stronger than syllogism. Science pretends to explain the miracle, but in the eyes of the masses, the miracle remains, seduces, and creates its own neophytes.
>
> A century from now, history may tell us that after the war a Messiah arose in Italy, who began speaking to fifty people and ended up evangelizing a million; that these first disciples then spread through Italy and with their faith, devotion, and sacrifice conquered the hearts of the masses; that their language was one in disuse, that it came from such a remote time that it had been forgotten—they spoke of duty when others spoke of rights, of discipline when all had abandoned themselves to license, of family when individualism

was triumphant, of property when wealth had become anonymous, of a fatherland when hatred divided its citizens and alien interests slipped through the frontiers, of religion when all denied it from fear of the ultimate judge. But in the end they won: because they returned good for evil; because they protected their very enemies; because every day they accomplished miracles of love; because every hour told tales of their humble heroism; because when men met them, they became better men; because through their activity Italy became more orderly, peaceful, prosperous, and great; because they had a joyful song in their hearts, and in their eyes shone their sacrifices; because they fell with a cry of faith, and for each man who fell, a hundred sprang up; and because when the truth shines in every part, not even an owl can gainsay it.

This is how Fascism won: through its militia . . . The chalice of sacrifice is offered to the best, and we must drink of it. Then, as Christ said when he drank from the sponge soaked in vinegar, we can say, *Consummatum est.* Its sacrifice is the triumph of others. What matters a single individual? What counts is the race, the stock; its renewal is vital for the good of the fatherland and the world. The Duce has spoken . . . His command is our law—or, better yet, is the unfolding of our own law, that which is already within us. From every part of the world people look to Italy as a beacon to lead mankind to salvation . . . We are the princes, those who cast the die among the new legions of civilization.[6]

The religious side of Fascism was strongly emphasized in the first period of government, from 1923 to 1926, mainly to legitimize its monopoly of patriotism and, as a consequence, its right to a monopoly on power. Every opponent of Fascism automatically became an enemy of the "religion of the fatherland." Hence Fascism could claim the right to persecute and banish those who would not convert to the national cult—that is, who did not accept the Fascist version of this religion. A proper Fascist, as Dario Lupi warned early in 1923, had made a total and definitive commitment:

He who joins us either becomes one of us in body and soul, in mind and flesh, or he will inexorably be cut off. For we know and feel ourselves in possession of the truth; for of all the ideologies, past and present . . . we know and feel ourselves to be part of the only movement in marvelous harmony with the historic time in which we live and with that time now being readied. For ours is the only movement that faithfully reflects the innermost layers of the souls and feelings of our own kind.[7]

The new political religion's tendency to integralism was already in full swing. As *Critica fascista* said on July 15, 1923:

As the Church was always right when it cast heretics out of the communion of true believers, even when these claimed to be of the same faith, so Fascism is right to excommunicate those with heretical views toward the fatherland. Thus Christ, whom some thought meek, almost a liberal, one day took up his scourge and chased the swindlers and moneylenders from the temple, for having desecrated it . . . Fascism is a closed party, not politically but religiously. It can accept only those who believe in the truth of its faith . . . As the Church has its religious dogmas, so Fascism has its own dogmas of national faith.[8]

With this premise, any illusion that a civil religion might come into being that could reconcile the cult of patriotism with that of liberty, as was the ideal of the patriots of the Risorgimento, vanished; simultaneously, the Fascist religion's intolerance grew, and alongside the increasingly Fascist nature of the state, the process of its sacralization now began. The Fascist faith, wrote Ettore Lolini, a convert to Fascism and a noted expert on the problems of a state bureaucracy, was like a "divine madness"; it was "either felt and accepted with heart and mind in all its irrational grandeur, or rejected and loathed and fought against with an equal faith." As Lolini pointed out, however, "only when the Fascist faith and ideal have permeated every institution of the Italian State will the Fascist Revolution have reached its full development."[9]

The New State Acquires a Political Theology

At its origin—at a certain popular level, and especially among the *squadristi*—Fascist religion was for the most part spontaneous, reflecting rebellious spontaneity: an immediate, aggressive, and anarchic emotional response, and a common belief not yet subordinate to the rules of a church. Before the March on Rome, that religion was not yet bound to obedience or to the infallibility of a leader. Once Fascism gained power, however, this spontaneity became incompatible with the need for discipline and unity, the chief preoccupations of a Fascist conception of the new state. *Squadristi* rebelliousness had to be overcome and suppressed wherever it arose; spontaneous symbols and rituals had to give way to an institutionalized, Fascist system of values and beliefs. To the "heroic period" of struggle—while the old, liberal order was being dismantled—there succeeded a "period of reconstruction" needed to build a new order. The country had to pass, so to speak, from religion as something lived in the immediate, to religion as a system of beliefs, as a faith defined and regulated according to the dogmas of a codified political theology.

"Revealed religion," wrote Giuseppe Bottai, "has reached the point where it must set down its codes and build its temples. We need church fathers and builders."[10] Faith "must be made systematic," asserted *Il popolo d'Italia*. "It must be brought down to precise tasks and defined objectives: that is the only way to create a new social order. To achieve this, nothing can be conceded to selfish ambitions, and hierarchies must be extremely firmly anchored in their functions."[11]

Fascist religion was institutionalized thanks in large part to the decisive contribution of idealist intellectuals who for years had been preaching that a crusade was needed to spiritualize politics, to elaborate a political theology. These were either the heirs of the ethical statism of the right or survivors of a painful experience of democracy, and they were in agreement that the state should take on the characteristics of a secular religion, and should therefore expend much of its energy in educating the masses to form a national consciousness.[12] In their eyes, Fascism seemed like a revelation of the long-coveted, long-sought new political religion. As one such intellectual, in charge of the Propaganda Office and deputy secretary of the Fascist party, wrote in 1925: "I joined the Fascist party out of a sense of duty and in the flush of a religious enthusiasm. It wasn't just the peril facing the fatherland, or love of our culture, that led me to do so, but hope for an Italian state that would become the subject of History, which seemed to me the life of God himself. For me, history is a religion; my faith is romantic idealism—that of the Risorgimento, on which Fascism fed."[13]

Romolo Murri, a former priest and promoter of "Christian democracy" and then a radical militant seeking a democratic and religious renewal of the state, saw Fascism as the answer to "an age-old spiritual problem: how to discover a faith that would arouse history in a personal way, some act that would give history a conscience and spiritual, universal worth . . . Today, as in the Risorgimento, the aim is to make Italians into one Nation and one State . . . to seek and firmly establish a vision of national unity . . . and an ethically valid State that would function in our very own consciences." Murri trusted the Fascist government's attempt to carry out a real religious reform in Italian politics, one that would lead to a new national state, because he saw in Fascism the energy and faith of a movement that "acted on conscience and history with enthusiasm, voluntary discipline, heroic dedication to its beliefs, and a religious spirit." Beyond that it was also "a notable example and a living expression of some of the qualities and needs of a contemporary religious conscience." Fascism tended to "invest politics with a mystical afflatus"; it waged an idealistic war against optimism, romantic individualism, Enlightenment ideology, and scientific materialism. Therefore, Murri concluded, Fascism, by maintaining its character as a "religion every bit as religious as political," was in a position to set in motion "that deeply personal religious renaissance that Italian history has invoked and awaited for five centuries."[14]

Like Murri, many other prominent figures involved in the cultural debates between radical nationalism and the modernist avant-garde of the Giolitti years also saw in Fascism the closest approximation to their ideals of a secular religion that would finally "form" the "soul" of the nation. The Fascists had a movement, after all, endowed with power, will, and a *man* who not only had known how to interpret "the fresh religious aspirations of our political conscience," but also was capable of creating a new state.[15] It was no coincidence that the first signs of the Mussolini/Duce myth appeared among these groups, and that certain of these intellectuals helped transform the myth into a cult.

The decisive contribution to Fascism's political theology was that of Giovanni Gentile and many of his followers. Viewing Fascism as a revival of the moral revolution of which Mazzini had dreamed, they gave the primitive religious feelings of early Fascism a much stronger cultural underpinning. Converted to Fascism in 1923, Gentile was, at least until the 1930s, the chief theologian of the new state. Even when his cultural leadership within the régime began to decline, his mark on the Fascist vision of the state remained strong and clear.[16]

Since the interventionist period, Gentile, as spiritual heir to the "prophets of the Risorgimento," felt a political need to give the Italian state a faith and a soul. To him, Fascism was a true religion because Fascists had "that religious feeling through which one takes life seriously"[17] and because it was "a cult born of the whole soul of the nation."[18] Fascism realized Mazzini's political religion in ways that were adapted to modern Italy; it had faced the challenge and survived an ordeal by sacrifice, being reborn through the blood it shed in the Great War. As a "son of the war" itself, Fascism was the "live and active conscience of the new national soul, that of the young Italy . . . that fought the war."[19] From its religiosity, Gentile derived the totalitarian character of Fascist doctrine, which was the expression of an "integral politics, a politics not to be distinguished from morality, from religion, or from all concepts of life."[20]

The task of resolving "the religious question", which had tormented the great figures of the Risorgimento, Gentile assigned to Fascism and its leader. It was their job to complete that uncompleted revolution by creating a new state in which, in totalitarian fashion, the masses would be integrated into the nation. "Step by step, the state should be ready to welcome all Italians into history and the civil state—in fact and not just in word, educating all of them, binding them all to the new faith."[21]

In the Gentilian concept appropriated by Fascism, the state was not only the educator of the masses but the creator of a nation that expressed the moral unity of the people. As such, it was a state that repudiated agnosticism and neutrality as far as values and beliefs were concerned; it faced these as a divine demiurge that "sought to remake not just the shape

---

of human life but also its content, man himself, his character, his faith."[22] More prosaically, *Il popolo d'Italia* declared that more than a party, Fascism was above all "a religion of the Fatherland and duty," which proposed to gather in the many still unconnected to politics and "make Italians of them."[23]

During the régime, formally defining Fascism as the religion of the state became one of the fundamental tenets of its culture; it was universal, endlessly repeated, and confirmed as a kind of ritual formulation in every self-portrait of Fascism, rudimentary or sophisticated. It was used at every level in Fascist propaganda and by all ranks in the hierarchy. As a popular journalist said of the régime in 1925, it was a moral force that gave Italians "order, discipline, a harmonious strength, a will to work, a spirit of sacrifice, a mystical love of country, blind obedience to a single man, and the courage to reform," because Fascism offered a cure for "the ills of modern society without destroying, as Bolshevism did, that society's millennial principles."[24] It was its courage when facing death, wrote Salvatore Gatto in 1928—then a young journalist, a Fascist and *squadrista* since 1919, and deputy secretary of the party in 1941—which proved that Fascism was a true religion, like Christianity: "Fascism is a civil and political religion because it has its own conception of the State and an original attitude toward life . . . Christian martyrs and the young heroes of the Fascist Revolution asserted a single, luminous reality through the years: only a religion can refute and wipe out attachment to mundane life."[25]

In 1932 Mussolini pronounced himself definitively in *The Doctrine of Fascism*: "Fascism is a religious conception of life, in which man is seen in his immanent relationship with a superior law, with an objective will, which transcends any individual and raises him to the status of an initiated member of a spiritual society."[26] This society found its organizing principles in the totalitarian state, in which the *idea of Fascism* was continually made concrete, thus becoming both an institution and a collective faith.

The "True Paradise"

As the party Secretary in Milan, Mario Giampaoli, wrote in 1929: "like the Christian ideal, the Fascist ideal is one in a state of perpetual becoming."[27] By this definition, it was easy to justify contradictions or shifts in certain orientations of Fascist ideology. The philosopher Balbino Giuliano, minister of national education, explained that Fascist religion had not been made rigid through the development of a definitive theology:

We are unable to determine, in its explicit entirety, the Fascist content of any particular idea, because this "Fascist content" partakes of the nature of any great religious idea. Like the sun, such ideas are ever-present, always themselves, and never anything else, but are not contained in any particular concept; from within themselves, they produce theories of concepts because, to repeat myself, these ideas are religious and not theological.[28]

Being syncretic, Fascism welcomed different orientations, but none of these could aspire to be the authentic interpretation of the "faith" or challenge the fundamentals of the Fascist religion. These fundamentals did not leave the "idea of Fascism" in a vaporous or fluid state. Both in theory and in practice they all converged toward the sacralization of the state, facing which the fluidity of the religion rigidified into a dogma that could not be interpreted elastically. Statements of Fascist doctrine, issued by Mussolini with the collaboration of Gentile, were peremptory about the sacred nature of the state vis-à-vis the individual. For the Fascist, "The State is all, and nothing human or spiritual exists, or has any value, without the State. In that sense, Fascism is totalitarian, and the Fascist State, as synthesis and unity underlying every value, interprets, develops, and potentializes people's lives . . . the State is an absolute, and compared to the State, all individuals and groups are relative."[29] Giuliano himself, speaking to students of the School of Mystical Fascism, had spoken of "a divine majesty in the State to which obedience is sweet."[30]

In the sacralization of the totalitarian state as supreme authority in politics, spiritual life, and morals, as the ultimate and only educator of the collectivity, one sees the major outline of the highest ideal of Fascist culture and what its vision of politics really was. In the way it conceived of the state this vision could formally acknowledge Rousseau as one of its precursors.[31] Camillo Pellizzi, one of the most sensitive interpreters of Fascist myths, imagined the state as being almost like "a mystical subject, an archangel of this world." He thought the gravest problem Italy faced was that of "reconstituting in ourselves a religious sense of the State."[32] The Italian statist tradition, and even the neo-absolutist statism of someone like Alfredo Rocco, despite his being the architect of the Fascist state, pales alongside some of the wilder panegyrists of the sacred state among the régime's politicians and intellectuals. Paolo Orano claimed that "the Fascist state can only be conceived of, believed, served, and glorified, religiously," for "adhering to Fascism is a mystical vocation carrying civil conduct over into a religious mission." Even Catholicism, for Orano, should help reinforce the conviction that the state was "omnipotent, the source of all good and of any rising national destiny . . . Anything useful in Catholicism, Fascism absorbs; it feeds on it and makes of the nation-state God's most glorious reign on earth."[33] Bottai himself, for all his frequent polemics against the dogmatism of the most intransigent Fascists, was one of the most passionate promulgators of the cult of the state, which he saw, following Gentile, as a supreme value in society, the highest and most complete manifestation of human spirituality, because in the state "man realizes the highest moral values of his life, and thus overcomes every form of particularism within himself: personal convenience, interests, and life itself, if necessary. It is in the State that we find the highest spiritual values: a continuity that extends beyond time, moral grandeur, and a mission to educate both oneself and others."[34] According to Bottai, "the powerful State is not just the secular branch of the divine, which lives in the mind, but the sign of a sacred authenticity of thought. A heroic State is the ground on which heroic thought expresses itself."[35] The sacred nature of the State naturally made the individual relative, "a transient element, a participant in an enormous achievement that transcends him; he brings his bit to it and then vanishes. His duty is to work with others to build a collective national life, an inexhaustible task."[36]

For philosophers, intellectuals, and party leaders, the exaltation of the state might have been simply a ritual act of dedication performed as a bureaucratic duty. But the idea of a sacred state was not confined to a circle of doctrinaires and bureaucrats. The idea pervaded and dominated the whole symbolic universe of Fascism; it permeated the institutions through which state and party operated to control the intended transformation of the collective consciousness; it slipped into every aspect of public life and education. It was as omnipresent as a divinity that absorbs everything about it, annihilating everything by subordinating it to its own superior collective essence. The Fascist party taught that "from the tenderest years onward, the idea of the State must impress itself on the minds of the young; a myth must be outlined that, with the passing of the years, becomes a form of civil discipline and active militia."[37] The state, Bottai declared, this time in his role as minister of education, had its own morality, "which endows all human activity, and even thought, with a need . . . day by day, to remake the Italian character."[38]

Students in elementary schools were taught that "paradise lies where God's duty is done, and God's will is perceived through the will of the State."[39] A young Fascist who grew up with the régime left an eloquent record of the intellectual climate in which the new generation was educated:

> Fascism was presented to me, and I presented it to myself, as a total concept, a religion, a divinity all its own: the State, with its own supreme worship;

war with its privations, its will to kill and be killed, its all-encompassing way of life, as "a state of idealistic high tension," with a constant disposition to the "supreme sacrifice" . . . The State was all. It was the divinity to which everything should be sacrificed.[40]

Every institution of the régime, from schools to labor syndicates, participated in the sacralization of the educator state and the propagation of the faith. The lead role, however, was taken by the party itself, whose task it was to nurture "the cult of the state among the people," to alter "the icy relationship between sovereign and people to one of religious devotion," the object being to transform "royal subjects into the faithful."[41]

The Religious Military Order

Fascist ideology, the theology of the state, was easily laid out in a "credo" that kept Fascism from having to face doctrinal conflicts. The only "true" interpretation lay in daily observance of the faith, which must be lived as religious, total dedication—at least in regard to the higher aims of life in this world—to the will of the state. To make the meaningfulness of a political militancy based on total obedience and dedication more sublime, Fascism defined the party as "a religious and military Order. It is religious because in its conscience it has a faith of its own; it is military because, obeying its own inner imperatives, it defends its faith and sacrifices itself for that faith. This is the mystical nature of Fascism, a militia of believers in a skeptical, weak-hearted world."[42]

Fascism did not hide the fact that in politics it sought to create a form of organization akin to that of the Catholic church, the chosen model for the construction of a totalitarian state. As Alfredo Rocco noted:

> One of the basic innovations of the Fascist State is that in some respects, like another centuries-old institution, the Catholic Church, it too has, parallel to the normal organization of its public powers, another organization with an infinity of institutions whose purpose is to bring the State nearer to the masses, to penetrate them, organize them, to look after their economic and spiritual well-being at a more intimate level, to be the channel and interpreter of their needs and aspirations.[43]

For totalitarian Fascism, the analogy with the church went well beyond its organizational and social aspects; it included the religious nature of the analogy.

The organization of the Fascist state, noted *Critica fascista*, "in some ways replicates certain of the main characteristics of Roman Catholic organization: power that collects and unifies the work of its members, marks it with its own character, makes of its own ends the highest goal of their lives as citizens, and does not tolerate civil or political heresy."[44] As a religious idea, wrote Carlo Scorza in 1931, when he was secretary of the organization of Fascist Youth (Fasci giovanili) and about to undertake a violent campaign against Catholic Action, Fascism learned from "the greatest and wisest teaching in recorded history," not that of meek and humble saints, "but of those great and imperishable pillars of the Church, its great saints, its pontiffs, bishops, and missionaries: political and warrior spirits who wielded both sword and cross, and used without distinction the stake and excommunication, torture and poison—not, of course, in pursuit of temporal or personal power, but on behalf of the Church's power and glory." As the "great new civic religion of the Fatherland," Fascism should draw inspiration from "this great school of pride and intransigence."[45] Scorza thought the party, through its youth organizations, should increasingly become an "armed religious order" modeled on the Society of Jesus and consecrated to the "Mussolini myth."[46]

An important part of the institutionalization of Fascist religion was played by Fascist party secretaries. Roberto Farinacci, secretary from 1925 to 1926, justified the integralist policy of the party, which helped install the régime with "Dominican faith." But the definitions of the institutional forms taken by the cult of the lictor were the work, above all, of Augusto Turati (secretary, 1926–1930). In his speeches, especially those to the Fascist Youth, this "new apostle of the religion of the Fatherland"[47] preached the need to "believe absolutely: to believe in Fascism, in the Duce, in the Revolution, as one might believe in the Divinity . . . We accept the Revolution with pride, we accept these dogmas with pride; even if we are shown they are wrong, we accept them without argument."[48] In 1929 Turati sponsored the publication of a catechism of "Fascist doctrine" to settle the orthodox interpretation of the "Fascist faith" against "twisted concepts and expressions" and to reaffirm that Fascism was based on "the subordination of all to the will of a Leader."[49]

His successor, Giovanni Giuriati (secretary, 1930–1931), intensified the fideistic and dogmatic side of Fascist religion, especially among the young. He developed the youth organization to form the missionaries and soldiers of the Fascist religion, according to the command of the Duce, who in 1930 coined the slogan "Believe, Obey, Fight" as a sort of viaticum for the recently constituted Fascist Youth. Finally, during the long secretaryship of Achille Starace (1931–1939), the formalization of the Fascist religion, through constantly proliferating and rather automatic rituals, together with a meticulous definition of the rules of life for a Fascist, reached its apogee—indeed sometimes overreaching the limits of the ridiculous in an exasperated search for a conformity of behavior such as to produce conformity of conscience and belief.

This regulatory tendency was not without its logic. The party probably did not fear ridicule: it was convinced that in the end, the uniform, or better yet, the style, the rules of moral and civic behavior, fixed by the rigid parameters of an orderly marking of the events of public life, together with many other occasions to exercise civic virtue and bear witness to the faith, would determine a change in character leading to the birth of the "new Italian."

In 1938 the party published a new catechism of the Fascist religion. In question-and-answer form, it was designed to give Fascists a "simple guide, such as might be needed for the cultivation of the mind as for the relationships of daily life."[50] As *Critica fascista* admonished, every generation should get used to considering it "the primer of its faith."[51]

In the Beginning Was the Faith

The process of institutionalizing the Fascist religion emphasized formal political participation in the party. In essence, this meant complying with its beliefs and adopting a life-style in strict conformity to the precepts put forth by the Duce, or by the party in his name.

The essence and aim of this life-style were summed up in its *faith,* a key word in the political language of Fascism: "The whole soul must be illuminated at the hearth of the Faith; one should believe in the Fatherland as one believes in God . . . this Italy of ours, already so divine as God gave it to us, must be made godlike to all," proclaimed *Il popolo d'Italia* on the morrow of the celebrations marking the first anniversary of the March on Rome.[52] The preamble to the party's new statute, drawn up in 1926, solemnly stated that Fascism was "above all a faith, with its own confessors."

Identifying the party as a military and religious order also helped stifle internal dissent;[53] it enabled the party to expel rebels as "betrayers of the faith" and to impose absolute obedience on its members. Signing up for the Fascist party involved more than adherence to a political program; it implied total dedication, sealed with an oath. The formula for this oath was significantly modified during the régime; allegiance was no longer to the country, as in the early days, but specifically to the Fascist cause: "I swear to obey without argument and serve with all my heart the orders of the Duce and, if necessary with my blood, the cause of the Fascist Revolution."[54] Later, following polemics with the church, the words "In the name of God and Italy" were added.[55] The variation was significant not only because Italy appeared alongside God to solemnize the oath, but also because it confirmed institutionalized Fascist militancy as a religious duty, based on faith and practiced with absolute obedience.

The Fascist oath, the *Dictionary of Politics* explains, "is no platonic adherence to an ideological system, but a deliberate, willed expression of intransigent loyalty to a doctrine that is not mere words but a way of life. It is both political credo and a 'call' to action with a deep idealistic content." When a Fascist takes his oath, "he makes an act of faith: his conscious and wholehearted acceptance of the Fascist order, with all that entails."[56] Any infringement of the oath was punished by expulsion; the offender was a "traitor to the cause" and was "banished from political life." This sanction, the equivalent of Catholic excommunication, was strengthened in 1929, and for "political life" substituted "banished from public life."[57]

The ideal "Fascist man" was the warrior-disciple of a religion, and that was the model proposed from infancy to each new generation as it joined one or another party organization. The perfect product of a Fascist education was "a six-year-old *Balilla* who swears loyalty to the Duce, marches in formation to the beat of a drum, doesn't hang on to his mother's skirts, who is frightened, but nonetheless dreams of fighting and dying for his country."[58] Young Fascists were above all exhorted to believe blindly in the Duce: "Always have faith. Mussolini gave you your faith . . . Whatever the Duce says is true. The Duce's words are not to be contested . . . Every morning, after your 'Credo' in God, recite your 'I believe' in Mussolini."[59]

The organ of the Fascist Youth proclaimed in 1932 that "Fascism is a way of life, and thus a religion. A good Fascist is religious. We believe in a mystical Fascism because it is a mystique with its martyrs, its devotees, and humbles a whole people before an idea."[60] "Faith" was the highest value for political militancy; it was the "Fascist man's" main quality, more important than intellectual capacity. Culture and intelligence counted for less than devotion to the dogmas of the Fascist religion. During the régime, at least in principle, it was ruled that "faith" should have precedence over "competence," because "faith has an integral value."[61] The official text on Fascist doctrine, as used in the politics courses by the party in forming new cadres, taught that "only faith can create a new reality."[62]

All of this was consistent with the concept of the party as a religious and military order. The party was the seminary in which the future apostles and fighters of the Fascist religion were formed, alongside the new leaders of the state-as-church. The principal party rituals make plain the similarity between Fascist and Catholic militancy. The Fascist "Calling to the Colors" (Leva Fascista), created in 1927, played a similar role to confirmation in the Catholic liturgy. It was a form of rite of passage in which young people drawn from the Youth movement confirmed their faith in Fascism and became "consecrated" as Fascists by being made party members.

The ceremony took place throughout Italy, but with the greatest solemnity in Rome, where it was held in the presence of the Duce. The young were presented with a symbolic party card and a rifle: "The former is the symbol of our faith; the latter the instrument of our power," proclaimed Mussolini at the inaugural "Calling to the Colors."[63] After the roll call of Fascist martyrs, the new recruits swore to "execute the Duce's orders without question" and to serve the cause of the Fascist revolution with all their strength, if necessary with their blood. The party secretary, who conferred the "highest Fascist chrism,"[64] was a "priest speaking in a mystical tongue, with a life-giving summons."[65] "Tomorrow," he said to the recruits, "I may ask you to account with your life or death for your every act, your every gesture, whether good or ill."[66]

The Keeper of the Sacred Flame

Beyond the personal convictions of the high priests of the régime, the role of the party in the institutionalization of the Fascist religion was also buttressed by more pragmatic considerations. It was how the party maintained and legitimized its primacy over other Fascist organizations. The party alone, on orders from the Duce, was responsible for safeguarding the "flame of the revolution." As the official texts for the party's courses in politics put it, the party acted within the Fascist state as "spiritual leavening, as a flame fed by the blood of the fallen."[67]

For both militants and the masses, the cult of the fallen played a fundamental role in the birth of early Fascist liturgy; it kept its place of honor in the cult of the lictor. Martyrdom for the "cause" was at the peak of Fascist moral values. Like every other religion, this was Fascism's way of transforming the problem of death: it exalted the communal feeling that integrated individuals into the group. He who died in the Fascist faith entered its mystical world and gained immortality in the collective memory through the liturgical celebration of the heroes and fallen. As the deputy secretary of the party, Arturo Marpicati, wrote:

> All great enterprises have their heroes; all faiths have their saints. The cult of heroes originates in the fact that even after death these live on as a benevolent force for the cause in which they fell. He who faces death for a cause can be certain of the continuity of his work beyond mortal life. It is for this certainty, sealed with his martyrdom, that he truly lives in the continuity of all generations: an immaterial force, but one of a power without limits.

In the Lictorial Palace (Palazzo littorio), seat of the National Fascist Party headquarters, there was a "votive chapel" in which burned an inextinguishable flame. It was lighted by the Duce himself, with fire offered by a *Balilla*:

> The flame illuminates the words with which Mussolini consigned the martyrs' glory to eternity. Overhead is the motto: *Believe, obey, fight*. To the side shine the words: *Fell for Fascism—shall live—in the hearts of the people—forever*. In front, solemn, is the Promise: *The sacrifice of the Black-Shirts consecrates—the Lictorial Revolution—certain of a future—in the glory of the motherland*.[68]

Every Fascist headquarters had a "sanctuary" in which the fallen were remembered, together with their banners, the relics of their martyrdom, and mementos of the "heroic period." To preserve through the centuries the memory of "the heroic sacrifice of those who died for the black-shirt revolution" (so the dedication read), an altar was built on the Capitoline Hill in 1926. Along with the Altar of the Fatherland, this was the spiritual heartland of all the ceremonies that took place in Piazza Venezia. The roll call, read on all Fascist anniversaries, periodically renewed the memory of the martyrs, and on the anniversary of their death Fascists went on pilgrimage to the fatal site, marked by a tablet or a monument. Where three Fascists had been killed in Milan, a "votive fountain" was built in memory of the martyrs as a symbol of the resurgence of fresh energy.

Public works of the régime were frequently named after a martyr. As frequent was the dedication of a tree, a symbol of life, of solid roots in the native soil and of rising to heaven. On occasion special shrines were built, as in Bologna, to bring the martyrs' bodies together in one place. The remains of Fascists killed in Florence were translated in 1934 to a sanctuary dedicated to them. There was a solemn ceremony broadcast throughout the country. "The new shrine," the organ of the Fascist Youth wrote, "suggests the exaltation of a good death."[69]

The priestly function of the party, to which party leaders were greatly attracted, was made manifest through powerful symbolic representations designed to make the party's role in civic life "sacred." Local party headquarters were thought of as "the churches of our faith," "the altars of that religion of the Fatherland," in which "we cultivate the memory of our dead" and "seek to purify souls."[70] The party venerated the sites or squares of early demonstrations as "sacred places," as it did the "Den" *(Covo)*, the first office occupied by Mussolini's newspaper, Piazza San Sepolcro, and Piazza Belgioioso.

Part of this priestly task was the custody and veneration of party symbols. As we have seen, the benediction of the pennants was from the beginning one of the most "sacred" of Fascist rituals. The pennants were always blessed in the name of the martyrs of Fascism; they were the symbols of the spiritual unity, including both the living and the dead, of a particular squad. Carlo Scorza, at the time federal party secretary in Lucca, reported that in 1928, during a ceremony in Valdottavo, as the pennants were about to be blessed, no priest was present. Scorza took three pennants in his hands and blessed them himself in the name of the martyrs of Fascism. In his speech he said:

> We have blessed our pennants ourselves because when we used to go out to get our throats cut, we didn't ask for any blessings, and not because what we were up to was irreligious. But after we've given their dignity back to priests, after having put the cross back in schools from which it had been banished, we have the right do without a blessing from God, although we all have Him in our hearts. Our blessing carries with it the blessing of all the mothers, wives, and orphans after the war. It carries the blessing of all the blood spilled, and you could take all the holy water in the world, and we still wouldn't have a more saintly blessing. Let these flags wave in the sun; you can be sure they are no less noble than any other. And when these black pennants belonging to the *Balilla* and the *Avanguardisti* face the tattered white emblems of Catholic circles whose program is unknown, our standards will certainly not be lowered.

Scorza concluded with a salute to the fallen: "Valdottavo should be a Fascist Altar . . . Two dead and four wounded have made this a holy place, and you people must be worthy of them."[71]

Throughout the régime the party symbols retained their sacred functions at all levels of the organization; given official status within the party, they were imposed as well on all Italians.[72] Particularly stringent regulations applied to the use of the lictorial fasces, badges, and the "black shirt" to protect their "sacred character" as emblems of the Fascist faith. Fascist pennants, according to a 1929 statute, were "a symbol of the faith." An Honor Guard of the Militia, with an officer in command, escorted then during official ceremonies. The pennants of the national party directorate and of provincial federations were likewise accorded full military honors.[73] Great symbolic significance was given the standards of the secretary general and the Duce, and special homage was accorded them during "sorties" for mass assemblies or meetings of party leaders.

The first of all such pennants, that of the Fasces of Milan, was given the homage due a holy relic. In 1932, on the anniversary of March 23, a special ceremony took place in the "sacred and historic" Piazza San Sepolcro, when a new banner took the place of the old. The speaker, folding "the glorious banner," invoked "our dead" who, "having agreed to receive the old flag, raised it over there, where, like the livid light of their sacrifice, it will shine forever, eternally feeding our faith." When the new flag was unfurled in the breeze, the crowd saluted "the old flag while the heroic patrol carried it on high, an eternal ensign marking their holocaust and our faith."[74]

The increased priestly role of the party in the lictorial rites, especially during the period of Starace's secretaryship, was part of a silent strategy to expand its power within the state. In 1932 Starace sought to make the symbolic presence of the party more resonant by decreeing—once again in imitation of the Catholic tradition—that every party headquarters should include a "lictorial tower with bells," which would be rung on party occasions. With its bells, "both mystical and popular," as the Fascist Youth organ explained, the party was invoking a centuries-old civic and religious tradition, thus making its "original and ever more lively form of religion" more expressive. It was a "political religion, deriving from a virile, Roman spiritual education, which can't help but integrate itself with the religion of the divinity."[75] With these moves the party laid claim to its function as keeper of the Fascist ideal and propagator of its faith.

Fasces and Cross

In asserting the holistic spirituality of the state in the pages he devoted to Fascist doctrine, Mussolini had no intention of placing a new god on the nation's altars, as Robespierre had done. He recognized "the God of ascetics, of saints, and of heroes, alongside God as he is seen and prayed to in the honest, basic hearts of the people." He added that the Fascist state had neither a theology nor a set of ethical principles. Nonetheless, by arrogating to the state its own morality, Fascism took over the fundamental function of religion—the right to define the meaning and ultimate aim of human existence for millions of men and women—and it did so according to its own totalitarian conception of politics, which made of the state the supreme and absolute value. A jurist explained that in the Fascist state, "the ethical principle defines religiosity, and it is not religion that determines its ethical imprint."[76] Gentile noted that the state controlled religion "for its own objectives, and in this respect governs it, the State at any given moment being able to contradict religion, especially in regard to peace and war."[77]

In reality Fascism did not limit itself to venerating the traditional God, "the patrimony of the religion of the fathers," but substantially intervened in the world of religion, constructing a universe of its own of myths, of rituals and symbols all centered on the sacred nature of the state. In this sense it rivaled the Catholic church in the formation and control of the Italian conscience. Aware, however, of the failure of other experimental civic religions that had challenged the established church, it cautiously avoided direct confrontation. Its attitude toward the church was more of a matter of political realism than ideological fanaticism; it practiced what we might call a syncretic form of cohabitation, looking to associate Catholicism with its own totalitarian project. As Armando Carlini observed, "Mussolini understood only the human and historical side" of religion. He was a "layman, a pure layman," and remained a close "disciple of Nietzsche." As such, "the ethics of Fascism as created by him is entirely a celebration of the basic principles of paganism."[78]

Mussolini had great regard for the value and power of religion in collective life; its faith and its mystico-symbolist tradition had deep roots in the consciousness of the masses. He was therefore convinced that Fascism, while laying claim to primacy in the politics and ethics of the Fascist state (which "is Catholic, but is also Fascist, indeed, above all, essentially Fascist")[79] should avoid a war of religion, for in this domain, it was highly probable that it would lose. In a secret and previously unpublished report to federal leaders early in 1930, Mussolini gave clear directions on this subject:

> There is no need to get all tied up with antireligiousness and give Catholics reason for unease. We need instead to multiply our efforts in education, sports and culture. Until priests start with triduums and processions and the rest, there's nothing we can do. A fight on this ground between Church and State, the State would lose. Catholic Action is another matter. There confrontation is a duty. When it comes to religion, maximum respect—which Fascism has always given. To win individual souls, we need the appropriate means, not exaggerating the difficulties or depressing ourselves by considering these difficulties as insurmountable. A Holy War in Italy? Never! Priests will never get the peasant to rise against the State . . . At most, consent; show ourselves deferential toward religious processions and the like, in anything that regards the salvation of the soul. Protestants save their own souls, but we are Catholics and we let priests do their work. On the other hand, when they try to interfere in politics, socially, in sport, then we fight them.[80]

Keeping to this realistic line, four years later the Duce was to reaffirm his convictions on state-church relations, allowing himself, to make his thoughts clearer, an ironic allusion to certain neopagan tendencies proliferating in Nazi Germany. At the time, the Duce did not much like Nazism. He chose a foreign forum for his declarations:

> In the Fascist concept of a totalitarian state, religion is absolutely free and, within its own sphere, independent. It never even remotely entered our heads to found a new religion of the State, or to subject the religion professed by all Italians to the State. The State's duty does not consist in writing a new

gospel or other dogmas, in overthrowing old gods substituting them with others, called "blood," "race," "Nordic," and things of the kind. The Fascist State does not consider that its duty requires it to intervene in religious matters, and this happens only when religion touches on the political or moral order of the State. . . . A State that has no desire to disseminate spiritual disturbance and create divisions between its people should beware of any intervention in strictly religious matters.[81]

Considering what we have seen of declarations about the Fascist religion and the sacred nature of the state, we are entitled to certain reservations about these statements of Mussolini's. Beyond his desire to avoid a war against religion because of a thoughtful and realistic evaluation of the risks involved in so doing, these statements are altogether too reticent, if not completely hypocritical, when compared with his more committed statements regarding the Fascist religion. At least in the sense that it never occurred to any Fascist to interfere in doctrinal matters, and even less so to advance any personal, reforming view of church theology, Fascism's interest in Catholicism can be called purely political, not theological. The privileged recognition of the church in the Lateran Treaty, as the refusal to open up religious arguments, was dictated by the desire to use traditional religion as an *instrumentum regni*. This, however, was no impediment to Fascism's emphatic repetition, on every possible occasion, of its claim to being a religious movement, to having a clear religious concept of politics, one that postulated the absolute of the state as against the relative of the individual, one that never ceased to claim for this religious state an unarguable right to define the morals of the citizen and the ultimate aim of his existence.

Whatever the declarations of principle, the Fascist régime displayed in an entirely coherent manner an enormous array of commitment and energy in order to intensify its totalitarian conquest of the country's conscience; it devoted great energy to the continual elaboration of its own forms of cult and secular religiosity; it intervened daily, with a meticulousness that was little short of obsessive, in matters of behavior, custom, civic morality, *style;* it sought unremittingly, through national education, omnipresent and dominant in every stage of a citizen's life, to accelerate the process of transforming the national character. Throughout the régime, but particularly in moments of tension, Fascism, as both government and party, waged a constant "war of symbols" against the church and Catholic organizations; it prohibited Catholic use of banners, standards, or insignia bearing the colors of the pontifical flag; it competed with the church by spreading the use of a civic bell tower in Fascist headquarters; in short, it stopped at nothing to propagandize its own religion.

This inevitably left the door open to potential conflicts between the totalitarian state and the church. In this respect it is interesting to recall what the party's *Dictionary of Politics* had to say under the entry "Church." The church, wrote one of the principal collaborators in the dictionary, "operates on human conscience to pass to that conscience its own ideal patrimony as a continuity"; it was "inevitable . . . that it should come up against the activity of the State, which, when it has a moral content that it wishes to put into action, must also have a profound effect on those same consciences. The element of dissent between Church and State, when the latter is animated by its own moral will, lies in the very reality of things." Such a dissidence could be resolved either by a compromise that recognized the reciprocal values and spheres of action of each, or by convergence, in which both were "different expressions of an identical human conscience, historically determined, which manifest themselves on two distinct planes." In the latter case, "religion is, in politics and the state, but the concrete form of the latter," a value as a "means to raise the spirituality of the people", an "essential element of the nation" in terms of the historical form in which it was shaped: "the concrete forms of religion, the organization of the Church, its rituals, the ethical principles of its work on earth, reflect the history of the people among whom it came into being."[82]

The totalitarian nature of Fascism, which viewed politics as the highest form of a complete life, naturally pushed it to blur the distinctions between the political and the religious, thus causing a grave problem to the marriage between Fascism and Catholicism. There was an inevitable ambiguity in the relationship between two faiths each of which, in its own domain, dealt with the ultimate meaning and ends of life. For instance, not all Fascists were inclined to interpret the sacred nature of the state in so radical a manner as to make it incompatible with Catholicism. Some, while allowing that Fascism was a civic and political religion, insisted on the primacy of Catholicism. Others had contradictory, elusive, or ambiguous attitudes in this regard and sought to reconcile their sincere faith in Fascism as a political religion with personal devotion to the church. The latter perhaps thought that their dilemma might be resolved by a symbiotic relationship between Catholicism and Fascism, each in its own way being *totalitarian* and *Italian* religions; they yearned for a joining of their forces to pursue the common objective, a "new civilization," its heart being in the holy city of the "religion of the fathers" and of the lictorial cult.

Bottai's position was typical in this regard. Having overcome a youthful Mazzinian anticlericalism, Bottai had rediscovered in 1922 that "the spiritual substratum of our race, in the highest expressions of its thought as in its humblest manifestations of life," was "undeniably Catholic." This made the Church of Rome a "factor in national life that could not be overlooked by anyone seeking to regenerate the life of the nation" and in the search for "ways to create a higher form of order for both individual and collective life." This was a problem that the "new morality born of the war" had "solved with anguish" for the new generation in Italy.[83] Along the same lines, Bottai developed, in a way that made sense to his personal, totalitarian vision, his own religious conception of Fascism, "which is not just a physical activity, but something rather more than a doctrine. It is a political and civic religion that does not exclude, but rather includes, the ecclesiastical, conferring on the latter a deep vital substance, a continuous connection to life itself, in all that is most worthy and noble. From this point of view, Fascism is simple, clear, linear: it is the religion of Italy."[84]

On the Catholic side, despite compromises, understandings, a common tone, and various convergences, those Catholic consciences most refractory to the wooing of Fascism and the seductions of an arranged marriage were not unaware of the basic insidiousness concealed in the proposed symbiosis between secular and religious totalitarianism. As early as 1924 one fiery Catholic polemicist had warned against a "Catholicism" co-opted by the "Fascist religion" and against "captious suggestions and carefully orchestrated manifestations" seeking to make the world believe in "the existence of a marriage . . . between universal Christianity and nationalist paganism." The truth was that Fascism, "by its totalitarian nature, self-centered, all-absorbing, tolerates no isolated, uncontrolled forces outside its own jealously guarded seraglio. It takes a dim view of a Church that proceeds freely down its clear and peaceful ways towards eternal life [and feels that] the Church, too, should conspire in this rebirth, in this new era, these parades and rallies, this *duce*-like pomp."[85]

Some years later Luigi Sturzo, forced into exile, gave further warning that Fascism was "a fundamentally pagan doctrine and opposed to Catholicism"; it was "statolatry and deified the nation." Fascism "admits neither discussion nor limitation: it wants to be worshiped for itself; it wants to create a *Fascist State*."[86] Even in the periods of greatest cordiality between state and church the highest levels of the church hierarchy remained fearful that the state's totalitarian supremacy and the political syncretism of the Fascist religion were likely to be a serious threat to the religious supremacy, the autonomy and the universality of the church. In 1931 Pius XI had to intervene with an encyclical to express the church's firm condemnation of Fascist "religiosity," the party oath, its worship of the state, its claim to a monopoly of the education of the younger generation, and its domination of private consciences.[87]

With an eye on a form of syncretic marriage, Fascist religion managed not to become a direct antagonist of Catholicism—notwithstanding the extremist, anticlerical wing of the party or partisans such as Julius Evola, who sought a traditionalist paganism[88]—because it had properly evaluated the risks in so doing to the stability of the régime, nonetheless tried to absorb the church into its own mythical universe. Catholicism, Fascists thought, could be syncretically absorbed into the Fascist religion as a "religion of the fathers," thus as a creation and component of the traditions of the "Italian race," and not, therefore, as a universal "religion of man" revealed by God. For Mussolini, Catholicism, born as an oriental sect, had become universal only by transplanting itself to Rome and putting down the foundations for its development in imperial traditions. Rome had "witnessed one of the religious miracles of history, through which an idea that ought to have destroyed the might of Rome was converted into a doctrine reflecting its greatness."[89] The Duce may have thought a similar miracle would take place in Fascist Rome. The church was not revered by Fascism as a depository of revealed, divine truth, but was recognized and respected as a *hierophant of Romanity*, a creation of the Italian race and possessing the vital patrimony of its traditions.

In an article called "Eternal Rome," written in a quasi-oracular style, Giovanni Gentile proposed his own rather special interpretation of the Romanity of Catholicism.[90] In terms of understanding the place assigned to Catholicism in the Fascist religion, to gain its support and to confirm the Fascist attempt, *qua* religion, to capture a fragment of eternity in human history, it was a significant essay. The chief characteristics of Romanity, Gentile wrote, were its universality and eternal nature. The "first eternal Rome" was imperial Rome, "creator of the State . . . that begins to act as a State, as the Be-all and End-all of men, outside of which no man can find anything of value." "A new Rome," that of Christianity, "attached itself to Rome-as-a-State, and from it drew new vigor and form." But the new Rome led to the undervaluation of the state and its subordination to the church, making a new Caesar of the Bishop of Rome and creating a "new empire—political, but above all, religious." It "create[d] a political religion by the very act with which it raise[d] political relations to the level of religiosity." For this reason, the "new Rome" was "the same old imperial Rome, spiritualized and raised to the level of religion," thus confirming its "effective eternity" even if the political Rome should fall apart and into decadence, because Roman civilization now continued to talk to the peoples of the world, spreading the spirit of Romanity throughout the world. Italy's political renaissance found it necessary to destroy papal Rome in order to create the new Rome of a united Italy, but at the same time felt anguish at thus losing the feeling of Rome's universality, Rome now becoming no more than "the seat of government of one state among many," by which it lost the right to speak to "and be heard by all civilized peoples." The "third Rome sought the Word with which it could save eternal Rome, and itself." Only with Fascism was this prayer vouchsafed, because, as Gentile argued, "Mussolini understood the greatness of the immanent and eternal, Roman and Christian, Italy," bringing back to life and recombining the cult of "Rome-as-a-State" and "Rome-as-a-Church," thus conferring on all Italians a universal mission.

With this vision of the relationship between Romanity, Catholicism, and Fascism, Gentile showed Fascism how it could, as a religion of the state, conquer both eternity and universality. It was to absorb within itself both the "State Rome" and the "Church Rome." From this synthesis it could build a new, universal civilization, in which Catholicism would be a constituent and inseparable part of Italian identity in the common search for Romanity.

The Modern Romans

The ideal of a Fascist religion, in fact, harked back to the religion of the "ancient City," and especially to the Roman religion, which sacralized political order in the cult of the state, allowing other cults only to the extent that these were not in conflict with the state religion. Before it was ever advanced by Fascism to give luster to its colonial conquests, the myth of Romanity had entered into Fascist culture, mainly to legitimize its totalitarian aspirations and create a new religion of the state.[91] A learned Romanist, and the main cultivator and propagandist of Romanity in the Fascist period, explained that the guiding principle of the Roman state lay in an "ethico-religious concept in which the essential reasons for the existence and power of the State are raised to the level of symbols of faith."[92]

> Roman civilization based its greatness on the vivid realization that an order existed to which every moment of human existence must be subjected . . . an order in which preeminence is reserved to political values, in the sense that whatever appearance life and history bear, including those of religion and ethics, the dominant moment . . . the essential end is that of their organization in the light of common interests and rising power. Religious precepts, ethical norms, judicial principles are no more than the development of this one original, fundamental, political reason.[93]

Fascism sought to bring "the spirit of Roman creative power" back to life, a power that "in the family, in religion, in military education, and in its laws had managed to instill sacred respect for the principle of the subordination of the individual to the collective."[94] In its totalitarian state,

Fascism sought to recreate that "intimate spiritual nexus between family and state, between state and religion, all in that perfect equilibrium" which had given "the Roman conscience a grounding in virtue, knowledge, and discipline, the secret of greatness."[95]

Along with the myth of the Duce, the myth of Rome was the most pervasive belief in the whole Fascist symbolic universe.[96] When Mussolini celebrated the Founding of Rome as a public holiday, he raised Romanity to the level of a myth that should give life to Fascism: "Rome is our point of departure and our reference; it is our symbol, or, if you wish, our myth."[97] Fascism's cult of Romanity was not moved by love and archaeological respect for some original identity in the past that ought to be recovered and restored; nor was its passion for archaeology animated by science, or even respectful of scientific requirements. In fact it didn't cavil at destroying sites or allowing arbitrary restorations or innovations—as in the building of the Piazzale Augusto Imperiale[98]—or hesitate to "create the monumental Rome of the Twentieth Century."[99]

Fascism practiced a kind of "symbolic archaeology," an updating of the vestiges of Romanity, inspired by the call of a once-upon-a-time "sacred center"; it wished to enter into communion with the "magic power" of Romanity in order to create, quite arbitrarily if need be, an urban and monumental cityscape that would embody in visual terms and in new "sacred spaces" the symbiosis between Fascism and Romanity; it sought a mix of ancient and modern, the resulting whole to be a celebration of the lictorial cult in the Eternal City, one that showed Fascism to be the inheritor and culmination of the Roman tradition.

A fine example of how the Fascist cult of Romanity was used to advance the lictorial cult was the 1937 Exposition devoted to the Fascist Revolution, inaugurated by Mussolini on September 23 as part of the celebration of the bimillennium of Augustus. It was an intentional statement of the symbiosis between Fascism and Romanity. The political motive for the Augustan Exposition, beyond its careful scientific organization, was to celebrate the everlasting and universal nature of Rome, which, said Giulio Quirino Giglioli, the creator and organizer of the exhibition, "under the leadership of the Duce . . . has once again taken up its destined [civilizing] mission" to the modern world.[100] Turning to Mussolini, he said: "Your work as *civis romanus* is present and life-giving—not merely in what you say, but in the spontaneous connection between so many of your deeds to those of the greatest Romans of two thousand and more years ago," and especially to Caesar and Augustus, symbolically conjoined in the figure of Mussolini.[101]

Visitors, who were to number nearly a million by closing day on November 7, 1938, could make a "journey through Roman civilization," illustrated with imposing documentation—plaster casts, photographs, reproductions of monuments and statues, drawings, models, copies of pictures, sculptures, and mosaics—and inscriptions from Latin writers alternating with those of Mussolini, this leading in turn to the display of Rome's influence and survival in Christianity and the Middle Ages, and concluding with Fascism.[102]

What Fascism was doing, according to Bottai, was transvaluing Romanity "into our own world and time," making it active and alive "in time, according to our times and in our own time." This was no "idea petrified in this or that traditional form, but alive and in action . . . belonging to our own current awareness of politics and history": "The return to Rome brought about by the Black-Shirt Revolution is . . . a renewal of the idea of Rome in the consciousness of the modern Italian; not a restoration but a renewal, a revolution in the very idea of Rome," and one that marked "the eternal name of Rome with the seal of 'Fascism'; by remaking the idea our own, we accept it, and confer on it the fresh originality of the modern world."[103]

Fascism thought of itself as a restatement of Romanity in the twentieth century; like the "State Rome" and "Church Rome," it aspired to conquer its own fragment of eternity, dropping the Rome of Mussolini into history. Fascist mythology invoked the eternity of Rome as a spiritual guarantee for a Fascist Italy. It placed Rome at the very start of its mythical representation of Italian history, in which the brief history of Fascism appeared as a hierophant of Romanity, coming into being after centuries of the "eclipse of our race, deeply lacerated in 1915."[104] The vision was of a millenarian cycle of the seasons of Italian civilization and derived from a mythical past greatness and power that projected itself, through Fascism, to an equally great and powerful future. In the Fascist religion, Rome took on the function of the paradigmatic archetype; it represented the *mythical era* of the Italian race,[105] ever reinvoked and renewed through myth, symbol, and ritual, to arrive at the educational model susceptible of forming a "New Italy." "The virtues of classical Rome, the doings of the Romans of old," said Mussolini, "are always in my mind. They are a heritage that I try to turn to good account. The matter I have to shape is still the same; and outside there is still Rome."[106]

The myth of Romanity was born of the "mystery of Roman continuity."[107] "This historical soil has a magic of its own," Mussolini asserted.[108] The remains of monuments gave this place chosen by destiny, where for the first time the miracle of the greatness of the "Latin spirit" had made itself manifest, an aura of the sacred; it was here that a new hierophant of Romanity, Catholicism, had asserted itself; and now, with Fascism, the third miracle marked here "the resurrection of our race."[109] Rome was the "center of inspiration, the foundation of construction, an unceasing symbol; it stood for uninterrupted commerce with an earthly divinity; it was a mystery celebrated in the very heart of the Mussolinian consciousness."[110]

The celebration of the founding of Rome was interpreted by the Fascists as an initiation rite that opened the way to communion with Romanity. Through this rite, which was animated "by a 'solar willpower,' an imperial will, a will to power . . . the new Italian could make spiritual contact with ancient Rome."[111] This "new man" took on a religious significance; he became the symbol of that *metanoia,* or change of feeling, of the Italian people, which Fascism wished to forge into worthy spiritual heirs of the Romans, invincible warriors, but likewise "formidable builders who could, as they had before, defied time."[112]

Fascism was obsessed with time. Mircea Eliade wrote that religion is an aspiration to immortality, born of desire to represent "time as a whole," to be able to live "by transforming successive time into a single eternal moment."[113] This same aspiration is a consistent theme in Fascism, although it translated that idea into terms appropriate to a culture that identified the immortality of a people with the myth of civilization—that is, its capacity to defy destiny's challenge by putting its own mark on history. That Mussolini command, "endure," meant more than just an opportunistic politics living each day for the day; it revealed a will to power sufficient to defy time. Its attitude toward death, its cult of the fallen, its futuristic impetus to action, the myth of a "continuous revolution," like its manic drive to be a political protagonist in the real world, were all manifestations of a will for power fighting against time and of a longing for immortality. Its insistence on the vital importance of faith derived from this same defiance: faith itself is a power against fate, and a spark of eternity.

"Destiny" was very important in the symbolic universe of the Fascists. In the context of a "sacred history," it evoked a dark divinity that reigned over the events of history. With its cyclical challenges, it put to trial the capacity of a people to give birth to a civilization and thus leave a lasting mark on history. For Fascism history was a perpetual struggle between destiny and will, a struggle that spanned the ever-wheeling cycle and the dawn of civilization. It was an unpredictable and inexorable deity, but the will could, in extraordinary circumstances, meet the challenge. The Duce believed that he possessed the gift of divining his own century; he was convinced he was living in one of those epoch-making cyclical revolutions, and that destiny offered the Italian people an opportunity once again to prove its strength and virtue. After centuries of decadence, Italians might now prepare a new civilization. But the challenge could be met only through faith in the Fascist religion and total submission to his own leadership: he would mold Italians and produce a race of rulers and conquerors:

> The great moment is not sounded at all hours or on all clocks. The wheel of destiny turns. The wise man is the vigilant man who grasps the moment as it passes before him . . . If I succeed, if Fascism succeeds, in molding the character of Italians as I wish, you may rest easy in the certainty that when the wheel of destiny is within grasp of our hands, we will be ready to seize it and bend it to our will.[114]

The educational project undertaken by the totalitarian state could be summed up as the desire to mold Italians into "modern Romans," capable of defying time and marking the course of events with the sign of the lictor. The meaning and function that Fascism assigned to the sacralization of politics are all summed up in that absurd experiment.

To realize that vision, to regenerate the Italian character, to create a "new Italy," wholly Fascist, the régime did not hesitate to engage in conflict with the church, as occurred before the Reconciliation and immediately afterward, in 1931 and 1938. The reason for the conflict was the same as always: the Fascist state claimed a monopoly on the education of the young, as of the whole collective; it claimed to teach them according to the values inherent in its own nationalistic and warlike morality; it admitted neither conditions nor limits to the total loyalty and dedication of every citizen to the state.[115]

4

The Liturgy of Collective Harmony

In our history of making Italians, Fascism is the greatest experiment of all.
—Benito Mussolini

The problem of every State and every revolution, every philosophy worthy of
the name, and every civilization is Man: that is, the shaping of the perfect citizen . . . Physical formation, spiritual formation, political formation: these are
tasks the State cannot allow to be entrusted to the goodwill of individual initiatives, for they are one of its principal tasks.
   One could say of Fascism that it takes Italians one by one and seeks to
mold them, every second of the day, to fit a national imperative. They have to
become perfected instruments so that they can achieve the aims of the State,
as was the case with Rome, which was the unchallenged master of this sort of
education; it knew how to impart a mystical value to its very name, which
was no longer that of a city but that of a divine entity; being a citizen of
Rome meant partaking of that divinity.
—Emilio Bodrero

A major part of the state's educational function operated by means of a
growing, insistent, capillary "propagation of the faith" through rituals
and mass demonstrations, and one of the Fascist religion's vital functions was the creation of a state liturgy that worked not just on members
of the party but on all Italians who were, willy-nilly, involved in the régime's periodic celebrations. Fascism followed its own logic in creating
this liturgy, and it showed a knowledgeable and realistic understanding
of the role of symbols and rituals in modern mass politics.
   In the period between Fascism's coming to power and the transformation of the régime, its rituals had taken on many different functions
related to the consolidation of the new political system. During the period
about to be discussed these became, above all, symbolic acts consecrating
the irrevocability of Fascist power, legitimizing Fascism as the savior of
the nation and sole interpreter of the general will of a "new Italy" born

in the war. With the intensification of its own ritual, even before it achieved an effective monopoly of power, Fascism took over and controlled "sacred spaces" in which it could celebrate the cult of the nation and integrate it into the cult of the lictor. Its rituals, moreover, were always a show of force, sometimes designed to terrorize its adversaries and impress the wavering, as well as—in a period in which the party was constantly being shaken by internal crises—to reinforce the sense of identity, coherence, and power of the Fascists themselves.

At the end of the 1920s, while the new régime was consolidating and developing the structures of its power, presided over by an effective police apparatus that was both preventive and repressive, Fascism imposed discipline on mass demonstrations, limiting and coordinating them, subjecting them to strict controls, and formalizing the cult of the lictor into a rigid ceremonial defined by the party. None of this, however, made the party any less interested in developing its own ritual system; on the contrary, it extended it, multiplying the demonstrations and now, above all, seeking to have them involve the masses outside the party.

In this new phase, while rituals and symbols continued to reinforce the bonds among the Fascists themselves, manifesting in Italy and beyond an image of the unity, compactness, and power of party and régime, these also served to highlight the majesty of the totalitarian state and to clothe the power of the Duce and his party in an aura of the sacral. In the broader sense, these same rites and symbols were also a means of propaganda, instruments with which to influence public opinion by summoning up its feelings, emotions, fantasies, and enthusiasm. In periods of economic crisis such collective rites, by creating excitement and enthusiasm, compensated for privation and hardship; behind a façade of order and efficiency, they occluded the difficulties of the régime and periodically distracted the masses from worrying problems abroad, reassuring them with a self-praising exhibition of power.

No analysis of the meaning and function of Fascist liturgy, however, should limit itself to these pragmatic and utilitarian functions. Although these were certainly present in the minds of those who created the liturgy, they cannot be considered typical of or exclusive to Fascist liturgy; they are present in any form of political liturgy, whether democratic or authoritarian. To understand what is specific to Fascist liturgy, we must turn our attention to another function of ritual and symbol and consider it as an expression of the Fascist religion itself. Political liturgy worked as a way to legitimize power and as a means to manipulate and control the masses, but it also expressed, and not in any marginal or contingent fashion, the beliefs, values, and aims of Fascist culture.

Political Myths and the Politics of Myth

The creation of a state liturgy was a direct consequence of the way Fascists' conviction that feeling, not reason, dominates among the masses, and that only an appeal to feeling, through myths that give a shape to their desires and incite them to action, will enable a political organization to utilize their energy to achieve its own aims. Fascism employed no mealy-mouthed, demagogic explanations. As the party's leader put it:

> For me the masses are but a herd of sheep, so long as they are unorganized. I am nowise antagonistic to them. All that I deny is that they are capable of ruling themselves. But if you would lead them, you must guide them by two reins, enthusiasm and interest. He who uses only one of these reins is in grave danger. The mystical and the political factors condition one another reciprocally. Either without the other is arid, withered and is stripped of its leaves by the wind.[1]

Though denying the masses the capacity to govern themselves, the Fascists well understood that the loyalty of the masses was one of the great forces in modern politics. It was indispensable to the consolidation of the régime's power and, above all, vital to the creation of a totalitarian state, for the "masses have become an active element in the modern community," and the relationship between governors and the governed, "given the present state of mind of the people, can in no way be reduced to 'domination,' but seeks 'participation' through the organization and formation of a collective spiritual unity."[2] In this view of mass politics, myth, a central idea in Fascist culture, present in the very idea of a totalitarian state as in the creation of that "new civilization" which Fascism sought, played a vital role.

As an ideology that specifically dismissed the primacy of reason and rational culture—even if in practical politics it did not renounce the rational use of irrationality—Fascism glorified mythical thought and elaborated its own concept of political mythology in the wake of Georges Sorel,[3] interpreting myth principally as an image and symbol capable of producing in the masses feeling, enthusiasm, and the will to act. "A myth," Mussolini said, "is a faith, a passion. It is not necessary that it be real. It is real in the sense that it is a dagger, a hope, faith, courage."[4]

This was a widespread view in Fascist culture. In fact it was an almost obligatory point of reference in every mention of the masses and their education. "Myths," wrote a contributor to the Lombard Fascist organ, "express a reason for pride that is common to the whole race united in memory of its past greatness. Myths offer an example of virtue which directly affects the sensibility, itself more open to persuasion."[5] Myth was a form of thought well adapted to being molded. As one governor in the earliest days of the Fascist government wrote, the "childlike spirit of the masses [is] an easily molded material ready to take on the seal and stamp of a new idea and a new spirit."[6]

On a somewhat higher intellectual level, many of the most significant thinkers of Fascist culture gave considerable thought to the question of myths. Giovanni Gentile, for instance, sought to justify Fascism's basic anti-intellectualism and use of dogmatic formulas by arguing that "formulas are not ideas and do not serve as ideas. They create myths, they build a consensus and blind, global loyalty; they set in motion the power of feeling and will." For this reason, they aroused and set in motion "those great bundles of men who overturn centuries-old historical positions. These are the live instruments of the kind of thinking that takes root and lives in a few guiding spirits, indeed in one, the Duce."[7]

Carlo Curcio, a historian of ideas and a committed Fascist, author of an essay on political mythology, wrote in the party's *Dictionary of Politics* that "a myth reveals its life-giving and formidable presence in great mass movements, especially those whose base is political and social. [Myths] have a decisive importance in the lives of peoples." Like "a representation, now painterly, now unconscious, of the world, or at least of some of its aspects," and regardless of whether their "content is true or false, useful or damaging," the myth, which may derive from a man or a movement, "when it truly touches the conviction of a large social stratum of the population with a mad faith, when it expresses an interpretation of history or life, incites those men who believe in it to actions that are sometimes heroic or superhuman. In the name of an absolute that allows no doubt, in a language that is both accessible and imperious, and for as long as it goes on living, myth becomes a faith, a religion, and is capable of the boldest enterprises." But to have the power to attract men, a myth "must always refer to men's needs or demands. It is intolerant, threatening, sure of itself; and yet also malleable and sometimes modifiable with time. It has its own life span, and this is often relative to the intrinsic range of its historical value, and thus to its intransigence, which does permit adaptations."[8] When these become "widespread and dominant" beliefs and convictions, noted Rodolfo De Mattei, a historian of political thought, "they create a collective consciousness and serve those who govern to lead national egotisms toward mass action."[9]

Fascism took this view. Myths were potent and indispensable engines of political action. Carlo Costamagna, one of the most integralist jurists of the régime, viewed myths as "subjective representations of reality capable of promoting an affirmation of the spirit quite independently of their experimental logical content." They were ideas that "give rise to opinions, feelings and willed determinations [that] make up the moving forces of political action."[10] A new state and civilization were founded and survived through myths that had become the collective faith of the masses. "The task facing the 'founders' is that of bringing to people those revelations that cause revolutions, promote the transformation of régimes, create states, and generate the civilizations of the world."[11] For the ideologues of Fascist "mysticism," who identified Fascism itself with the myth of Mussolini, all the great events that had transformed history were mythical events created through faith.[12]

Within Fascist culture, myths were not a form of thinking confined to an archaic world or to the primitive mind, but a structured form of human thought, expressed primarily in artistic creation and religious movements, but just as relevant in the world of politics. Thus Giuseppe Bottai, responding to the creation of political myths "that besiege our civilization," thought them a characteristic of modernity. There was a "need for myths," particularly among and for the masses: "in order to offer and clarify an ideal to be realized, [they are] an aspiration that touches and unifies their own feelings." It was up to politicians to elaborate myths that responded to the needs of the masses.[13]

The need for political myths felt by the "founders of civilization," as the Fascists thought themselves, inevitably involved the use of rites and symbols. This was a subject on which Mussolini certainly remembered the lesson of Gustave Le Bon, an author whom he greatly admired: "A religious or political belief is based on faith, but it would not last without ritual and symbolism."[14] Fascism was well aware of the interconnections among myths, rituals, and symbols; they were a necessary condition for inculcating and sustaining a collective faith. "A fine symbol," wrote Camillo Pellizzi, "has greater weight" with the human spirit "than a mediocre fact."[15] A revolution, noted a Fascist party leader in 1927, is also identified "by the power of its symbols and the beauty of its rituals."[16]

Fascists did not of course limit the political importance of symbolism to its aesthetic aspects. Ways of visualizing and dramatizing myths, symbols, and rituals were necessary to make the mythology of the "Fascist religion" accessible to the masses and to convert them to the new faith. According to the Fascist sociologist Roberto Michels, political symbols are born of the need to make the attraction of authority concrete in a visible way; they are "the link between Authority and the masses, among whom they maintain its prestige."[17] The masses, said the author of a treatise on the Fascist concept of the state, "need spirituality, religious feeling, a catechism, ritual."[18]

Proceeding from these suppositions about culture, whatever their personal convictions and beliefs, Fascists recognized that religion, as a system of beliefs, myths, and rituals, had a dominant social role in collective life. It was a unifying spiritual force. Such a force was ever more needed in a society that—after the historical, social, and cultural rifts caused by centuries-long political and geographical fragmentation—was now troubled by new rifts: class warfare, the ideological conflicts accompanying industrialization and modernization, and the arrival of the masses on the political scene. Restoring order to society presupposed, as far as Fascists were concerned, imposing an authoritarian discipline; but effective nationalization of the people required cultural integration in those ways most likely to influence the masses.

Compared to the liberal ruling class, Fascism took up the problem of forging a moral unity among the Italian people with greater conscious, practical knowledge and a greater *democratic sensibility*—that is, a "totalitarian democracy."[19] It went ahead resolutely with indoctrination and conversion, using totalitarian methods, convinced that modern society could not realistically hope to nationalize the masses while still trying to reconcile individual freedom with the moral unity of the nation. Only by sacrificing liberty, and through the collective conversion of individuals and the masses to the Fascist religion, could it achieve unity.

The state should work full-time as if it were a major re-educational institution. It should forcibly eliminate any form of mass culture opposed to the primacy of the state, and accompany that with experimental new forms of collective culture. The aim was to achieve a totalitarian integration of the masses according to the values and objectives of Fascism and its culture. For Fascism, the conversion of the masses to its own myths was an indispensable and necessary condition, not only to consolidate its own power, already well protected by its police system, but in order to realize a far grander totalitarian project—the regeneration of the Italian people into a "harmonious whole."

Totalitarian integration was a process of "continuous revolution" which required that the collectivity—its politics, its production, and its "free time"—be organized in capillary fashion and that the masses be constantly mobilized. Totalitarian pedagogy had a fundamental conviction: "without political activity, a man's civic virtues grow deformed. Fascist policy requires constant mobilization."[20] Only by socializing its own system of myths and beliefs, by making the Fascist religion a habit of mind, a civic ethic, a style of life for the country as a whole, could one obtain the active and lasting integration of the masses into a totalitarian state, transforming the people into a moral community animated by a single faith.

One of the chief vehicles for propagating its myths among the people, to instill and keep alive its faith in Fascist religion, was to adopt a system of rituals and symbols that could influence the masses, as all religions had done.

The Degenerate Disciples of Rousseau

Yet again the Fascists followed the precepts of the author of *Crowd Psychology:* "National holidays, major anniversaries, flags, statues, official pomp, magistrates' robes, the apparatus of justice with its symbolic scales, are the surest buttresses of tradition and of the community of feeling on which the strength of a nation is based."[21] A mass liturgy was as important as a totalitarian organization to promote the mobilization of the masses and conquer their consent—understood not as free and critical participation, but as partaking of the faith. Through ritual, constant catechetical indoctrination by the party and the state, the Fascist religion must become an essential component of the mentality and character of all Italians; it had to be transformed into tradition and custom, to arouse and give substance to the participation of the masses in the life of the régime. To this end, said Mussolini, a mass liturgy should also have a "festive" element: "Music and women allure the crowd and make it more pliable. The Roman greeting, songs and formulas, anniversary commemorations, and the like—all are essential to fan the flames of the enthusiasm that keeps a movement in being. It was just the same in ancient Rome."[22] At least in his days as a socialist militant, Mussolini must have had some familiarity with the historiography of the French Revolution, and in speaking of ritual and symbol probably had in mind Michelet's suggestive pages on the revolutionary festivities and cults. But he probably also had in mind the use of symbol and ritual in Bolshevik Russia. A Soviet diplomat, referring to the "quite confidential" relations between Mussolini and Stalin in the 1930s, revealed that Mussolini had requested and obtained of Stalin the stage plan for the May Day celebrations in Red Square as well as those for the anniversary of the October Revolution. These he had copied, as the same diplomat was able to observe when he attended a Fascist demonstration with Mussolini present.[23]

Probably referring to this experience, Mussolini said that "the would-be revolutionist while using old traditions must refashion them. He must create new festivals, new gestures, new forms, which will themselves in turn become traditional. The airplane festival is new today. In half a century it will be encrusted with the patina of tradition."[24]

For its own liturgy, the Fascist revolution lacked a great artist like Jacques-Louis David, who choreographed the great popular festivals of the French Revolution. Nonetheless, in certain ways the organizers of the lictorial cult, with their mass propaganda, can be considered as the degenerate successors, however spurious, of the Rousseau tradition, applying his prescriptions for the popular festivities that would accompany the construction of a "Virtuous Republic." Just as it had sacralized the "Educator State" when it created its political liturgy, Fascism followed the wide-open road laid down by the French Revolution—all the while vulgarly ridiculing the "immortal principles of '89" and Jacobinism's rational utopianism and egalitarianism.[25] A contributor to Mussolini's journal in 1922 had in fact made explicit reference to the cults of the French Revolution:

> A few dogmas are worth more than prolix dissertations. More effective in creating feeling than any dogma is its external choreography, its ceremonial and ritual. Visible performances irresistibly arouse powerful feelings . . . During the French Revolution, the religious exaltation of the people showed itself in a picturesque form of secular rite. Something of the sort is to be seen today in the Fascist ranks.[26]

At the time this invocation of the French Revolution seemed neither unjustifiable nor unseemly. At the end of 1924 one French journalist, president of the Association of Foreign Correspondents in Rome, studied the political symbolism of the Fascists with considerable acumen. He found a number of analogies between the French and the Fascist revolutions, to the point where he spoke of a real link between Fascism and Jacobinism. Like the Jacobins, wrote De Nolva, Fascism sought to create a virtuous world; to achieve it, Fascism had to claim that a revolutionary dictatorship was both necessary and legitimate and should be devoted to the cult of the Fatherland.[27]

The Ritual of the Mass Communion

Having solidly established its power, Fascism continued to devote itself to the elaboration of a national liturgy that would correspond to its myths, rites, and symbols. This was a fundamental part of its totalitarian design to create a "new Italy." Its activity in this area developed, as we have seen, with the creation of an organic system of rituals, celebrations, and collective manifestations to celebrate the "Fascist" year according to a rhythm dictated by the Fascist "calendar." But alongside these periodical holidays celebrating unity, the monarchy, and the Great War, the anniversaries of the Founding of Rome and the revolution, there were other mass events, ranging from consecrations to exhibitions, from parades to huge assemblies organized on special occasions—as, for instance, those connected with the Ethiopian campaign—encounters with the Duce during his periodic tours of Italy, his countless appearances on the balcony of Palazzo Venezia to satisfy the demands of the crowds.

This inexhaustible and spectacular orchestration of a collective enthusiasm involved millions of Italian men, women, and children and likewise fascinated travelers from abroad sympathetic to Fascism and even disenchanted observers who were not in thrall to the rhetoric or the myth of the Duce. An American scholar defined these rituals and ceremonies "as a new Fascist art of age-old celebrations."[28] Another wrote that mass manifestations were the chief industry of Fascist Italy, and that it would be unjust to those who organized and made them happen not to include them in the country's production statistics.[29]

Mass celebrations of the lictorial cult took place under the leadership of the party and the close supervision of the police apparatus, which made sure there was no risk of disturbance, particularly in major cities. On the eve of every such demonstration, the necessary measures were taken to ensure "that established ceremonies should not be interrupted by subversive demonstrations or incidents." There would be "a rapid and widespread search for suspect individuals," a close watch kept on foreigners, an intensification of "border patrols for special measures to be adopted in regard to the security of railroads, works of art, bridges, viaducts, and sites important to national defense or the nation's economic life."[30]

The essential form of such lictorial rites can be illustrated by those of the anniversary of the March on Rome in 1926, celebrated "by the great mass of the Italian people incorporated into the Fasces, the Militia, syndicates, youth organizations," together with the decorated, mutilees, veterans, and "all the other organizations associated with the Régime." The celebration had a "strongly military character" to show "the powerful array of forces behind the Fascist Revolution ready to defend its life and development against anyone."[31] The procession was headed by widowed mothers and orphans of those who had fallen in the war, the decorated, and mutilees. After paying homage to the fallen, the procession moved on to attach the Fascist symbol to new public works.

The party further ordered that all ceremonies should be "marked by the greatest possible austerity and sobriety. To this end, banquets and lavish receptions are prohibited." Speeches should be limited to the reading of a symbolic message from the Duce and a listing of the works accomplished by Fascism, read by the federal party secretary "without rhetorical flourishes."[32]

Fascists were required to don their black shirts and meet in their headquarters "for more intimate assemblies among members" to recall the party's martyrs. To glorify the Duce, by then on his way to becoming a living myth, a film dedicated to him would be "simultaneously projected" in all the main cities and in the colonies. He would be shown in "a luminous and vital vision that will instill an ever greater love for Italy."[33] The entire ritual of the anniversary was interpreted as a renewal of "the oath of loyalty to the Idea." "A whole people, at one with the mind and passion of its leader, celebrated the beginning of a new year of struggle and hope," commented the orders for November 7, 1926.

There were no substantial modifications in subsequent years. On the eve of each anniversary the party made its dispositions for the celebrations, divided into two parts: ritual and festivities, to distinguish the "sacred" from the "profane." The service, generally in the morning, included both religious and military ceremonies: a mass in memory of those who died during the war or in the revolution; a parade before the civilian and military authorities, involving all the Fascist organizations and the veterans' groups; homage at the various monuments to the fallen in both the revolution and the Great War; a reading of the Duce's message; his radio message broadcast in the piazza.

The festival part took place in the afternoon and included country walks, dances, songs, and musical entertainment. All this was staged in ways that mixed old and new symbolisms. There were flags, public buildings were lit; the bells in the "civic towers" were rung for a half-hour; there were public illuminations in the squares and streets, spotlighted fasces and inscriptions in praise of the Duce; torchlight processions and bonfires on the "peaks of the Alps and the Apennines." The ritual choreography of the ceremonies in the capital was a symbolic mix of the ancient and the modern, with military parades among Roman ruins, flights of planes, and huge assemblies in the Colosseum. On these anniversaries Fascists were obliged to wear their black shirts, the uniform of the groups they belonged to, and their decorations. In the evening they were to meet in their headquarters in a "brotherhood of memory and determination."[34] On March 23, from 1932 on, a place of honor was kept for the *Sansepolcristi*,[35] who wore a special insignia issued by the Duce. Ceremonies on October 28 characteristically included the inauguration of public works completed in each province. These were loaded with symbolic significance, in that the idea of construction, in the minds of Fascists, evoked Romanity, vital activity, the concrete feeling of achieving something, the will to "endure," as a continual defiance of time, of faith in the future.

The most solemn of all the lictorial cults naturally took place in Piazza Venezia in Rome with the Duce present, in front of the Altar of the Fatherland and the Palazzo Venezia (which by 1929 had become the Duce's office). As one of the great bards of the Duce's myth wrote, Fascism had rehabilitated the piazza as a place of worship. Piazza Venezia, located between the temples of ancient Rome and those of the new Italian state, was the "sacred center" of the Fascist revolution; it was the "Piazza of the Revolution, synthesis of all the piazzas of Italy," a place of constant pilgrimage and huge assemblies that "beg for the Duce to appear and speak, all of which raises tension to the highest possible degree."[36]

The ceremonies in the capital, in addition to the routine military parades of the Fascist forces and the Duce's speech, sometimes included other rituals. Thus in 1928 the Duce officiated, at two Roman altars from the Diocletian Baths set up in front of the Altar of the Fatherland, at a public burning of bonds worth 140 million lire as "a symbol of the people's offering to the public Treasury."[37] The great assemblies to support the Ethiopian campaign, especially the "Day of Faith," were probably the two moments of greatest unity of feeling between the régime and the Italian people, the closest to that moment of mystical communion which Fascism would have wished to see transformed into a permanent part of the collective life of the nation.

This sort of choreography was not limited just to political rituals, but extended to all the organized manifestations of collective life, from popular festivals to sport and exhibitions. Fascism took over traditional festivities by inserting its own system of myths, symbols, and rituals—as it did, for instance, with its "Fascist Epiphany,"[38] with the distribution of presents to poor children to make them feel, "with the smile of a kind present, the affectionate care of their Fascist nation."[39] In 1931, as part of "a vast program of Winter Relief," the Fascist Epiphany in Milan included a Christmas Day distribution of gifts in the name of the Duce, to be known as "the Duce's Christmas."[40]

By the end of the 1930s, Achille Starace's zeal for reforming bourgeois habits that did not fit in with the lictorial cult had reached the point of putting out circulars prohibiting the exchange of greetings on New Year's Day because the Fascist year began on October 29. There were even rumors that Italy's traditional New Year's Eve festivities would be abolished, as a result, word had it, "of an anti-Catholic Germany, which replaces and denatures Christmas with its new religion of Nature."[41]

Despite frequent solicitations from Nazi Germany, Fascist Italy never moved in that direction. The Italian mass mentality was still distrustful or recalcitrant about overtly ideological messages, so Fascism incorporated syncretically into the lictorial cult the whole complex of already-existing manifestations of collective life, sifting them through Fascist religious myths, thinking these more likely to influence Italians.

Even traditional rural festivals were permeated with Fascist symbolism. The wine harvest, celebrated on the last Sunday in September, was given fresh life by the régime, which saw it as a way to promote production by "persuading the people to consume the delicious and health-giving fruit of the vine."[42] The harvest became an occasion on which to emphasize the "Romanity" of Fascism by restoring the truly Italian nature of "harvest festivals" and those "healthy traditions of the earth and its fertility." Such festivals "overcome time; they bring together the new races that create and reconstruct the ancient races of the Mediterranean, whose law was to build and produce in a real world." According to the organ of the Fascist Youth, the wine harvest was "very similar to that of the Romans, who did not admit barbarian influences in their rituals and did not want orgiastic contamination of the joyful festival of the wine harvest."[43]

In its Fascist incarnation this festival, like others linked to agricultural production and peasant labor, was not just a "colorful and cheerful folkloric show, but a healthy and vigorous expression of rural life, of the luxuriant fertility of our vines."[44] The régime promoted it as a "joyous and festive ritual" that added "high symbolic worth" to its commercial importance; it "broke down the barriers between winemaking and the vine, between city life and rural." Thus, even the wine harvest was pressed into the service of the liturgy of the "collective harmony." It was the "great autumnal festivity for the whole nation" and was celebrated in the open air.[45]

Fascism supported all the traditions related to nature and rural life, but unlike Nazi mystical romanticism it did not create a "religion of Nature."[46] Nature, in the lictorial cult, was Nature dominated, domesticated, redeemed, and fecundated by the work of man. Of the 207 carts that paraded before the Duce for the wine harvest of 1931, among the first was a group representing the reclamation of the Maccarese region, which well symbolized this idea of Nature as a "work of redemption." The first cart contained a section of swamp, choked with reeds and malarial; the others showed the process of draining and reclamation; the last showed "a stupendous vision of a harvest of opulent grapes in plump clusters."[47]

Nature as such was no part of Fascist religion, but it was ever-present as a place for its rituals: "The new life of our new Italy must be brought out of the seclusion in which the people of another time muffled and impoverished it; it must be brought into light and air. To move physically is also to move spiritually."[48]

Fascism's glorification of collective life encouraged intense and widespread support of gymnastics and sports. These, too, were put to work for the "propagation of faith" because, as the commission set up to prepare a project for the physical education and military preparedness of the fatherland wrote, "the cultivation of physical strength is always connected to the nation; where there is an ideal of national redemption, love of physical exercise is immediately present."[49] Considerable resources were devoted to gymnastics and sport. These were used to finance the construction of gymnasia, stadia, and camps. All became part of the lictorial cult and of the mass education and training of the "new Italy," building the body and tempering the character of a virile, virtuous citizen, a true believer and a warrior for his country.

One of the first of the new stadia was the Lictorial Stadium in Bologna, begun in 1927 thanks to Leandro Arpinati, the local Fascist leader, to whom *Il popolo d'Italia* attributed a "visionary and practical" temperament, and who was "a propitiator and champion of secular and ecclesiastical religions."[50] An equestrian statue of the Duce graced the Bologna amphitheater in memory of the speech Mussolini had given there the year before to 50,000 black-shirts assembled "in the great, bare, barely-outlined ellipsis, as a Roman population entered on the foundations of a future city." In the most grandiose of all Fascism's sporting complexes, the Mussolini Forum, the huge approach plaza was dominated by a tall marble monolith on which the Duce's name was inscribed, "to project into the future his name and his era."[51]

Renato Ricci, the future president of the *Balilla,* had in mind even more grandiose monuments to glorify the lictorial cult. He proposed a giant bronze statue of Fascism that, as he wrote the Duce, "would make the legendary Colossus of Rhodes look tiny in comparison." The statue was to have been three times as tall as the Statue of Liberty, and to have arisen in an area five times the size of Piazza Venezia, to be called the "Assembly of the People." It was to extend over 120,000 square meters and hold 300,000 people. The project, on which work had already begun, was abandoned because of the Ethiopian War and the League of Nations sanctions.[52]

Sport was supposed to "rouse the passions of the people, and not just make sporting champions."[53] It was another part of the totalitarian mobilization of the people, designed to overcome a mentality of private, personal isolation and replace it with a sense of "human communion"[54] while also encouraging sporting competition as preparation for leadership in international competition. Sport should be "encouraged as a genuine service and civic duty"; it should be undertaken by any "good Fascist citizen" wishing to be an integral art of a people whom the Duce had declared to be "the body of the state" and its dynamic coefficient, the state being, by that same definition, "the soul of the body."[55]

Physical education and sport had a preponderant part in the totalitarian reform project, directed particularly at the training of the citizen-soldier.

The giant gymnastic displays, especially those held periodically in the capital with the Duce present, were just so many further events to celebrate the lictorial cult. The choreography of the various heats, the mass demonstrations, processions, and choruses, the Duce's speech, were all part of a ritual and symbolic cultural event; by their very spectacle they helped spread Fascist myths among the participants and their public.

No collective manifestation was without its purpose as a means of indoctrination and as part of the lictorial cult. Exhibitions or shows of any sort organized by the régime were used for Fascist propaganda. This was very much the case with the celebrations of a decade of Fascist power, which involved the greatest deployment of ritual activities and mass ceremonies, all for the purpose of intensifying propaganda among the masses, which were showing signs of increasing dissatisfaction as a result of the "great crisis" of the Depression.

The year 1932 saw many exhibitions mounted, ranging from agricultural machinery to reclamation, from fruit-growing to baking, from the fiftieth anniversary of Garibaldi's death to the exhibition honoring the Fascist revolution. All of these, *Il popolo d'Italia* explained, were based on a single idea, "a healthy educational purpose," which transformed these from events connected to "groups, cenacles, little academies estranged from the life of the people and marred by intellectualism and dilettantism" that often had "purely commercial or advertising purposes," into "integrated manifestations of the national education which the Fascist State has taken on and is carrying out, in schools, sports fields, among youth and leisure organizations, and in the most varied sorts of initiatives such as, to mention just one in the news, that of 'popular trains.'"[56]

A New Italian for a New Civilization

The Fascists boasted that they had reinvented what one might call an aesthetic of the masses. "Before Fascism, public manifestations were extremely unaesthetic. Fascism has restored to the cities of Italy that 'art of movement and of human groups' of which the Fiume Statutes speak. Our processions, when they wind through the street or form in squares in the piazze, are worthy of our cities, and their beauty adds to the beauty of stone and marble"; they give the people "the brotherly love of 'civic events,' and this is also love of the city, of tradition, and hence of the fatherland." They reawakened in the people "a love for improvised songs and choruses." Fascist festivals were "great choral occasions."[57]

Propaganda, at every anniversary or collective festival, drew attention to the difference in spirit and style from those celebrated under the liberal régime, which were characterized by a waning patriotism and fear of crowds, a ceremonial looking to the past. The Fascists maintained that their rituals were projected toward the future; they took in the different stages and triumphs of a "permanent revolution" laying the foundations of a "new culture." "Unlike the old democracies," Fascism was "not concerned with commemorating the past," but continued its march forward with "eyes to the future." "Everything in the old individualistic and libertarian culture is cracking, and Italy has been summoned to give a new order to nations that seek salvation."[58] The script for Fascist rituals included piazzas thronged with applauding crowds of men, women, and children of every class, all celebrating together, in mystical exaltation, the glory of Fascism and its leader. The Italian "Labor Day," which for many years had been celebrated by "threatening crowds" and had been the "incubus of the ruling class," was now transformed into a "partisan" and "national" holiday, an expression of "the new weave that keeps the organization of our civil consortium solidly together."[59]

Fascism laid claim to having redeemed the crowd and transformed it into a *liturgical* mass that participated with joy and faith in the celebration of the rites of the new régime. As *Gioventù fascista* asserted at the end of the celebrations of the régime's first decade:

> With Fascism, a crowd has become a harmony of souls, a perfect fit of citizens actively participating in the great life of the State . . . The streets of Rome were thronged with this new crowd; in great waves it seemed to replicate the generous breath of Fascism. Symbolically, it looked like the vast and solid base of a huge pyramid on whose pinnacle, alone and all-powerful, stood Mussolini . . . This was no crowd misled by demagogic-romantic hallucinations; this was a crowd with self-knowledge, aware of its obedience, its faith, and its fighting mettle, a crowd serene and secure, trusting in its Leader, in a State, and in an increasingly noble passion, ever more life-giving: Fascism. This was no faceless throng, but an image given shape and order by spirits educated in the epic of these new times; not an amorphous mass, but an amalgam of fresh values and intelligence.[60]

In this glorification of ritual and symbolism as a manifestation of faith, no small part was played by the Fascist mania for *style*, for reforming dress, an obsession that grew increasingly manifest from the late 1920s onward, especially during Starace's secretaryship—even to the very end, in the agony of the collapse of the régime. With all its organizations and at every level of the hierarchy, the régime devoted itself to this campaign to reform how people dressed. Quite apart from its indisputably ridiculous aspects, the question of style was one of intricate motivations, mainly traceable back to the prime role that Fascism assigned to liturgy in the making of a "new man." On the eve of the March on Rome, Mussolini charged democracy with having "deprived popular life of style," while "Fascism has given 'style'—that is, a form of behavior, color, power, the picturesque, the unexpected, the mythical—back to the people."[61] "In the absence of symbolism," he reiterated the following year, "it [the form of life] would be a casual matter, undifferentiated."[62]

By its very nature as a religious movement Fascism, explained one of the régime's educators, had given new luster and life to myths, symbols, and rituals; it had restored style to mass politics. Style was the expression of order and discipline governed by faith; in a world convulsed by the tragedy of war and in a new era seeking to define itself while being undermined by grave economic and moral crises, menaced by the incubus of a return to chaos, style indicated a triumph over disarray and uncertainty. "Style puts the soul under the influence of what is noble in the spirit."[63]

Understood this way, style was an expression of Fascist religion; one could say that it was religion translated into costume, a living witness of its ethic, its rule, its "asceticism." For "when we speak of a Fascist style we mean a victory of the spirit . . . What else is it but a rigorous definition that comes with the facts of Fascist doctrine?" Once again, Fascist politics used the church model: "A religious ceremony, the celebration of a ritual, are essentially definitions, that is: a visible attachment to and a public profession of one's faith . . . With style, ceremony, and Fascist ritual, politics moves from definition to the human and living and becomes a source of joy."[64]

The demagogic orchestration and missionary fanaticism of Fascism was linked with what one propagandist called "a passion for crowds."[65] Manipulation of public opinion, searching for consensus, aesthetic preference for "the art of huge collective parades," all seem inspired by a will for power designed to act on the body social, to mold it, transform it, and make of it—as though it were a work of art—in Mussolini's term, a "collective harmony," a body politic with one faith and one set of morals, entirely devoted to the state made divine. A will to form the mass was at the heart of totalitarian Fascist politics and derived from the political culture of the revolution and the experience of war. As Bottai wrote in 1928, "Everyone of us has been a leader or a follower, a molder of life, an assembler of intelligible, mature energies."[66] Mussolini, who liked to compare politics and art, defined a politician as an artist who shapes human material. In every Fascist, from Giovanni Gentile to Achille Starace, from the Duce down to the lowest member of the party hierarchy, dwelled the ambition to be someone who shaped life.

The notion of "molding the masses," a Fascist version of the revolutionary myth of moral regeneration, was obsessively present in the politics of Mussolini and Fascism:

> The Fascist era will truly begin the day on which all the people have been molded, exalting Fascism by its faith and making it a giant in its hopes.
>
> For this to be possible, for Fascism to be able to win and grasp, right down to their roots, the consciousness and will of Italians, it must create its own atmosphere and ambience, it must tap the whole strength of the nation, right down to its most hidden energies . . .
>
> It is work for titans, but work to be done by the most talented men of the Fascist revolution. All the works of art and cultural currents of the past have to be examined through the lens of Fascism; we must recreate, with and in the political religion that we practice daily, the world as we feel it and live it; we must bend what was real in the past to what is real in our own times, times that are loftier, clearer, and truer because they form part of us and are closer to us, because they are ourselves![67]

Once again, probably without realizing it, Fascism moved in the footsteps of the French Revolution, repeating slogans of political education inspired by the notion of the moral regeneration of the masses, the concept of the state as educator, the myth of the "New Man," the sacred nature of the fatherland, and, to use Mathiez's useful term, the "passion for unity." Thus Rousseau's civic religion was translated into a modern totalitarianism that did not believe in man's natural goodness or his perfectibility—in the sense of his progressive emancipation toward a free and rational conscience—but instead in the malleability of his character, as an expression of a historical tradition, of the customs, beliefs, and ethic of a whole people. With myth, the moral force of a faith, and the educational influence of liturgy, the state had the power to act on the *character* of man and transform it.

In part, Fascism inherited this problem of "making Italians" from the founding fathers of Italian unification. Now they were convinced they had the right instruments to carry it through. Their own future depended on reforming the character of Italians, on ridding them of their defects, forging them into a new people, both virtuous and vigorous, true "citizen soldiers." Such a collective transformation was indeed a visionary project, but the régime pursued it with ever-greater determination and fanatical intransigence in the 1930s.

Fascism was no longer an interpreter of the nation but the creator of a new nation: "Under Fascism, this nation is being born . . . Fascism is creating the customs from which a nation is born, the Fascist nation."[68] Every one of the régime's organizations, from the party itself to the National Leisure Organization, the youth organizations, the *Balilla* and Fascist Youth, combined into a single organization, the Young Italian Lictors (Gioventù italiana del littorio), applied itself zealously to the task of indoctrinating the masses and the young according to the ideals, the ethics, and the dogmas of the Fascism.

Culture, too, was mobilized, for "Fascist culture must be life and the expression of life; it must create a species of man, a new man, a whole man, one who is the same man in his family, in society, and in the State."[69] The school was naturally one of the places where the "propagation of the faith" was most intensely and assiduously practiced, through catechetical indoctrination with Fascist religion, which worked its way into all teaching materials, and by constant liturgical observance to celebrate the rites of the nation and the revolution.

In the early 1930s a Communist party informer wrote concerning the schools:

> Classrooms have become a many-hued exhibition of the photographic and symbolic paraphernalia of the régime. Studying is unimportant. What count are parades, uniforms, insignia, official camps. Serious and dignified teachers tremble or knuckle under . . . The régime says it wants very few "cultural officers," just a few indispensable sergeants and corporals; it wants to make a higher cultural level and a future for the great mass of people impossible; for these people primary school is just a propaganda unit designed to put people's minds to sleep.
>
> Thanks to the prohibition of discussion and the political suspicions that cloud minds in schools, the little good that the [Gentile] reform contained has been submerged. A single problem dominates schools: *making them Fascist*. It matters little whether this, in open contrast with the concepts that current Gentilism expresses toward education, is stated by the régime's representatives as "molding, shaping, or forging"; the end result is schools that are instruments of political propaganda and political domination.[70]

The régime constantly sought new forms of mobilization and propaganda in order to intensify its "molding" of the masses. In 1932 "Sunday meetings" were created, at which party speakers exercised their "apostolate of propaganda"[71] in every commune, expounding "the ideas and details of Fascist ethics,"[72] lauding the political merits of the régime, collecting workers' complaints about their straitened economic circumstances, and promising them "that they would bring their various needs to the attention of those responsible in Rome."[73]

In 1935 "Fascist Saturdays" were established to accompany the forty-hour work-week. The free Saturday afternoons were to be dedicated to "the political education and military training of the Régime's organizations."[74] Each of the two main educational activities to form the "New Man" had its own day, thus acquiring, as the organ of the Fascist Youth put it, "a religious character whose effects cannot help but reverberate in the idea every Fascist should have of his life." It was a way of "reducing the *political illiteracy* that parallels *physical illiteracy*. It is beginning to be understood that to be *Italian* means being *Fascist,* and being Fascist means being a *whole man*."[75]

It is very likely that this constant intrusion of totalitarian training in the life of Italians caused resistance and adverse reactions, especially among those who least identified themselves with Fascist mythology and were least disposed to allow themselves to be integrated into a totalitarian community. News of discontent and impatience with the totalitarian impetus that the régime had given the mobilization of the masses reached higher levels of authority from many sources, although much of it was due to a worsening economic situation and to increasing anxiety and fear because of the threat of war in Europe. A police informer in Florence reported on January 5, 1939:

> I hear many people say that the Fascist Régime has incorporated into its various organizations just about every category of citizen and tends to discount and control all their activities. It is pointed out that this desire to regulate individual activity in every aspect suppresses any kind of freedom and suffocates individual initiative, for which reason people do not easily tolerate the limits imposed on them and the interference of the Régime in every sphere of activity, especially where they do not consider such interference justified. I hear it said everywhere that this squeezing becomes ever more intolerable.
>
> For the present everyone is supportive and out of fear does not openly state his objection openly; but in the event of a failure that could shake the Régime, there could be a violent reaction to this kind of constriction.[76]

For all that, various signs were not wanting that totalitarian politics had successfully worked its ideology among the masses. A Communist militant wrote in 1932 that "Fascism has managed to influence a fair part of the masses with its ideology, and only by fighting within its organizations and unmasking them do we have any chance to make workers understand how they have been deceived."[77] It was particularly the young who were exposed to Fascist propaganda: "The fresh blood of the people, the yeast of a new life, our hopes for tomorrow . . . are besieged and throttled by the régime, which manipulates them as it pleases. First there's the *Balilla,* then the *Avanguardisti,* the Militia, then gymnastics, trips, camps, with warlike and religious lectures." They are brought up in "a happy, blessed, animal state of unconsciousness, heedless of the future, indifferent, as enemies of their fathers, brothers, and workmates."[78]

This unremitting mobilization on behalf of the collective rituals of the régime could indeed give rise to feelings of satiety or impatience in some;

in others, more motivated, it brought out an enthusiasm for participation, or at least of attraction for these forms of collective activity. As Giaime Pintor noted in his diary:

> Saturday afternoon, in our Militia uniforms, we turned out for practical instruction in the university gardens. The hours we lost in these meetings and all the other special tasks to which we were assigned caused a fair amount of grumbling. But they were not just a waste of time; they were an example of collective life and served to tighten some bonds among us. The most tedious moments during the year were meetings to study the "Roman goose-step" [this was the period in which Starace was getting ready to "have an effect on customs"] in preparation for Hitler's arrival in Rome. For days on end we were removed from civilian life and led to exercises in the suburbs of Rome. Long waits, orders and counterorders, a complex of inertia and weariness within the organizations marked those days and contributed to creating a first legend. Leaving home at dawn, with the milkmen making their rounds through Rome, cold dawns over the Villa Glori, afternoons in working-class districts in which we had nothing to do but fool about with serving-girls and eat ice cream, were a picturesque form of education. But above all, we got into the heart of the spectacular complexity of a totalitarian regime: we learned how to be part of the tens of thousands of men who marched in parades, to march to traditional music, and to enjoy the impersonality which one enjoys in uniform.
>
> We missed not one parade during Hitler's visit to Rome.[79]

Thanks to its network of informants, the régime was kept up-to-date on public reaction to its campaigns, and it was certainly aware of their negative effects. Nonetheless, there was no question of desisting or declaring a brief truce in order to quell the rising tide of complaint and irritation. By its very nature as a religion and by its totalitarian logic, Fascism could not in fact give up propaganda and mobilization; if anything, it intensified its campaign and remained convinced that radical surgery on the Italian character was required if a "new man" was to be brought into being.

After the fall of Fascism, one disillusioned true believer wrote that "the Fascist mystique" condemned Italians to "enthusiasm."[80] Despite all the negative reactions, the campaigns continued, not just from sheer love of spectacle, but because the conversion of the masses to the lictorial cult required them. All these rituals and meetings and athletic meets and propaganda sessions were considered the instruments through which a gradual but continuous education in "collective harmony" could be achieved: "These great periodic manifestations . . . are extraordinarily useful; they are indispensable to instilling in all a sense of movement forward toward the goal of those civic virtues that Fascism has fostered in the country."[81]

The sober, martial rites of the anniversaries of the revolution were symbolic of strength and discipline; rural festivals glorified the country's hard work and cooperation between classes; solidarity galas showed that the régime cared for its poor; the great assemblies consecrated the union of the people with the government and the Duce; memorial rites for Fascist martyrs and dignitaries of the régime testified to the immortality of Fascist true believers within an everlasting totalitarian state. But the mainspring of all Fascist ritual was the myth of a totalitarian community, a people united in a single faith. "Faith" thus came to assume an inherent value as the one egalitarian principle in a society which, for all that the régime claimed it wished to do by "bridging the gulf" between classes inside a political system based on strict hierarchy, still retained its social divisions.

The symbol of this egalitarianism was to be the uniform, the black shirt, the common participation of all in celebrating the lictorial cult. This was the way Fascism sought to resolve the antithesis between the individual and the mass. The individual was to be integrated into the totalitarian community, thus transforming the masses by the "practice of a way of life that achieves a collective consciousness." This could be managed through "cohesive ways of living destined to create a collective spirit," ways that would "pass from the stage of being momentary to being permanent and ingrained," through collective events that "form a continuous chain of life-styles advancing a collective sense of life and becoming a part of a psychological groundwork of our people."[82]

> Popular assemblies, mass sports, the vibrant, living crowd in the stadium, choral song, popular theatre, country outings, and camping are all expressions of collective life, designed to give the nation a sense of being one. This welding into a unit is the defining result, national in its collective sense of life, and also directed toward obliterating regional differences.
>
> Wherever possible, create a great arc of Italians, all of them molded within our boundaries into a single soul and fit for some worldwide mission, a deed of empire.

To achieve this aim, every aspect of life, especially among the young, had to be ever more intensively subjected to a collectivist training "whose immediate objective is the mass, not the individual, which aims not at the creation of a constellation of geniuses, but rather at giving a framework of elements, morally balanced and all leading to a level of preparation, even if sometimes mediocre, still apt to serve the revolution and making people feel that they are living cells in a revolutionary organism." The lictorial rites went hand in hand with the educational goals and organizational regimentation of the state; they mattered because they "instill in the mass, and especially in its soul, the inseparable dynamic between individual and group, and thus with the State, the true exemplar of the group, in the sense that it responds not just to economic goals, but also to social, political, moral, and religious goals."

Training for a "collective harmony" was based on the supposition that conversion to the common faith of the Fascist religion would morally— beyond disparities in social conditions, economic opportunities, and differences in gender and age—unite all Italians. Fascism thought it had found the formula with which to solve, in Bottai's words, "the problem of the Italian people . . . not through some economic formula, but through the glorification of the brotherhood of the masses, all fused into a single will, a single passion, a single most noble purpose."[83] While sacrificing individual liberty to the totalitarian community, Fascism aimed to realize "the most extraordinary dreams of those utopians who believe in a people happy at its work and glorious and joyful in its diversions."[84]

By totalitarian logic, in such a community only those who did not believe in the sacred nature of the fatherland and the state, who lacked faith and were not given to sacrificing their own welfare for the common good, would refuse to be included. These were therefore not just anti-Fascists, but also the bourgeois with his individualistic morality, his skeptical, materialist nature.

The attack on the bourgeoisie, which was a constant undercurrent in Fascist preaching, and which took off in the second half of the 1930s, was motivated less by an unlikely attempt to abolish class differences than by the ideal that a "good citizen" in a Fascist state was a "social individual," while the "egocentrism of the individual only segregates him from context of the State. Bad citizens should be confined or isolated."[85]

The equality of all citizens before the law—already much reduced by the liberticidal legislation that marked the régime's accession to power and laid the groundwork for discrimination between "good" and "bad" citizens as designated by Fascism—was bound to undergo further alterations. To reinforce and safeguard the totalitarian community of "good citizens," Fascism did not exclude, as Mussolini's paper pointed out in 1927, "further legislation that, taking into account the moral imperatives of this new era, would provide radical sanctions for those who persist in maintaining their separateness from the fundamental aims of Fascist life."[86] Given this prospect, it was totally coherent within totalitarian logic to radicalize the principle of discrimination to the point of adopting anti-Semitic legislation in the framework of new laws "for the defense of the race." This was just a further fanaticization of the lictorial cult.

5

The Temples of the faith

What does the Church have at hand with which to create the Saint of Saints and about Him the House of God?

A few sublime spiritual truths, and the quotidian divine simplicity of bread and wine. In the rarest and most precious cases, some fragment of a relic, which is not shown publicly, but whose invisible, revealed presence shows in a halo of more visible glory about the place that preserves it.

Fascism—for all the distance between the human, however heroic, and the divine—has risen to these great examples. As the Church did, Fascism has entrusted art with the task of conveying and glorifying, in physical and even spiritual form, deeds of the spirit. The task of making this mythological symbol concrete rightly fell to architecture, the most concrete and most symbolic of the arts.

—M. G. Sarfatti

Art, too, was supposed to play a role in celebrating the lictorial cult and the Mussolini myth. Fascism allowed artists, at least those who were not openly anti-Fascist, freedom of inquiry and expression within the field of aesthetics; it differed from Bolshevism and Nazism by not seeking to impose an official "State art." "Nothing could be further from my thoughts," said Mussolini at the Twentieth Century Exhibition on March 26, 1923, "than to encourage anything like a State art," for art "is individual."[1] This agnostic position was somewhat modified when Fascism took power. Not that any official aesthetic canons for a "State art" were laid down, but rather that artists were called upon to create a new, "Fascist art." Now that Italy was morally united, Mussolini said in Perugia on October 5, 1926, the ground had been laid "for a renaissance of a high art that could be both traditional and modern. We have to create; otherwise we will simply be exploiting our great past. We need to create a new art for our times, a Fascist art."[2]

Although it did not canonize an official state aesthetic, Fascism did make it plain that only an art integrated with the totalitarian state and designed to assist in the education of the masses could be considered Fascist art. In art as in politics, the enemy was individualism, which opted out of the fusing of the "collective harmony" and generated among artists skepticism, neutrality, indifference to the state and to the Fascist religion.

A Militant Artist for the "Collective Harmony"

Artists were exhorted to leave the ivory tower of an aestheticism exclusively concerned with the cult of art and convert to the Fascist faith, to become propagandists of the lictorial cult and participate in the life of the "collective harmony." In the specific field of art, they should contribute to representing the myths of the Fascist epic and the creation of the symbols and monuments of the "new culture." Individualism "has a brief life span," said Giuseppe Bottai, discussing the "artist in the State," "because it soon dies of isolation. A more homogeneous State, harnessed to history, bundles them into the fasces of collective energies."[3]

Bottai, who was one of the most convinced and active supporters of the "social purpose" of art integrated into the politics of the totalitarian state, made it quite clear what the state required of artists:

> We ask artists to deal with subjects whose moral commitment is no less than that which every Fascist puts into the performance of his duty. We do not ask them to chronicle the heroic deeds of Fascism. We know that our reality is also their reality, and we want our artists not to read daily newspapers but instead to look into the very depths of the human soul. All we ask of artists is that they be actors and not spectators; protagonists in the dramatic, epic, religious events of this most ancient and very new Italy, not members of the chorus. Only by an act of faith, incumbent on all, artists and critics, will art and politics cease to be mutually incongruous activities and finally be reconciled on the epic plane of history, to apply a solid seal to that totalitarian unity of ideals which for so many poets and artists has been only a utopia, but which the Duce has founded once and for all.[4]

The freedom of aesthetic inquiry originally conceded was quickly brought back into orthodox Fascist religious lines by that same Bottai when he said that the artist "who wishes to participate consciously in the ideal life of Italy will examine his own ideas in the light of Fascist doctrine and practice, and will rebuild his own mental structure along lines set down by them. An essential condition is that in this self-examination he not substitute some personal conception for those affirmed by Fascist policy."[5] This call for a return to orthodoxy took on a somewhat sinister resonance when Bottai made reference to certain "pollutions" of Italian art in the past thirty years, to "certain artists . . . infected by Jewish elements," to "certain fleeting flirtations . . . with Dadaism and Surrealism" from which "real artists were immune." Other artists, Bottai added, were no bother: "their various sour little cenacles have never seriously troubled the judgment of honest people."[6]

The notion of a political function for art goes back to the very origins of Fascism. The duty of an artist "in this time of national resurrection." wrote a young Fascist in 1924, is to enter "the conscious and subconscious of the masses, to seek out their spirit, to make it flower out of the complex material of which, through so many events, it was for years a prisoner."[7] For the most vigorous recruiters of artists to the Fascist cause, the masses would be the principal beneficiaries of a pedagogical Fascist art. The artist in the "Fascist era," wrote Valentino Piccoli, should be inspired by the "spiritual grandeur and the political function of art." Like all the great Italian artists, he should gain his inspiration from "the halo of perfection that surrounds a whole people, from an awareness of the historical mission of this sacred Italy of ours."[8] "Race" was the fountain from which the artist should obtain inspiration, so that he could be simultaneously "the historian and the prophet of the people from which he has emerged." The artist was "the only one who, with his characteristic sensibility for his own being, draws his vitality from the living sources of the race and can at the same time luminously point a finger to the nation's future. When the soul of the artist and that of the people are one, then a national art will have come into being."[9]

Nor was the Fascist appeal unheard. One may argue about whether or not a "Fascist art" existed, but there were certainly artists who worked, as artists, to give shape to Fascist mythology as they themselves lived and interpreted it—at least until the time when, as the myths to which they had subscribed crumbled, they lost their illusions or became anti-Fascists. Such was the case of Giuseppe Pagano, an artist in perpetual conflict with the traditional Romanism that obtained in much of the regime's architecture. A Fascist as of 1920, a *squadrista* and a teacher in the School of Mystical Fascism until 1941, he went over to the anti-Fascist cause at the end of 1942 and died in a Nazi concentration camp after having refused to join the Social Republic.[10]

There were certainly artists who responded to the appeal for opportunistic reasons, but others—including some far from minor artists— became Fascists not only because they accepted its political ideology, but because they interpreted it in religious terms as expressing a new Italy. They enthusiastically accepted that art had a political task to perform in creating the new state. Some of the chief protagonists of the modernist avant-garde were among the earliest Fascists, and remained loyal throughout the régime, for they considered the movement headed by Mussolini as itself a vanguard: starting with politics, Fascism could bring

about their own ideal of a *total revolution*. Their revolution was a "spiritual" revolution, and in its wake would come not only a "new art" but
also a new life-style, a "New Man."[11]

For Ardengo Soffici the myths, rituals and symbolism of Fascism were
a manifestation of a new "Fascist religiosity" through which the long-
cherished secular religion of the "new Italy" would finally come into being.[12] Such painters did not disdain the theory or practice of a "propaganda aesthetic" destined to spread Fascist myths for the education of the
masses. "In every period, up to the very threshold of our own," as the
painter Basilio Cascella explained to the Duce, "Art, above and beyond
any discussion, has served to glorify the Throne and the Church with all
the means at its disposal . . . The Church has always known how to use
art for its own ends; it has never so far abandoned that tradition. The
State, on the other hand, has overlooked this potent medium, leaving art
to itself through an ill-conceived scruple about freedom." Instead, the
state should use art "as if it were a Religion, which stands above differences of principles and of feelings. It should establish, if I may be permitted the analogy, a sort of parallel to the papal Society for the Propagation of the Faith."[13]

As in the great periods of the church, artists were called on to illustrate
and glorify the myths of the Fascist religion. This was true not only of
the figurative arts, but of any form of art that involved a mass audience—
as, for instance and primarily, the theater. According to Pier Luigi Rosso
di San Secondo, it fell to Fascist Italy to restore "the civic, religious, and
poetic values of the theater, considered as the high expression of a whole
people," as it had been in ancient Greece.[14] Anton Giulio Bragaglia
thought that the culture that Fascism wished to create must have a "high
spiritual, religious, and moral fervor," for "the religion of beauty fits well
with the religion of God and of the State" and could fill the people's need
to "be guided by high ideals that act on the soul as faith and manly
enthusiasm." With the Greek and Roman models in mind, Bragaglia saw
the theater "assuming that splendid function of forming a sensibility and
aesthetic consciousness among the masses."[15]

This aesthetic "sensibilization" of the collectivity was the task to which
the Carri di Tespi, or Touring Thespians, created in 1929 by the National
Leisure Organization (Organizzazione nazionale Dopolavoro; OND), devoted itself; the group traveled throughout Italy putting on performances
to "raise the artistic sense of the lower classes and the mass of workers."[16]
In 1936 the Ministry of Popular Culture set up "Theater Saturdays" under
the sponsorship of the OND to subsidize rural and mass attendance at
theatrical performances.[17] These aimed, by putting on public performances, to create "that unity in the public on which the great theater of the

classical past was based," thus building "a new public, bringing to the theater the most diverse strata of society," and involving them in a collective passion such as was seen in sporting events.[18]

Especially among the young, however, there were those who wanted a far greater political content for the "mass theater." The propagandist function of the theater could be understood in two ways: either as "a revolutionary educational activity intended to arouse in the public feelings and concepts that were not those of the society in which the author works," or "as revolutionary work that did not seek to create in its public the consciousness of a new order," but rather made audiences understand the values of a new "universal ethos" that Fascism had already "created empirically." "Faith in the gods in ancient Greece, medieval piety, the cult of Honor in the theater of France's Great Century are the historical links that bound together and unified the people." It was "from the revelation and glorification of these forces that the Greek theater, the sacred theater of the middle ages, and the theater of Corneille and Racine were born." If a new ethos came into being with Fascism among the masses, it was up to the "theater of the masses" to carry out "the political function of revealing that essence to the people."[19]

Taking it for granted that Fascism had achieved a "fusion of minds, the like of which had not been seen in millennia," another apologist of Mussolini's "mass theater" explained that now at last a writer could "achieve unison with the masses . . . portraying for the people the sublime spectacle of the passionate revolution" that Fascism had created.[20]

These were indeed the criteria used by many playwrights who staged Fascist theater. Mostly they dramatized events in the revolutionary epic or Fascist myths, showing them as a real religion. For the most part, these were works of little artistic worth. They simply presented the chief events of Fascism as a movement governed by faith and founded and guided by a leader of genius. This leader had saved Italy from disorder and chaos; he had fought against the factionalism that had so lacerated the unity of the fatherland and against the materialistic degradations of socialism. It was Mussolini who had redeemed Italians, united them into one family in harmony with their common Fascist fatherland; and it was he who would lead them, a warriorlike, civilizing people, marching toward a radiant future.

The historical background to these dramas might be Italy immediately after the Great War, the feats of the *squadristi,* the Fascist Revolution, the social policy of the régime, or military interventions in Africa or Spain. The Fascists, many of whom were portrayed as repentant socialists, converted to and redeemed by the "Word" of Mussolini, were incarnations of the Good: they were pure and idealistic men, the heirs and successors to the volunteers of the Risorgimento; they acted solely out of faith in Fascism and the Duce; they were ready to sacrifice themselves for the safety and greatness of the fatherland, all under the emblem of the lictor. Some of these plays ended with a vision of the Duce spread-eagled against the sky at the head of his black-shirts, or with the apparition of luminous fasces, a radiant annunciation of the dawn of a new era. Their very titles— *Fascist Dawn, Aurora, Fascist Martyrs, Light in Darkness, Toward the Light, Regeneration, A People on the March, Italy under Way*—show the epic nature of this Fascist dramaturgy.

Redemption was the title of one of the earlier and uglier examples of Fascist theater. Written by Roberto Farinacci and staged in 1927, it told the story of a socialist who, having realized the materialism, the lack of religious faith, and the unworthiness of his comrades, repents and is converted to Fascism.[21] Only when he is mortally wounded during the mobilization of the March on Rome and sheds his blood for the Fascist revolution does his squadron leader give him his party card and accept him into the bosom of his squadron as hero and martyr. Mussolini, too, enjoyed collaborating on historical dramas with protagonists such as Caesar, Napoleon, and Cavour. These were solitary heroes, surrounded by incomprehension and betrayal, struggling against destiny to achieve their goal of greatness.[22]

Similar motives inspired Fascists in the figurative arts. Out of all the polemics among the various artistic movements as to which should be recognized as "authentic" representatives of a "Fascist style," the common driving force was the social and political function of art. Whatever their aesthetic orientation—whether it was to repeat the classical models of traditional Romanity or to seek out a Fascist "modernity"—all these artists created works designed to propagandize Fascist religion. The figurative and architectonic matrix used to celebrate the lictorial cult, though inspired by contrasting, and sometimes even opposed, aesthetic directions, may today be judged in various ways on purely artistic grounds. But they all have a common aim: to create a religious monumentality inspired by the myths of Fascism.

Of the artists engaged in the construction of the Fascist symbolic universe, Mario Sironi is perhaps the most representative.[23] His long collaboration as an illustrator in Mussolini's newspaper, in frescos, as exhibition architect and art critic, produced the most considerable and original aesthetic representation of the Fascist myths and epic. His was the work of a convinced but tormented faith that led him to subscribe even to the Social Republic. At the end of 1942 he was thanking Mussolini for having sent him a photograph inscribed "to the comrade of times both old and new." In his reply, Sironi repeated his loyalty. "Nothing," he wrote, "could have given me greater joy than Your remembering my 'old times'—that is, of my faraway, burnished, fiery, and absolute loyalty. And thus it remains in these 'new times.' For if all my pride rests in that, it is that I have lived and suffered for that loyalty, and it is from that, too, that arise all my greatest hopes. May God protect You, and with You, all of us."[24]

When Mussolini was asked to nominate Sironi to the Academy, the men who wrote to him presented Sironi as being not only "the only artist who will leave a profound mark on Your Era" but as "devoted, faithful, and a mystic."[25] Sironi was dramatically attracted to and won over by the mystical side of Fascism, which tied in with his own idea of the modern: "a period of grandiose myths and gigantic upheavals."[26] The role assigned by Fascism to the artist in the building of a "new society" was one that Sironi felt as a mission: "This is a time of faith," he wrote in 1929. "It is important to build."[27] Sironi saw Fascism as the dawning of a great period in Italian art. Fascist art should "reconnect us with our great past and . . . regain its leadership";[28] it should follow earlier painting's "grandiose unfolding of vast styles, the classical, the medieval, the renaissance."[29] This was the way to give birth to a new Italian style, as monumental and decorative as the great art of the classical period, one that would express the myths and symbols that would evoke "the complex orchestration of modern life."[30] This was the way to restore prestige and vigor to the political and educational functions of art, which Sironi saw as characteristic of the classical tradition in Italian art.

"Italy," Sironi wrote, "along with all its many 'unsanctionable' merits, has this unrivaled experience of art, which has worked its way out in strict dependence on events and political life."[31] Because Fascism was inaugurating a new era in Italian civilization, art should live and interpret this new sense of life and make it known to the masses. Through "the unity of the arts [Fascist art will] bring sculpture and painting back to their Mediterranean, sun-filled, decorative, and architectonic purposes."[32] In forms both modern and archaic it would find ways adequate to express, in a fashion severe, dramatic, and limited to the essentials, "the pagan and constructive primitiveness of the modern age."[33]

This would create a new *style,* Sironi explained, "because rather than working through a 'subject' (the Communist idea), or through suggesting a 'milieu,' it is through style that Fascist art will succeed in leaving a fresh mark on the soul of the people."[34] Sironi's remarks on style are in perfect harmony with the notion of "life-style" that crops up in all forms of Fascist pedagogical liturgy:

> Fascism is a style of life; it is the way Italians live. There is no possible formula that can fully express it, much less contain it. Equally, there is no formula that can fully express, much less contain, what is meant by Fascist

Art—that is, an art that is the expression, in plastic form, of the Fascist spirit.

Fascist Art will be delineated bit by bit, as the result of long, hard labor by the best. What ought to be and must be done as of now is to clear away the problems posed to artists by the many errors that surround them.

In the Fascist State, art has a social, an educational function. Such an art must convey the ethic of our time. It must give unity of style and grandeur to *common life*. In that way art will revert to what it was in its greatest periods, at the peaks of civilization: *a perfect instrument for spiritual government*.

The individualistic concept of "art for art's sake" has been superseded. From this it follows that there is a deep incompatibility between the aims of Fascist Art and those other forms of art that devolve from the arbitrary, from singularity, from the particular aesthetic of a group, a cenacle, or an academy. The anxiety that still troubles European art is the product of a protracted decomposition of the spirit. After years and years of technical exercises and fastidious nordic introspection concerning naturalistic phenomena, modern painting feels the need of a superior spiritual synthesis.[35]

Sironi thought Fascism was achieving a new life-style that gave form and order to the chaos of modernity by molding the consciousness of the masses and integrating them into a common life. His strong emphasis on the pedagogical function of art as part of political activity fits perfectly into the scheme of totalitarian politics. It is congruent with its overriding will to mold the minds of the people, with its desire to create a "harmonious collective," with an all-encompassing, unified, choral view of the popular mind—all states of being that art should contribute to forming while also becoming their highest form of expression. Sironi thought the artist should abandon his egocentrism and become a "militant"; he should serve "an ethical idea and subordinate his own individuality to the collective task." With "an intimate sense of dedication to that common task," the artist "should once again become a man among men, as he was at the height of our culture."[36] He saw Fascist artists as the "soldiers of the millennium," marching "toward the future in a world full of warrior songs," as the modern heirs of the religious and decorative arts of the Mediterranean peoples, from Egyptians and Etruscans to Romans and Byzantines.

The Epic of the Revolution

Much of Fascist art, not just Sironi's, provided an epical and mythical transformation of Fascism for educational consumption. The moral force that inspired the militant artist and made him devoted to the collective task was, in Sironi's eyes, the religious sense of life that Fascism had instilled into the régime's great collective set-pieces. "There is no country like Italy," he wrote, "in which art is a communion of minds, a sense of religion that is part of and accompanies every high point of our social life and culture." Art was "the constant handmaid of so many great epochs; it wove their stories into myths and legends as art." It sublimated the history of their glorious events. Major art shows should set aside their old elitist, bourgeois, and commercial functions and become "art festivals . . . universal . . . and popular," something "that really counts and commits people to the higher life of the national spirit, a place in which are reca-pitulated not only individual values, but also aspirations to the ideal, the more vast and creative orientations of the common culture."[37]

The most important and effective realization of Sironi's ideal of Fascist art as the sublimation of history "in the form of myth and legend" was the great Exhibition of the Fascist Revolution which opened in Rome on October 28, 1932, as part of the celebrations of the first decade of Fascist rule, and in which Sironi played a major part.[38] It was certainly the most accomplished and suggestive sculptural and figurative synthesis of the régime's mythic and symbolic universe. The Exhibition, Margherita Sar-fatti wrote, interpreting its purpose and meaning with her usual sensibil-ity, was not just "a collection of historical materials, but history in action through its translation—mythical but true, indeed the only truth—into symbol and allegory," a transformation that only artists could perform.[39] Participants in this project and its realization included some of the finest Italian painters, sculptors, and architects, artists such as Enrico Pram-polini, Giuseppe Terragni, Antonio Valente, Adalberto Libera, Achille Funi, Marino Marini, Domiano Rambelli, Leo Longanesi, M. Bartoli, and Miño Maccari.[40]

The idea for the Exhibition, to celebrate the tenth anniversary of the founding of the party, came from Dino Alfieri, president of the National Institute for Fascist Culture in Milan. Alfieri suggested an exhibition that might "make people relive fifteen years of the history of the Italian peo-ple," from intervention to the Fascist régime. The original proposal, out-lined by Antonio Monti, the director of the Museum of Risorgimento History in Milan, was to retrace the stages of national renewal through the war and the Fascist revolution.[41] Alfieri, in his reply, said that the exhibition must be not just a documentary representation, but also an epic evocation of the beginning of a new era; it should contain "both a panoramic overview and an apotheosis, a logical demonstration" of what Fascism had achieved.[42] The idea was then developed and controlled by the party.[43] The whole project was given further definition and approval by the party directorate on July 14, 1931.

The Exhibition was divided into four thematic sections: the State, Labor, Arms, and the Spirit. This final section was to have shown "the spiritual patrimony of the Italian people, illuminated by the abnegation and sacrifice that mark it as heroic." "Our spirit is our faith, which dominates events," explained Alfieri, "and the creative, active, achieving part of the spirit is will power." Therefore, "the visitor to this Exhibition should throughout feel the emanation of a superior will, that which gives life and molds men, the will of the Leader in which all the mysterious powers of our race converge."[44]

As the Exhibition was nearing the end of the planning stage, the project was transformed from a history of the Italian people into a glorification of Fascism and its leader, to which no part of the original plan had been devoted. The idea of devoting the Exhibition to a review of the achievements of Fascism was also canvassed, but this was postponed for a future exhibition,[45] and only a part was dedicated to Fascist institutions. Mussolini, ever more attracted by the idea, which he followed closely through its preparatory stages, decided that the Exhibition would be devoted to the "Fascist revolution" and be inaugurated in Rome on the tenth anniversary of Fascism's coming to power.[46]

Preparations advanced at a feverish pace between August 5 and October 22, 1932, the day of the inauguration, though not without argument and difficulty, including some economic problems. The penny-pinching administrative secretary foresaw a "real economic disaster."[47] Mussolini and the party secretary made supplementary appropriations available to continue with construction. The collection of materials through the various federal secretaries was under way, and an appeal had been sent out to all party members to busy themselves with research. The result was an enthusiastic response and a flood of documents and curiosa, letters, newspapers, photographs, manifestos, squadron pennants, relics of "Fascist martyrs," as well as red flags and other "trophies" and documents taken from their adversaries by the Fascist in their raids.[48] Touted as the greatest event of the Decennial celebrations by an effectively orchestrated propaganda machine, directed in particular toward Fascists, the Exhibition developed a special "religious" aura from the very start. This found a genuine response. Fascists were invited to make a contribution "for the success of the event, which will glorify the sacrifices and the faith of all Black-Shirts, including those currently far from home."[49]

Preparing the Exhibition involved a collective effort like that of building "a secular, ephemeral cathedral"[50] dedicated to the self-glorification of the Fascists. The Exhibition, according to an article in *Gioventù fascista,* was meant to serve Fascist believers, "not as a museum catalogue or a display of furnishings" but as an "outpouring of feeling to move hearts. We feel fanatical, for without fanaticism we cannot feel close to each other." For those artists summoned to take part, it had to be made clear "that the idea is to express a faith, which must be represented with the kind of fervor that, regardless of any professional deficiencies, can arouse religious feeling."[51]

As far as aesthetics were concerned, the organizers had orders from Mussolini to "be up-to-date, ultramodern, and bold, without any melancholy souvenirs in the style of the past";[52] it should be "full of vigor, and theatrical," and should celebrate the dynamically modern and revolutionary nature of Fascism. It must in no way resemble "Giolitti's frock coat."[53] The Exhibition was conceived and carried out in a modernist, futurist style and made an ostentatious statement against architectural traditionalism. The Umbertine façade of the Exhibition palazzo on Via Nazionale was completely redone to hide its nineteenth-century monumentality, described as "full of empty conceit, of grandiosity without style, of tasteless ornamentation," and unworthy to represent a revolution "that heralded the beginning of a new era."[54] Both the interior and the exterior of the palazzo were radically transformed by their architectural and dramatic redecoration.

Discarding various proposals for the façade, including one of a "Romanizing solemnity, stitched together with imitation travertine marble," and another that displayed a form of "mannerist baroque"—for "the great periods [of architecture] did not imitate the past, a procedure that inevitably leads to mediocrity, but rather created few forms and made original statements"—the project was assigned to Mario De Renzi and Adalberto Libera, the bold and original modernity of whose design seemed the most adequate to "represent our own inspiriting and dynamic, unsettled and feverish times."[55]

On inauguration day, the new façade was revealed to be a huge cube whose "geometric purity" symbolized "the synthesis of the totalitarian and integralist concepts of the Fascist régime," while its somber red, evocative of revolution, recalled a Roman tradition of Pompeian red. The façade was broken up by four polished, twenty-five-meter-high fasces, stylized into mechanical- and metallic-looking columns. These were linked to the marquee over the entrance, on which was displayed, in black metal, "Exhibition of the Fascist Revolution." The stylization of the façade, which made it look like some futuristic industrial chimney or the funnels of a liner, gave new meaning to the ancient Roman symbol of authority, and linked the myth of Romanity to Fascist revolutionary modernism.[56] Each side of the façade was decorated with a giant red-and-white sheet-metal X. The Roman numeral, emblem of the Decennial, was also featured on the main entrance and inside the Exhibition hall, as a magical symbol and augury that celebrated "the first of the ten anticipated and certain decades" of the Fascist revolution.[57] The overall effect of the façade, enhanced by lighting at night, was that of a fortress or of some inexorable fighting machine, and this warlike aspect was reinforced by the Militia Honor Guard drawn up before the Exhibition with helmet and rifle.

The steps leading up to the building, under their giant metal arch, seemed the entrance to a church. This sacred metaphor was reinforced, right after the entrance—flanked by two fasces of polished zinc—by the text of the Fascist oath, which the visitor could read, lit on a tablet, as he walked up the stairs. Inside, too, religiosity was all-pervasive. A well-conceived series of images, lights, colors, and sounds created "the atmosphere of the times, all fire and fever, tumultuous, lyrical, resplendent." They "suggest fantasy, excite the imagination and divert the mind. The visitor will be overwhelmed and shaken to the depths."[58]

The overall themes of the Exhibition, set out year by year, ran through the various rooms "like some huge symphony whose movements begin with the tragic time between July 1914 and May 1915, to conclude with the imperial apotheosis marked by the march of the Black-Shirts along the consular roads that lead to Rome." The central motif of the whole symphony lay in the "weighty, dominant, and determining figure of the Duce." His was the "main theme into which are inserted, with all the dynamism of an overwhelming crescendo, all the various episodes and figures, facts and documents, people and events" that "make up this vast whole designed to move the soul and exalt the heart."[59] In such surroundings, the assembled documentary material became a symbolic element designed to "give the visitor an intimation of vitality and feeling."[60] As Sironi wrote, the Exhibition was the symbolic expression of an idea; its "monumental realism, expressed openly and directly . . . generated feelings as powerful as any drama."[61]

The visitor, who had to follow a prescribed course through the nineteen ground-floor rooms of the Exhibition (the second floor was devoted to the institutions of the régime), was assaulted by waves of symbols and myths. Pictures, documents, stylized casts, sculptures, frescos, huge letters and photomontages brought back both people and events as a "demonstration" of the Fascist revolution and its future.[62] The succession of themes illustrated in the different rooms assumed the function of the successive liturgical "stations" of a sacred history, recounting the birth and origin of the Fascist religion as successively revealed by its prophet, its messiah, and its founder.[63]

In the first two rooms, the eve of intervention was shown as Mussolini's annunciation of a new faith in an Italy characterized by "political atavisms incapable of self-renewal, economics without principles, a state without authority, an art without expression, a public opinion that lacked leaders, and parties without ideals."[64] The whole area was dominated by a giant red fasces (referring to the assembly of the Fasces of Revolutionary Action in January 1915), and this symbol, in many aesthetic guises, persisted throughout the Exhibition. On a column stood a head of Mussolini in relief, the work of the sculptor Rambelli, whose rough-hewn and austere carving portrayed the Duce as a "fighting ascete."[65] Hanging overhead was a giant reproduction of the first issue of *Il popolo d'Italia,* the newspaper that was portrayed throughout as the symbolic gospel of the new faith.[66]

The next rooms were devoted to the war, shown as "creative and heroic," as an event that was both sacrificial and purifying and that gave "the strongest elements in the Risorgimento" new vigor, bringing about "the unique, precise, incomparable, and definitive miracle" of Fascism.[67] In a setting that was "majestic and solemn as a temple or a sanctuary," "unadorned and naked as in a Pantheon," rose a massive and imperious image of the Soldier King, this too the work of Rambelli, and a large bas-relief of an armed and winged Italy, by Marino Marini, whose crude and archaizing shapes brought to mind "a race inspired by the future without betraying its origins . . . a millennial culture that joins the ancient to the contemporary and perpetuates itself in its will for power and freedom of harmony."[68]

The rooms dedicated to 1919 and 1920—with their background of a postwar Italy prey to disorder and chaos, neatly demarcated in red and black—offered the story of the heroic handful of early Fascists, led by their chief, who fought to defend victory and to reaffirm the sacred nature of the fatherland against the assaults of Bolshevism. The "ever-returning Beast," as Mussolini had defined it, figured as a monstrous anthropoid, cloaked in red and topped with a Phrygian bonnet, which "with its twisted paws trampled on the sacrifice of war and victory." Next to it was a photograph of a "huge head with a stupid, mocking smile, all but suffocating in a great red flag about its neck," symbolizing the people prey to "the Bolshevik orgy."[69]

The rooms for 1921–1923 portrayed the rise of Fascism and the triumphal march to power. Against a dynamic, sweeping backdrop, a rich collection of documents and images of the *squadristi,* of the flags of their adversaries, trophies of punitive expeditions, and especially of portraits, souvenirs, and relics of the "Fascist martyrs," blood-soaked garments and flags, gave these political events a sacred character. A "gigantic, symbolic representation," bathed in dazzling light, created by the architect Giuseppe Terragni, showed a drummer and a forest of hands outlined against a blow-up of a Fascist "rally." The hands rose in the Roman salute powered by three turbines representing "the strength and will of the people—disciplined by its faith," reaching for power. An aura of "heroism and the sacred" was provided by a Mussolini inscription, dedicated to a fallen Fascist and containing a line from Giosué Carducci ("With his blood, he feeds the moving wheel"), to "indicate the holy nature of the Fascist martyrology that made possible and destined the triumph of the Revolution."[70]

In the rooms devoted to the March on Rome, which were suffused with the colors of the Italian flag, Sironi had, in his imposing, severe, austere, monumental style, recreated the victory of Fascism: through photographs of the squadrons on the march and an enormous bas-relief portraying a Roman sword striking through chains, an eagle in full flight, two Fascist warriors raising Roman insignia on high, and, as a symbolic climax to this triumphant march, the Arch of Vittorio Veneto, "whose glory contained the rise of the Fasces, the Exalter of the Fatherland . . . the Roman symbol, sculpted in travertine marble and rising to the red-tiled arch like a huge, living flame."[71]

Having thus taken part in the transfiguration into "legend and myth" of the Fascist revolution, the visitor passed through the portico of the *Salon d'honneur*—designed and realized by Sironi and dominated by a high relief of Mussolini the Soldier—and stepped into a narrow space that reconstructed "the Editor's austere cubbyhole at *Il popolo d'Italia*."[72] He then moved through the Gallery of the Fasces—flanked by rows of squadron pennants and powerful fasces-shaped pillars, each bearing a date from 1914 to 1922, likewise the work of Sironi—and subsequently through a doorway surmounted by a statue of Italia bearing the fasces and the star of Victory, where he entered the room devoted to the Duce. This was designed by Leo Longanesi and, in contrast to the dramatic settings of the other exhibition rooms, offered a sober but no less hagiographic account of Mussolini's life.

This room was the high point in a mythical transformation of Mussolini to which the visitor had been subjected from the very beginning of the Exhibition. The Fascist version of Italian history was epical in nature; thus Mussolini's development had about it a teleological character that came to its completion with his advent to power. "Everything is born in Him. Everyone turns to Him. Every morning Italy wakes up with Him . . . His great life contains a bit of every Italian's life."[73] All the figures of Italian history in the preceding rooms, from Garibaldi to Battisti and D'Annunzio, had been presented as precursors, prophets, messengers, and apostles of the Word of Mussolini; they had been cast in an epic dominated by the divine intuition of Mussolini, "the Determinator." The events portrayed seemed a creative emanation of the Duce's will. On him the Exhibition conferred the mystical sacred character of "the one hero of our times." As relics of an already legendary life, offered to the veneration of all with religious devotion, were pictures of the Duce's parents, photographs, documents, and other memorabilia of the "hero," such as the bloody stretcher and crutch from the time when he had been wounded in the war, and the blood-soaked handkerchief from the attempt on his life on April 7, 1926.

The sacredness of the Mussolini room was emphasized by its function as an antechamber to the "Altar of Sacrifice of the Hundreds upon Hundreds of Black-Shirts."[74] The "Martyrs' Sanctuary" was the mystical center of the Exhibition, the *sancta sanctorum* of Fascist religion. It attributed to "the sacrifice of the Fallen the ultimate pantheon, the crown of immortality"; it was "the sacred symbol of the capacity of a race for sacrifice, of its certainty in the future, defended and guaranteed by the invincible spirit of the Dead." The room itself was a round crypt with a large cupola, flanked by two lesser domes, from which flowed a blue light. Here the architects Adalberto Libera and Antonio Valente (although Mussolini himself participated in the final design of the room)[75] had created a symbolic visual representation of the Fascist roll call to the memory of the martyrs:

> From a blood-red pedestal rises a metallic Cross, a warlike cross made of metal, which seems as though suspended in the spent light of the crypt. On that symbol of sacrifice and faith, the Cross, appear the words of the ritual: the Roll Call. An inscription recalls the supreme justification for the sacrifice: "For the Immortal Fatherland." As the living silently invoke the departed, now, in the deep blue light of the Sanctuary, the martyrs reply: "Present." A thousand and one voices are caught in the glimmer, and that light echoes to infinity the voices of those who gave of themselves more than was ever asked, those who now show the way to the tireless legions.
>
> Along the bottom of the walls, arranged like battalions on the march, are the pennants of the action squads. Each bears the name of a martyr, and for every void the barbarian enemy caused in the ranks of the Black-Shirts, a new squad sprang into being, bearing as a mark of its faith the name of the Martyr, ever-present among the living as both example and spur.
>
> In the unreal atmosphere of that Sanctuary one can hear, as though borne from a mysterious distance, the song of the Revolution. A Militia-man stands guard, immobile.[76]

On leaving the Sanctuary the visitor had to pass once again through the Mussolini room. The effect was to reemphasize the mystical union between the Duce and the martyrs, the supreme inhabitants of the Fascist empyrean. At this point, the visitor left behind the mystical aura of the epic and went upstairs, where everything was calmer and more consonant with the disciplined, constructive spirit of the régime. In synthetic form, through didactic illustrations, the visitor could observe the organizations and achievements of Fascism.

Pilgrimages to the Temple

Outside Italy the Exhibition was widely hailed for its aesthetic value, while at home it was a huge success. Its visitors were so numerous that the closing date, April 21, 1933, had first to be postponed until October and then again until the following October. In its two years the Exhibition was seen by 3,854,927 people, and among the many foreigners who came to see it were Le Corbusier, André Gide, Maurice Denis, and Paul Valéry. This considerable attendance was the result of intense publicity throughout Italy, set in motion by the party and nourished by numerous enthusiastic comments in the press and by foreigners. Special prices made trips to the Exhibition and a visit to the capital possible. Many wanted to show their zeal for the Fascist faith and hoped to see the Duce in person; curiosity was also greatly aroused by the publicity campaign and by word of mouth. All these factors multiplied the number of daily visits—by individuals, but especially by organized groups of workers, students, teachers, members of the armed forces, professionals, and so on. It reached the point that the party had to take special measures to control the flow of visitors to the capital, limiting groups to five hundred and requiring approval from the various secretaries of individual federations.[77]

The fact that 1934 was also a Holy Year increased the number of visitors and indirectly contributed to the religious aura that the Exhibition's sponsors had hoped to promote. But one should not underestimate the genuine enthusiasm that moved Fascists particularly. Stimulated by the many celebrations and rituals surrounding the Decennial, they visited the Exhibition to drink in the events in which they had themselves been protagonists while also enjoying the self-glorification of an epic. According to one Tuscan visitor, people moved about inside the Exhibition with "a murmur worthy of some solemn ceremony in Saint Peter's."[78] A Sardinian noted "the wonderful feeling induced by the sacred, meditative atmosphere." He described it as "living among memories that communicate with overwhelming eloquence the presence and words of the Duce."[79] "Temple" and "Altar" are two of the most frequently recurring terms used to describe the Exhibition in the press or in comments made by ordinary visitors.

"Conceived as a cathedral whose very walls speak," wrote Margherita Sarfatti, "for the first time in the modern world [the Exhibition] brings an event in recent history into the fervent atmosphere of affirmation and of a religious ceremonial."[80] Another commentator said that "if the Temple has become an Altar, and that Altar is identified with Ritual, [it is because] of the sincerity of the Faith in which profession is made and with which it is professed," and to the way in which its artifacts expressed that Faith.[81]

In this overall atmosphere, for Fascists a visit to the Exhibition became a pilgrimage to the Eternal City, to render, in the words of the president of the Naples section of the *Balilla*, "devout and deferential homage to the Temple of our Revolution."[82] One correspondent suggested that a visit to the Exhibition should be made obligatory as a rite of purification, "because there are still people who think of themselves as highly cultivated who need, indeed greatly need, to go to the Exhibition and examine their own consciences, people who live in circumstances that only Fascist Generosity would allow . . . people who can manage a Roman salute [but] who live in malicious, closed circles—in short, despicable people."[83]

There were also hundreds of "pilgrims" from every part of Italy and from abroad who, animated by a spirit of adventure, curiosity, exhibition, or Fascist dedication, made the trip to Rome on foot or on bicycle. One such actually stopped to pay homage to the tomb of the Duce's parents in Predappio. A man with one leg amputated rode his bicycle from Brescia, while a group of Red Cross workers came from Santa Margherita Ligure dragging behind them a bed on wheels. A young Romagnolo Fascist, lacking the money for the trip, traveled from Cesenatico to Rome by bicycle.[84]

The Exhibition was particularly important in the lictorial cult. Not only was it a mythical dramatization of the revolution, it was also the occasion for a special, if ephemeral, ritual that brought into being an extraordinary *cult event*. Its "sacred space" was the Exhibition itself, and its protagonist the liturgical mass of the innumerable visitors—the groups that attended the changing of the Honor Guard and took part in the rituals before the entrance, which included marches, songs, music, and acclamations of the Duce and Fascism. The chronicler of the Exhibition, who was—as commander of the special Militia detachment assigned to the Exhibition—an eyewitness, gave an impressionistic vision of the crowd's movement: "Throngs of people converging on the threshold, a silent Honor Guard, steely grey fasces, rays of passionate color; from time to time, as the perfectly ordinary crowd climbs the stairs, the sound of a chorus or a fanfare; pennants, banners, flags; greetings to the DUCE, full-throated and frequent; a whole murmur of rituals, a rhythm of symbols."[85]

The liturgy of the Exhibition, as it could be called, began with the ritual inauguration before a vast throng, in which Mussolini and other hierarchs took part. The Duce was greeted with the singing of the Fascist hymn by a Militia band, by the Riflemen and 180 Militia consuls aligned with the standards of their legions, the Quadrumvirs and the national party leadership. In the entrance, by the Oath incised in the wall, he was saluted by a detachment of *Avanguardisti* rigidly at attention and by the orphan children of fallen Fascists. A young man recited the ritual oath and posed the traditional question, "Do you so swear?" to which the whole detachment replied as one, "I so swear." After walking through the various rooms with his entourage, as though in procession, Mussolini spoke a few words of praise for the organizers, halted before the relics of the fallen martyrs, and rendered homage, at attention, and in deep silence, to the martyrs' sanctuary.[86]

In the two years it stayed open, there was a ritual Changing of the Guard several times daily. This was executed not just by the Militia but also by family members of the fallen, by mutilees, fighting forces, the *Sansepolcristi*, and organizations of manufacturers and professionals. As the chronicler pointed out, this demonstrated, "through a profoundly symbolic act, the closest possible spiritual bond between the citizen and Fascism, the citizen and his government, between each Italian and the consciousness of his welfare and that of the Fatherland." This liturgy was a form of "second life for the Exhibition . . . a life sublimated in the symbolism and ritual of this Changing of the Guard, for which everyone readies himself as though for renewed profession of faith, a veneration of the Martyrs and their Cause: the [event] clothes all this with sanctity."[87]

The closing of the Exhibition on October 28, 1934, was celebrated with even greater ceremony than the inauguration. The ceremony began in the morning before a huge and dense throng. The tricolored Italian flag and the black flag of Fascism were raised on two of the fasces of the façade. Then throughout the day the Changing of the Guard was taken in turns by the *Sansepolcristi*, the organizers and builders of the Exhibition, members of the Academy, members of the government, and Fascist party leaders.

Mussolini, who had recently revisited the Exhibition, arrived in the evening accompanied by the party secretary. Followed by his ministers, by the Great Council and the Directorate, the Duce repaired to the Sanctuary, where the party banner had been placed next to the cross. There, standing at attention for some minutes, he gave the Roman salute. He made his way out preceded by the party banner and escorted by the *Sansepolcristi*. At the head of the entrance stairs he appeared before the throng while reflectors lit up the lictorial fasces. In the total silence, Starace delivered the "Salute to the Duce," eliciting from the crowd and the massed Fascists the ritual response, "To us!" Immediately afterward a *Balilla* approached the Duce and, having given the Roman salute, took his oath, the responses to which were given by the crowd and the Fascist ranks. Starace then declared the Exhibition closed and ordered the dismissal of the Guard of Honor. After the Salute to the Colors, followed by trumpet fanfares and volleys from the Riflemen, the singing of the national and Fascist anthems by a Roman girls' chorus and the crowd, the event closed with a salute to the Duce among many-colored torches and fireworks.[88]

The symbolic-liturgical interpretation offered by Fascist publicists called the Exhibition an epic glorification of the Fascist revolution celebrated by the Italian people. It was the people, as visitors, who had joined in this choral act of devotion. "The guiding and animating idea of this great structure," wrote the painter Gianfilippo Usellini, "the idea that makes it come alive in past and present history, is that of the spiritual unity of the Italian people, of an Italian way, and how it permeated from one man to a tiny minority, then to a whole people and its future. It is the idea of a modern Italian, of a modern Italian culture that, taking the place of the antagonisms and the negative attitudes of the past, affirms itself and acts as a new moral and political equilibrium."[89]

Beyond aesthetic matters, most writers commented on the educational and "popular" nature of the Exhibition. It had offered the public the "mysterious breath" of "a soul in continual contact with the visitor."[90] In the Sironi sense, the Exhibition had been a celebration of "living together" of artist and people. The hundreds of thousands of visitors, representing every level of society, every kind of person and every profession, were seen as a living symbol of the "collective harmony." By their pilgrimage they had attested to their Fascist faith. The crowd had formed an integral part of the liturgy of the Exhibition.

As the most extreme of all the writers noted of its symbolic and epic meaning, "Between the Exhibition of the Revolution and the People there is a now a high-tension current. This appears to be, and is, fed by a force not easily defined, a force mysterious, mystical, religious. It is without a doubt the most interesting phenomenon of collective psychology in this century."[91] In a slightly more restrained form, but with an equally enthusiastic "sense of community," Bottai hailed the Exhibition as the most impressive of all the celebrations and assemblies for the Decennial, during which one could observe the mystical unity between the Leader "and the sea of human . . . bodies all breathing as one," a mass in which "the idea was made flesh."[92]

Carried by the wave of feeling and enthusiasm raised by the success of the Exhibition, the Fascists appealed to have it made permanent: "as a basilica, the EXHIBITION of our VICTORY:"

Pilgrims of Love and Faith, on every journey, at every call from IMPERIAL ROME, we would visit, with fresh curiosity and renewed passion, the reliquary of our struggle; and, as in a church, our faithful and Fascist hearts would become ever freer of anxiety, ever more hopeful, and readier for whatever sacrifices are demanded of us.

If the DUCE so desires, if Your Excellency so wishes, the EXHIBITION of the REVOLUTION will become our Temple, ever open, ever guarded by Black-Shirts, and ever welcoming, as a refuge of fervent passion, for all those who believed, believe, and continue fervently to believe in the DUCE, and will, tomorrow, believe in our destined imperial future.[93]

One of the Exhibition's organizers took up the proposal, arguing that "the faith of each and all who build something should not be demolished, but should serve future generations as a sacred place in which they can gather and nourish their faith and shape their consciences." By so doing, the party would have "completed a huge and permanent task on behalf of Fascist propaganda among Italians and in the world."[94] In fact even before the Exhibition closed, Mussolini had decided that it ought to have a continued life, announcing that "the permanent home of the Museum of the Fascist Revolution, built in 'a modern, monumental style,' will arise on the Via dell'Impero."[95]

Eternalizing the "Age of Mussolini"

Like every time-honored religion, the Fascist religion sought to glorify its faith and mark its culture by erecting lasting temples and monuments. Fascism was possessed by a real mania for monumentality, which it saw as the material form of the myth and a perennial glorification of its religion. To this end, it entrusted architects with the task of building its cult-centers, such as the various Fascist headquarters, and the monumental buildings destined to perpetuate the glory of Mussolini and Fascism. It is, however, unlikely that this Fascist sense of the monumental derived from a romantic fascination with ruins such as had, according to Hitler's architect Albert Speer, inspired the monumental visions of the Nazi leader. Hitler, Speer says, liked to imagine the effect on future generations of the remains of Nazi monuments.[96]

In Fascist vitalism, monumentality was glorified as an instance of the "great struggle between the creative energy of the mind and the brute needs of nature." In this struggle, although monuments would seem to indicate the triumph of nature, "constructive art" represented "the most sublime and direct victory of mind over nature." But even in ruins the human spirit prevailed. "The ruins of monuments are aesthetically attractive because they give the viewer a living intuition of time's incessant process, and of the organic continuity of history." As such they were an incitement to give "fresh grandeur to a resurrected Fatherland."[97]

Mussolini himself sought to clarify the meaning of monumentality as an integral part of Fascism when he noted that monuments "unless warmed by the beating hearts of the people are just tombstones, cold, bare, and lifeless. These perennial symbols of our memory need to be hemmed about with our faith, and the sureness and solidity of our intentions."[98] A permanent setting for the celebration of the lictorial cult and the régime's ceremonies was needed, so that it would not be forced, on occasion, to use "absurd bits of fake roads, some of them recently built, to which the city decorators had to have resort" during Hitler's visit in 1938.[99]

Fascist monumentality, Sironi argued, "is the voice of the Leader heard over the voices of the many. It is the expression of Faith as opposed to the gesture of the interests, and is intended to give a face, a visible and clear expression to that faith, to its power, its amplitude, its force."[100] Sironi conceived of a monumental style which would be the "architectonic expression of Fascist society, of the State, Religion, its Leadership, of its dominant symbols . . . which would sum up in an over-arching unity the character of our culture."[101] Mussolini himself paraded his passion for architecture, which he called "the greatest of the arts, for it is an epitome of all the others."[102]

Even in this area the argument between classicists and modernists became a competition to determine which would have the privilege of defining the "Fascist style" best suited to immortalize the lictorial cult, and "capture, with the inspiration of art, and in stone, cement, steel, and the most durable materials in nature, the giant footprint of Mussolini, so that those to come can be astounded."[103] One Fascist ideologue, for instance, argued against architectural rationalism. Fascist culture, he wrote, should opt for "a 'lasting' architecture," one in which stone and the "monumental function" of public buildings prevailed. It should emphasize the kind of "language that speaks to men's minds in the form of memory and glorification," the kind of "atmosphere that these create around themselves; the way their constant presence slowly modifies the character of the generations to come." "Monumental architecture, which lasts for centuries," he wrote, "is a symbol of the permanence of the state."[104]

When it came to the political function of architecture, the ideas of the principal advocates of modern rationalism—such as Tarragni, Giuseppe Pagano, Valente—were not so very different. "Today," the architect Gio Ponti wrote in 1932, only politics and architecture "seek to discern, serve, and express" the human aspiration to a "new order."[105] The myth of "construction" through which Fascism symbolized its "Roman" determination to survive the challenge of time, "assaulting history" to create a new order, could hardly leave architects indifferent. Not unnaturally, they were the chief believers in this myth. As the architects Gaetano Minucci and Libera affirmed, architecture was "the fundamental art and science chosen to define and fix in time the nature and history of a particular period."[106]

For those artists seeking to shape a "Fascist style" through architecture and monuments, their guiding principle called, first and foremost, for a high symbolic and religious content. Their idea was to create "sacred spaces" in which to celebrate the cult of the lictor; by so doing they were helping, through the constant suggestiveness of public buildings, to give the "new Italian" a tangible faith in Fascist religion. Expressing the values and defining the form of the "new civilization" was the architect's main task.

It was as though architects had been unleashed by the first years of Fascist power and the ensuing euphoria. Projects of all sorts, ambitious or modest and pointless, tumbled across Mussolini's desk. Architects were among the first to try to immortalize the Fascist revolution for the future. One such project was the pharaonic Eternale Mole Littoria (Everlasting Lictorial Tower), in Rome, which Mario Palantini suggested in 1924 to Mussolini, who at the time seemed impressed by the idea. This "symbolic monument" was intended to "eternalize, in Eternal Rome, the Fascist Revolution, the Black-Shirt epic, and the grandiose achievements of the Duce." In the perfervid mind of its author, however, this building must have represented a synthesis of the Italian civilization that had culminated in the advent of Fascism. "It is not immodest or exaggerated," he wrote, "to state that the Mole might worthily become our third great national monument: after Saint Peter's and Catholicism, the Altar of the Fatherland and the Risorgimento, the Mole Littoria and the Fascist Revolution."[107] The structure was conceived of as the headquarters for the party as well as for various patriotic, military, cultural, commercial, and professional organizations; as housing special permanent exhibits, meeting rooms, gymnasia, thermal baths, an "Augusteo Mussoliniano" for important patriotic occasions, congresses of all sorts, concerts, festivals, and so on; as providing space for libraries, reading rooms, and a Fascist museum. The whole was to be topped with "a superpowerful lighthouse, symbol of the eternal light emanating from Rome."[108]

The Eternal Mole was never built, but the idea of "eternalizing" the Fascist revolution through symbolic architecture was something of an *idée fixe* for Mussolini and the party. Fascism gave a powerful impulse to "sacred" architectural symbolism by building temples to its cult. In both the old and the "new" towns created by Fascism, architects and city planners were busy scattering lictorial symbols. The fasces became a fundamental part of "permanent" or ephemeral architecture. They appeared everywhere—on monuments and buildings, in exhibitions. It appears that

Mussolini himself suggested and outlined the Victory monument built in Bolzano by Marcello Piacentini, a triumphal arch at the foot of the Alps. It consisted of fourteen columns in the shape of fasces, with the ax as capitol, and was designed to "glorify in everlasting marble" the martyrs of Trieste and Trent, "here venerated as saints on an altar."[109]

In 1927 the party had urged that "houses" or asylums be built rather than monuments; each of these "Houses of Italy's New Life" would have borne the name and an account of the exploits of one of the fallen, and in the proposed model schools children would have been taught to honor the memory of those who had fallen for their country.[110] But instead the régime continued to build a great number of monuments to celebrate victory, those who had fallen in the Great War, Fascist martyrs, and heroes of Italian and Fascist history.

The party ascribed considerable cultural value to the *Casa del Fascio,* or local headquarters. As the center of party life it contained a sanctuary dedicated to Fascists who had died in action; in this "mystical temple" these were venerated and "glorified in mutual meditation."[111] Every local party felt it necessary to have a headquarters adequate for party functions, and worthy to host religious ceremonies, for, as the federal secretary for Turin put it, "A Faith needs a Temple."[112]

In its second decade in power the party spurred the construction of these local Fascist centers, which were supposed to glorify the party's dominant role in public life. It asked the federations themselves to raise the money. The structures, their location, and their aesthetics went beyond their bureaucratic purposes as the center of all party organizations; the Fascists also took into account their educational and propagandistic objectives. The party insisted particularly on their symbolic aspect, in which special prominence was given to their "lictorial towers," symbolizing dominance and resembling the communal towers of the Middle Ages. Their bells were designed to rival those of the churches. Besides containing the party's offices, these centers were the heart of the political and social life of the "collective harmony," a place of veneration for the cult of the Fascist martyrs, and a place where people could be indoctrinated into the dogmas of the Fascist religion.

Giuseppe Terragni was inspired by this idea when he built his Fascist center in Como: "In a house dedicated to the people," he wrote, "certain moral, political, and propagandistic considerations arise, and these combine all the purposes for creating a headquarters for local party organizations." These should no longer be, as in the early period, "a hideout, a refuge, or a little fortress," but rather should become "houses, schools, Temples."[113] Built in the rationalist style, the building was an exemplary "symbolic idealization of Fascism."[114] It was explicitly inspired by the

Mussolinian metaphor that "Fascism is a glass house." Its construction was such as to give the public an immediate sense of the full integration of the party into the lives of the people and of the direct communication between the masses and their leaders. Its spiritual center was the sanctuary, symbol of the spiritual content which underlay "Fascist mysticism." Seeking to give it a high sense of memorial religiosity, Teragni designed it as an open cell formed by three monolithic walls of red granite reminiscent of the primitive royal or religious edifices of Mycenae or Egypt.

The Casa Littoria, the new seat of the national party secretariat, was to have been one of the most important expressions of the architectonic symbolism of Fascism, at once sacred and profane. The decision to make the Exhibition of the Revolution permanent, with a perpetual abode for "the Sanctuary of the Black-Shirt Epic,"[115] led to the idea of erecting a giant monument to house the party offices and those of its ancillary organizations as well as the Exhibition of the Revolution and the Martyrs' Sanctuary. The party launched a public subscription to finance the building, for "the Casa Littoria should be the House of all Italians; erected by the whole nation, it will gather unto itself all that incomparable energy which the national spirit offers the Fascist Revolution—this revolution which, unlike any other, conquers time, makes it its own, and moves straight into the future."[116]

Mussolini's wish was that the building should rise opposite the Massenzio Basilica on the new Via dell'Impero, solemnly inaugurated on October 28, 1932. This road through the Roman forums linked Piazza Venezia to the Colosseum. The building should also be set back from the road, as the competition's specifications put it, in order not to obstruct "the view of the whole complex of the Colosseum from Piazza Venezia." The setback would permit "an esplanade raised over the Via dell'Impero to accommodate mass assemblies at solemn events." This too was to be so situated as "not to obstruct the clear view of the Palazzo from the Via dell'Impero." At the appropriate place on the esplanade, there should be "a tribune or rostrum from which the Duce could speak." In color, the building should be in harmony with the surrounding monuments, and its design should reflect "the greatness and power that Fascism has given the renewal of national life in continuity with the Roman tradition. The great structure should be worthy of transmitting to posterity, in a permanent and universal fashion, the era of Mussolini."[117]

By inserting its own monument between the monuments of Rome and the vast Vittorio Emanuele monument, the party's ambition was to create a symbolic architectonic and urbanistic synthesis with which to immortalize Fascism, as the artifact of a new civilization bringing back to life, in the twentieth century, the glories of Rome. The Casa Littoria would also have created a huge "sacred space" between the Colosseum and Piazza Venezia, in which great assemblies and parades could be held for the celebration of the lictorial cult.

The monumental grandiosity of the project aroused heated debate—over the site and the design of the building—between traditionalists and modernists, polemics that were not confined to the architects themselves but spilled over into the Chamber of Deputies, where the supporters and detractors of modernism confronted each other. Beyond this argument, however, the most significant Italian architects on both sides, aroused by the "religious" nature of the project, took the risk of competing over the choice of a symbolism adequate to synthesize the traditionalism and modernity of the Fascist myth: the epic of the revolution and the corporate state; the cult of Romanity and the Duce; devotion to Catholicism and to the Fascist religion; the Italianism and the universality of Fascism.[118]

Common to all the projects was the sacred nature of the edifice as a "temple of the revolution," "the lictorial temple," "the monument to the Faith." Likewise, all the competitors used a form of symbolic syncretism derived from Roman, Christian, and Fascist tradition, to glorify that sacrality. One project was based on the idea of a marriage between Catholicism and Fascism, decorating the proposed palace with an enormous bas-relief featuring Pius XI and Mussolini kneeling before the Virgin in "mystical prayer," with columns representing patron saints such as John Bosco and Benedict as symbols of the *Balilla* and the corporations respectively. This, however, was an isolated case. Most of the projects limited reference to Catholicism to the symbol of the cross and a chapel, while otherwise in every possible way concentrating on the sacred nature of Fascism itself, its symbol, and its leader.

One architect suggested a distinction between two parts of the building: the lictorial palace proper and a second building for exhibitions. Both were huge and symbolic of "the new idea that moves the New Man." Like "two steps toward the sacred," the two parts would be united by an "ideal link," a "Sacred Enclosure." For exhibitions, the architect had designed a "great flight of steps to Calvary" that, turning about an illuminated cross within the round "Tower of Sacrifice" would "convey the pilgrim . . . from one station of the cross to the next . . . while the walls showed the various stages of a mystical asceticism." The Fascist martyrs were venerated in a sanctuary below, this also tenuously illuminated by the cross, and closing off "the ideal cycle that joins the death of the Nazarene to Man redeemed and purified in soul by the Ethic of Fascism." In such surroundings visiting would be, "for the faithful, repeating the path taken by the Martyrs and Precursors, a place to retemper the soul."[119]

Some projects gave special prominence to the concept of a tower as symbolic of power and rule. One architect planned a tower, symbolizing the "Genius of the Duce," that rose eighty-eight meters over the Via dell'Impero, high above all the neighboring monuments; it had a big "M" that "illuminated by night would cast its light in imperishable memory of the Founder of the Corporate State."[120] Light was symbolically important in various projects; it represented the shining future of the "new civilization" that showed the way to salvation for all of humanity. Alongside the remains of the monuments of Imperial Rome—a "first light" in which "the life of modern civilization shines in all its splendor" would be encircled by the sacred buildings from which sprang the "second light" that redeemed mankind—would rise the Eternale Mole Littoria. This particular project was inspired by the Fascist conception of itself "as a beacon of contemporary culture," shining to illuminate "the hard-earned conquest of a superior civilization." Another project proposed a huge lictorial fasces, complete with ax, to stand before the palace on the Via dell'Impero; it could be lit up for solemn occasions. The architect Palanti envisioned a palace shaped like a ship, symbolizing the "Mussolini course," pointed toward the whole world. He had also devised a system of lights and reflectors that would project light over the whole façade, creating "truly fantastic effects, like a real ship, isolated from the ground and traveling alone and detached." From the ship rose a tower shaped like a fasces, its tribune shaped like an ax, "in harmony with the incisive speech of the Duce."[121]

The glorification of the Duce, as the divinity to which the Casa Littoria was dedicated, was part of every project. "May this symbolic work rise and become the Altar of the Idea," wrote one designer, "a palace from which the will of the Duce, the force of His convictions, the fascination of His Person, will continue to radiate."[122] In another proposal, the palace was to be "an iconographic projection of a huge plough with which the first farmer of Italy, Benito Mussolini, the new Romulus, turns over the sacred furrow of the new Via dell'Impero." In this scheme, "the classical figure of the Duce, symbolizing the greyhound awaited by the people, rises like a giant thrusting his aerial prow, symbol of modern Rome: the flying ship to illuminate the world with its new light, Fascist Civilization." The whole building, he wrote, is "saturated with Him, with Mussolini. Every stone should illustrate and glorify His work."[123]

Both Terragni and Sironi also took part in this symbolic divinization of Mussolini. The two men were part of a group that submitted two projects, the first of which, inspired by "concepts of universality, unity, power, and wisdom, and in direct relationship with the imperial traditions of the Roman Forum," proposed an architectural complex in different units that gave the "main role to 'The Exhibition of the Revolution and

Sanctuary,' crystallized in an everlasting, templelike building." This structure was to be separate from the purely administrative part. On the top floor of the Palace of the Revolution would be the Duce's room and that of the party secretary, "looking out on the Via dell'Impero in a position of command. On top, as a continuation of the Great Hall, is the podium from which the Duce can show Himself. Everyone can see him. Against the sky, He is like a God. There is no one above Him. The whole façade is a hymn to His power, His genius. From all parts of the great avenue which is the heart of Rome, the heartbeat of the world, from Piazza Venezia to the arches of the Colosseum, He will be alone, on high, in the light. He will face the acclaiming throng: of all, with all."[124] The façade of the palace was also devoted to Mussolini: "Built mostly of granite, it will have only one window: Yours, on which will be inscribed the sacred words of the Oath."[125]

From roughly a hundred projects, twelve were chosen by a committee chaired by the secretary of the party, who announced a further competition in 1937.[126] This second stage called for a monumental building that would house the party directorate, with the offices of the Duce and the party secretary, the Lictorial Tower with its sanctuary for the party's relics, and offices for the party's subsidiary organizations. The competition was won by Enrico Del Debbio, Arnaldo Foschini, and Vittorio Morpurgo, but their project had to be further modified because Mussolini decided that the palace should be built not on the Via dell'Impero but near the Foro Mussolini, thus "bringing materially significantly closer the center from which proceeds and is diffused the spirit of the Fascist idea, and the fields on which the youth of Italy prepares its bodies for the greater glory of the Fatherland."[127] Work was begun on October 28, 1938, but construction was suspended because of the war, although for a brief time the party moved its headquarters there.[128]

A similar fate befell the régime's most ambitious project: the Universal Roman Exposition (Esposizione universale romana), known as EUR, first mooted in 1936 in the wake of the enthusiasm aroused by the rebirth of the empire, on the Roman "hills of destiny."[129] Conceived of as a "cultural Olympiad" among nations to illustrate the contributions made by the different countries to the progress of humanity, the EUR was intended to celebrate the superiority of Italy by showing its twenty-seven centuries of history, from ancient Rome through "the age of Mussolini who, unlike any other political genius, knew and knows how to allow Italians to live in an exhilarating atmosphere of Romanity."[130]

The Exposition was to open in 1942, during the twentieth-anniversary celebrations of the régime, but was postponed, because of the war, until after the expected triumph of the Axis. This postponement caused a substantial revision of the original idea: the "cultural Olympiad" became instead a "Peace Exposition," and it was given a more markedly political character designed to show, in the form of a "gentlemanly competition" between the two hegemonic empires of the Europe of the Axis,[131] the universal superiority of Fascism's "new culture" from which the principles and institutions of the New Order were expected to emerge.

The EUR involved far more than an ephemeral exposition. From the very beginning, Mussolini had decided to transform it into a permanent architectonic complex and make of it the nucleus of a "new city" designed to represent "a hierarchically organized collective, directed and led by an ordering mind."[132] The EUR was to be the monumental center of Mussolini's new Rome, the modern capital of the empire and of the "new civilization." "Whoever, arriving from Rome or the sea, finds himself on the Via dell'Impero . . . will see, opening before his eyes, in white marble and golden travertine, the new city, alive with water and greenery, a city worthy of flanking the old, but with this much more: that in its sober and powerful architecture, this new city is able to welcome the many-faceted and dynamic life of today and tomorrow."[133] The new city, combining usefulness and monumentality, would also have been a place of worship, festivity, and diversion for the masses.

The whole of Italy's humanistic, artistic, and scientific community was mobilized for this ambitious project. The architects had the hardest task, that of creating a "stage setting with magic"[134] to afford the public "a grandiose spectacle or display, accomplished by moving people through a permanent scenic decor," architectural, sculptural, and muralistic, "of outstanding visual effectiveness, such as to strike and impress the on-looker's imagination." It should reach into the "visitor's memory through fantasy," to show "the people the magical continuity, universality and contemporaneity of Italian civilization, our privilege and the distinctive sign of that primacy among peoples that Gioberti exalted."[135]

The political and propagandist purpose of EUR's monumentality, as presented by its designers and commentators, together with explicit symbolic and cult references, in fact underlay the whole urbanistic, architectonic, and decorative conception of the new city, which sought to "glorify a sacred backdrop inspired by Fascist values."[136] The lictorial cult was to have a new "sacred center" for the self-glorification of Fascism and the Italian people, and this would be accomplished by transforming history into myth in the symbolic form of a grandiose and solemn monumentality: "like a theater of fabulous architectures, born of evocation . . . of effective expression, of unheard-of dimensions, of a magic realism" that would repeat no past models but rather produce "an architectural ecstasy that would transpose the classical into lyrical and abstract *evocations*."[137]

The Exhibition of Romanity and other exhibitions devoted to Fascist institutions and various social, cultural, manufacturing, economic, and scientific aspects of Fascist Italy were all to have permanent installations in the "new city," but the dominant theme remained "the glorification and celebration of the new order brought into being by Fascism." In the section of the Exposition devoted to the party, besides the Martyrs' Sanctuary, an imposing altar based on the Augustan Ara Pacis (Altar of Peace) was planned, "to represent the triumph of the Fascist idea and consecrate peace among peoples with the arrival of a New Era."[138] From within the altar a powerful source of light was to project a "huge fasces of light into the Roman sky."[139] Powerful reflectors would also have been brought into play to illuminate the great Arch of the Empire, a 40-meter-high structure in aluminum and steel. This was to have been the sacred axis of the new city, a sort of peace rainbow, a triumphant symbol of the new Pax Romana to ensue from the Axis victory, achieved under the emblem of the lictor.[140]

Light and color were to play a decisive role in the symbolic architecture and religious significance of the EUR. The Mediterranean sun-bleached white of the monuments and their lighting-effects, turning night into day, would confer a sacred aura on the city; they were symbols of the victory over darkness and chaos represented by the Fascist religion, which would now spread the values of a new civilization over Mussolini's Rome. Religiosity and art "meet on the same 'mystic' plane which from the start (though with increasing intensity in the war years) marked the Exposition as a city of representations and effects of light."[141] In this respect, the monumentality of the EUR was another example of the myth of Romanity acting as a form of syncretic symbolism between Fascism and Catholicism.

The Exposition was to have a large section devoted to the contribution of the church in shaping Italian civilization, and the faithful were assigned a church dedicated to Saints Peter and Paul. The true religious center of the EUR and of the new city, however, was the palace that was to be the permanent home of the Exposition of Italian Culture, from Augustus Caesar to Mussolini. This, wrote Emilio Cecchi, "was the stuff of religion; it could not be celebrated in any other way than with religious reverence."[142] It was so powerful that it gave the building a sacred attribute—almost the "Temple of the Race," as one group of architects described it.[143]

The project chosen for this sacred symbolic function—the so-called Square Colosseum, with its four faces pierced by Roman arches, repeated "with a rhythmic insistence" that, besides being "a clear expression of the Roman Italian national character, seeks to affirm an eternal essence"[144]— was by three architects, G. Guerrini, Ernesto La Padula, and Mario Romano. As in a Roman temple, the decorations would have shown, in frescos and sculpture, the myths, values, and heroes of the lictorial cult. A prominent part of the Exposition was to be dedicated to the cult of the representative great men of what Mussolini called "a people of poets, artists, heroes, saints, thinkers, scientists, navigators, transmigrators." Displayed on the walls of this Fascist Pantheon, the public could venerate the heroes of Italian civilization, from Caesar, founder of the first empire, to Mussolini, founder of the second. The Mussolini room was planned as a glorification of the Duce, who "sums up in himself the deepest aspirations of the race . . . In him end nearly two millennia of history. Since Augustus Caesar, only today has Rome had a universal political mission . . . The exaltation of our Leader should set the highest possible tone of spirituality."[145]

6
Italy's New God

So I can't say anything else on account of I can't put it into words, I couldn't go to school no more, and I believe the Duce will forgive the mistakes I make on these three pages. I've nothing more to say except my heart says long live the head of our government, long live the man of steel, the Lion and the Savior of Italy from Bolshevism, long live the new God of Italy and of this new Italy.

I was born a peasant and I'll die one next December I'm coming back to my beautiful country and my beautiful land where I was born and grew up and with my wife and two sons.

—S. M. to Mussolini, Struthers (Ohio), March 26, 1930

For more than twenty years something that has been beating in my heart has suddenly stopped: a Love, a loyalty, a devotion. Now I am alone, without my Leader . . . In a man's life a Leader is everything: origin and end, cause and purpose, point of departure and finish line; if he falls, there is a terrible solitude within. I would like to find him again, my Leader; put him back at the center of my world, reorder it, this world of mine, by him. O fear! Fear that this will no longer work!

Now I know what fear is: the sudden loss of a reason for living.

—Giuseppe Bottai

The symbolic universe of Fascist religion centered upon the myth and cult of the Duce; these were assuredly the most spectacular and popular aspects of the lictorial cult. But Fascist religion did not begin with the myth of Mussolini; rather, it was created out of the collective experience of a movement that considered itself invested with a missionary charisma of its own, one that was in fact not, in its beginnings, identified with Mussolini. Many traditions from the past flowed together in forming the way the Fascist religion saw itself; and Fascist mythology, which derived in part from these older traditions and in part from its own experience, was much richer and more complex than the Mussolini myth, even though the latter occupied the foreground.

The Mussolini myth came into being within the environment of the Fascist religion once the latter had been institutionalized. Even if the Duce's figure was "numinous" on its own, thanks to his charismatic personality, his myth should therefore properly be considered a derivative of the Fascist religion. But there is no doubt that the myth of the man—also nurtured outside the Fascist environment—contributed greatly to the growth and value of the fideistic dimension of Fascism. The very existence of this dimension, moreover, contributed to reinforcing the charismatic role of the leader, thus glorifying the myth until it worked its way into the heart of the lictorial cult. The persona of the Duce, as a fundamental component of the mythical and symbolic universe of Fascism—which it effectively became after 1925—cannot be seen independently of Fascist religion.

The Myth and the Cult

To understand Mussolinism within the lictorial cult, it is important to distinguish the myth, or rather the myths, of Mussolini from the cult of the Duce. A personality cult always has a mythological basis, but the myth of a man is not always accompanied by ritual acts of dedication and devotion. In the case of other charismatic leaders, such as Stalin and Hitler, myth and cult developed simultaneously within their movements, and as a function of these movements. In Mussolini's case, however, not only did the myth precede the cult, but it showed up in a number of guises even before the birth of Fascism and before his rise to power.

In fact there are a number of different "myths" that correspond to different periods of his life. They originate in differing environments and different political and cultural contexts. Each of these myths, however, created a charismatic aura around the man and laid the groundwork for the Fascist myth of Mussolini and the creation of a cult of his personality during the years of the régime.[1]

First one could mention a *socialist myth*, created when Mussolini was only twenty-nine, when, from being an unknown, provincial, socialist party leader, he suddenly appeared on the national scene as the "new man" of the revolutionary faction that took over the party at its national congress in Reggio Emilia in July 1912. Mussolini became the idol of the socialist masses, the very model of a revolutionary leader, the symbol of a new and intransigent socialism that had liquidated reformism and was marching resolutely toward revolution. Then, when Mussolini chose intervention, the socialist myth collapsed and was transformed into the anti-myth of the corrupt traitor who had sold out.

Meanwhile, between 1912 and 1914, alongside the socialist myth, another myth was in the process of formation among those intellectuals, grouped around Giuseppe Prezzolini's *La Voce* and Gaetano Salvemini's *Unità,* who fought in the united anti-Giolittian front.[2] For Prezzolini, Mussolini was "a *man*, and stands out in a world of half-men."[3] Salvemini admired the young socialist leader as a "strong and direct man," a serious revolutionary, of the kind who "say what they mean and do as they say, and therefore bear within them a part of Italy's future destiny."[4]

This myth endured, and indeed grew stronger after the collapse of the socialist myth, for Mussolini's choice of intervention was considered a proof of the *myth of the new man* in Italian politics, the man whose personal political drama symbolized, as the futurist painter Carlo Carrà wrote on November 15, 1914, "the drama of our whole generation."[5] From having been the idol of the socialist masses, Mussolini became the hero of the political and cultural avant-garde of interventionism; he was the future *renovator of the nation.* "You, Benito Mussolini," wrote a young southerner at the end of 1914 "must give Italy a new people."[6]

This second myth remained attached to Mussolini right into the postwar period, but its attractiveness remained limited to the "fighting elites," such as the *Arditi,* the futurists, and the rump of interventionists with whom Mussolini created the Fascist party. Although the use of the term *Duce,* typical of the language of the Italian left, was already used for Mussolini in his socialist period, the birth of the cult of the Duce did not coincide with the birth or growth of Fascism. For a majority of the first Fascists, at least until 1921, the *Duce*—that is, the charismatic leader of the "Italian revolution"—was not Mussolini but Gabriele D'Annunzio. It was to D'Annunzio that the various revolutionary nationalist movements turned, especially during the Fiume adventure.

Within the organization of the Fascist movement itself, although Mussolini was the most prestigious of its leaders because he was a national figure and because he edited an influential daily, he was only a member of its propaganda bureau and its executive committee. Nor was his authority undisputed or worshipped like that of a charismatic leader. The Fascists who knew him thought of him as a "comrade" or "our friend Benito," while others called him "Professor Mussolini."[7]

When Fascism became a mass movement, Mussolini had to face a genuine revolt by the various *squadristi* leaders against his claim to being recognized as founder and leader of Fascism. Only after the November 1921 party congress, which authorized Fascism's becoming a party rather than a movement, was Mussolini accepted as the *duce* of Fascism. Even that recognition, however, was far from giving him any dictatorial power such as Hitler achieved within the National Socialist party in the same year.[8] There Mussolini imposed himself as much through his political knowhow as through any recognition by the Fascists that he had exceptional charismatic gifts. He was accepted as Leader and Duce only once the anti-Mussolini revolt and the attempt to draft D'Annunzio was quashed. At that point the provincial leaders realized that none of them could seriously challenge Mussolini for the leadership and at the same time maintain unity. Mussolini was the only one capable of keeping in line all the little local potentates who made up the Fascist movement at the time; therefore, he was the only one able to keep them in some sort of precarious unity.

Even after Fascism came to power, there arose fresh internal resistance to Mussolini's claim to exercise, through his authority as prime minister, absolute and indisputable authority as Fascism's leader, to whom therefore absolute obedience was required. In the various crises that shook the party from 1923 to 1925, there were Fascists who rejected the identification of Fascism with Mussolinism. In 1924 Camillo Pellizzi felt it necessary to remind Mussolini that "a major political movement or a nation on the march is not ever to be totally summed up in one individual or Leader. Thus Fascism is not summed up in You."[9]

Nonetheless, these very crises helped the rise of the *myth of the Duce*. He was glorified, spontaneously and instrumentally, as the one unifying factor in Fascism and as the only point of reference superior to the local Fascist potentates. In the rivalry among Fascist leaders, all of them eventually had recourse to Mussolini's authority to legitimize their actions, thus simply adding to his authority. As the Fascist régime was being built, Mussolini's authority ceased to be challenged. This phenomenon in turn contributed to his mythological status as the necessary element of coherence and stability in the balance of forces that made up the régime, as well as the supreme arbiter and mediator between the various little duces, all of whom could overcome their rival ambitions only by submitting to the authority of the Duce.[10]

As the regime advanced, at each stage the Duce's position was codified in the party's or the state's statutes in ways that progressively enhanced his superior position as the leader of Fascism. In the 1926 statute, the Duce appears for the first time at the head of the party hierarchy, as "Supreme Guide". The first catechism of Fascist doctrine, prepared by Augusto Turati and destined for the young and the public as a whole, concluded with a series of questions and answers about the Duce and with the Fascist Oath, defined as "the Italian's duty toward Mussolini and toward the Fascist Revolution."[11] By the time of the 1932 statute, Mussolini had been elevated over the party hierarchy into a separate position, and by 1938 he was formally identified as the "Head of the National Fascist Party." In the same year a new catechism was issued by the party, duly brought up to date with a section titled "Defense of the Race," in which Mussolini was described as "the creator of Fascism, the restorer of civil society, chief of the Italian people and founder of the empire."[12]

As the statutory system of the régime's institutions was consistently revised, the figure of the Duce acquired a juridical meaning, for the word *Duce* now meant not only "the leader of the party" but also "the Leader of Fascism, the Guide, the Supreme Head of the Régime, which is henceforward indissolubly linked to the State."[13] The myth of Mussolini was thus fully integrated into the juridical and institutional structure of the Fascist state, which—given the scope and force of the attributes reserved for Mussolini as both "myth" and "leader," in practice, in legislation, and in the theology and liturgy of the Fascist state—now took on the aspect of what I have characterized elsewhere as "totalitarian caesarism."[14]

However, the affirmation and institutionalization of the myth of the Duce were by no means due solely to events within the party. That myth, as it emerged in the wake of the March on Rome, was made of multiple strands, some of them quite distinct from Fascism. As others have correctly observed, it is necessary to make a clear distinction between strictly Fascist manifestations of the myth and cult of the Duce, which have a political and an ideological basis, and generically popular manifestations, which often had no such basis.[15]

The Cult of the Leader

The foundations of the cult of the Duce as absolute and undisputed leader of Fascism were laid with the institutionalization of the Fascist religion, which transformed the relationship between the Duce and Fascists into a charismatic relationship in which the latter gave him dedication and obedience based on faith and on his historic mission as founder and chief interpreter of Fascism. In this sense Augusto Turati, party secretary from 1926 to 1930, was the founder of the cult. As he began the "Mussolinizing" of Fascism, Turati placed the Duce on the altar of the lictorial cult where he was offered for the veneration of the Fascist masses. Mussolini, according to Turati, was the chief "the Revolution wanted between 1914 and 1922. In October he brought it about, and ever since he has guided it. One Leader, the only Leader, from whom all power flows. One Steersman, the only Steersman, whose place no below-decks rabble can take."[16] With his "brilliant and powerful mind," he was, said Turati, "intent on molding the new Italian people, bent body and soul to a new tomorrow."[17] The Duce was also "the finest, the strongest, the best of the sons" of Mother Italy.[18]

The formalization of the cult of the Duce, however, was the work of Achille Starace, who multiplied the rituals and formulae of devotion in a variety of ways, such as stipulating that the word *Duce* should always be written in capital letters, and noting the ceremonial to be followed when the Duce appeared in public, the "Salute to the Duce."[19]

With the establishment of the lictorial cult, the glorification of the person of Mussolini became the main activity of the "consensus factory,"[20] which worked ever more intensely to propagandize the myth and cult of the Duce among the masses, making his image omnipresent and showing him as the "hero with the thousand faces." The expansion of Mussolini's personal greatness now knew no limits of space or time. His sanctification as prophet, savior, creator, and guide of the nation in the Exhibition of the Fascist Revolution was merely one aspect of his mythic transfiguration. He was shown as towering over the Italian scene, as the *summum* and synthesis of every form of greatness, the greatest thinker and man of action of all time. He was statesman, legislator, philosopher, writer, artist, universal genius and prophet, messiah, apostle, infallible teacher, God's emissary, elect bearer of destiny, the man announced by the prophets of the Risorgimento—by Francesco Crispi, by Alfredo Oriani, by Georges Sorel, Cesare Battisti, and Enrico Corradini. His greatness was described by analogy to Caesar and Augustus, Machiavelli and Napoleon, Socrates and Plato, Mazzini and Garibaldi, not excluding Saint Francis of Assisi, Christ, and God himself, for, as Asvero Gravelli wrote, "God and history today mean Mussolini."[21] An anonymous informer wrote in a secret report: "Fascism is a religion, a religion that has found its God. Popular zeal by the faithful should bring the people that much closer to the Duce's moral stature, and make it certain that people need not say to themselves, as Spinoza did: if he had not been found [*sic!*], they would have searched for me."[22]

For one of the most extravagant of these bards of the Duce's cult, Mussolini was "the myth of the Hero" incarnate:

> His figure, already a monolith, stands out in the contemporary world, in history, in predictions of the future; it dominates men and things, as a prince among statesmen, as the genius of our race, as savior of Italy, in reality and myth, as a Roman of imperial Rome, as the personification and synthesis of the Idea-People, as the great initiate . . . From the start he followed in the steps of the Hero, who alone set out to conquer his own world, which exists first and only in the workings of his mind . . . the myth of the Hero is a projection of all the myths of divinity . . . [He] is all Hero, resplendent as the sun; the inspiring and creative Genius; the Leader who conquers and fascinates; He is the massive totality of myth and reality . . . The Revolution is Him; He is the Revolution.[23]

This glorification of Mussolini as a living deity became a dominant part of transforming the new generations into Fascists. Mussolini was presented to them as the greatest of all the great men in history, as a new

Caesar, the Leader to whom one owed one's life, body and soul. The *Avanguardista Handbook,* which accompanied the young on the outings organized by the *Balilla,* read: "You, as an *Avanguardista,* would not exist, were it not that before you, with you, and after you, He and only He is."[24] An aura of sanctity likewise surrounded devotions to his parents and his birthplace in Predappio, which became a place of pilgrimage for the youth organizations.

In 1930 the School of Mystical Fascism was founded by university students who wanted to devote themselves full-time to the cult of Mussolini, drinking deep of the man whom they considered to be the fount of Fascist religion: "The source, the one, unique source of mysticism is indeed Mussolini, Mussolini only and exclusively."[25] These mystics, who had elected Mussolini's brother Arnaldo as their spiritual guide, meditated on the Duce's writings and speeches; they were inspired to conduct their lives with total dedication as an ideal, even to sacrificing their lives. Even marriage and procreation were seen among them as an act of obedience and devotion to the Duce. Some of the principal scholars in Mussolinian mysticism, like their founder, Niccolò Giani, died in the war for which they had volunteered. The school confusedly blended the Catholic and Fascist religions; it offered lecture cycles inspired by the Duce's thought and on the problems of history and Italian life, which they illustrated and developed as they elaborated a mystical vision of the Fascist religion. In 1940 the School added courses in mysticism for elementary-school teachers who wanted to "give fresh life to their faith in the spiritual values and principles of the Revolution, drawing on the Mussolini myth for the direction of their pedagogical activity."[26]

These educational and cathartic activities were thought to be inherent to the essence of the cult of the Duce because, as was explained, there was no part of national life that was not impregnated with "Mussolinian teaching." "We are overjoyed to see the divine spectacle of a people drawing ever closer to the light, a people that listens to the Word of the Duce, which every day becomes action, blood, flesh, rhythm, the light of life, a religious mission. And while it fascinates us with its high, heroic content, it shows us the only way to rise, through the perennial fervor of its devotion to its Roman fatherland, to the summits of God."[27] Mussolini was the "prototype of the New Italian"; he was the "living and working model of the moral and political individuality we should emulate."[28] A noted Machiavelli scholar asserted that Mussolini educated Italians "just by looking them in the eye," and the younger generation aspired to "model itself on the living example of the LEADER."[29]

Beyond the more grotesque and risible aspects of its manifestations, the cult of the Duce fitted in well, and with its own logical purpose, into the proposed education for a "collective harmony" and the future new civilization. For Fascists a new civilization was the work of a founder-leader who, under the influence of a myth, shaped a collectivity. To the Fascists, Mussolini appeared a quite extraordinary founder, and was also himself a living myth that worked as a molding force on the minds of the masses, instilling in them a new faith and transforming them into a moral community organized in totalitarian fashion. According to Paolo Orano, Mussolini's capital discovery was of a "patriotism pushed to the point of mysticism, of sainthood, martyrdom, and faith considered as the building blocks of a civil construction." Hence, "Mussolinism is religion," in the sense that faith in the Duce was "the preparatory phase of an Italian religiousness, a religious Italianism."[30]

The Duce and the Hierarchs

Though participating in the cult of Mussolini with varying degrees of genuine faith and conviction, and though considering Mussolinism by their cultural lights an essential and even determining factor in laying the foundations for a new civilization, the Fascists who believed in their movement as the political religion of a new civilization did not dissolve the one in the other. The function of the Duce as living myth within Fascist religion was clearly, if exaggeratedly, formulated in *Critica fascista:*

> The religious sentiment of any people needs a point of concentration. From time immemorial Italy has needed major figures who arose and assumed the status of national symbols, who acquired divine status and served as unifying myths and movers of our history ... I believe and assert that neither Cavour, nor Mazzini, nor Garibaldi will be comparable to Mussolini in the light of history. None of these three attained that constructive universality or had the whole human personality of Mussolini; none of them put together such a unanimous consensus or possessed such powers of fascination; none was burdened by such responsibility or had such a vast field of action.
>
> The Mussolini myth will last as long as that of Romulus and Remus and Caesar. It will be impossible to use the Duce's name as the banner of one party against another; he will be the symbol of the whole nation alone against the world.[31]

It is precisely as symbol and living myth, incarnating Fascist religion, that the cult of Mussolini took root after the régime came to power, when the last challenges of riotous and rebellious Fascist chieftains had been overcome and he could impose himself, totally permeating Fascist thinking and culture with his personality.

Besides the obvious political, propagandistic, and functional conditions, there were other cultural and ideological conditions that tied in with the logic of Fascism as a religion. In fact it is in the context of mythical thinking that Fascism elaborated its own conception of a charismatic leader. In Giovanni Gentile's political theology, Mussolini was invested with the charisma that derived from his being the living incarnation of the "Fascist idea"; that idea was worked out in history through his personality. The Duce, Gentile asserted, was "a hero, a providential and privileged spirit in whom thought has become flesh and vibrates constantly to the potent rhythm of a youthful and exuberant life."[32]

Mussolini's charisma acquired a far greater hold over his collaborators after his accession to power. On March 10, 1923, Giovanni Giurati wrote him professing his "firm faith that you are the Hound whose advent Dante prophesied."[33] When Giuseppe Bottai was dismissed in July 1932 as minister of corporations, he told Mussolini he accepted his decision "with serenity," but that "sometimes I still feel a nostalgia for my Leader, his presence, his orders. I will try to overcome that feeling, thinking that in my private life, as for so many years now, Mussolini will continue to act as a constant force for betterment and perfection."[34]

Certainly in the power relationship between the Duce and the hierarchs who contended with one another to find the keys to his heart, similar testimonials could be ascribed to sheer opportunism, to ambition, interests and even fear. But the publication of the intimate and autobiographical writings of a number of leading Fascist figures after the collapse of the myth and the death of their authors—such as Bottai's diary and Tullio Cianetti's memoirs—allows us to see that when the cult began, there was a sincere and spontaneous devotion to him, typical of a culture that believed in the mythology of heroes and the cult of the leader as a major force in history.

Another case is that of Giurati. At the beginning of the 1930s Giurati distanced himself from power and from Mussolini. His brief and trying experience as party secretary had led him to disillusionment with Mussolini, and he did not join the Social Republic. Reflecting on the cult of the Duce after the fall of the régime, Giurati confirmed that he had truly believed Mussolini "was the man destined to give life to Dante's idea: that the two great symbols, the Eagle and the Cross, would be brought together again in Rome, and that moral and civil disorder, heresy and war, would be put to flight, not just from Italy but from the whole world."[35] Bottai, as he was about to leave for the war zone in 1941 on Mussolini's orders, noted in his diary: "My Leader failed, as I was leaving, to say farewell as man to man, for which my faithful follower's soul yearned. But faithful to him I remain . . . and I dedicate my death to him. Like that of countless other soldiers it should serve to enrich his spirit for the moral renewal of our Italy."[36]

The destiny of that first generation of Fascists was tied to Mussolini's. Although they recognized the man's limits and his progressive self-absorption as Mussolini increasingly became a prisoner of his own myth, hierarchs such as Dino Grandi, Bottai, Italo Balbo, Roberto Farinacci, Giuseppe Bastianini, and Tullio Cianetti felt that they owed it to Mussolini that while still young, immersed in an anomalous future within the petty bourgeoisie, they had been lifted up into *historical time*, transformed into makers of history. They were convinced that they were undertaking, with Mussolini and thanks to him, a great enterprise that would mark an epoch in the history of civilization.

Typical is the case of Cianetti, the son of a sharecropper, who ascended through the ranks of the syndicalist movement to become, in May 1943, minister of corporations. In his memoirs Cianetti shows, with the lively sensibility of an eyewitness, how powerful Mussolini's charisma was and how it steadily declined during the Second World War. Although he had been much disabused by Mussolini, he writes that when he was elevated to the heights of a régime in its death-throes, he was filled with enthusiasm:

> "I am a Minister of Mussolini's!" I said to myself, "I work alongside one of the great men of history, an authentic historical figure. I have greatly loved this fascinating man, and I love him still. Disillusionments have not been wanting in these twenty-one years, but life is not made just of roses. Mussolini is probably the most disconcerting of all the condottieri we know about. He speaks like a genius, then falls into the most childish banalities; he sets off with great firmness, then plays about like a spoiled child; he preaches like one of the great initiates and then leaves you dumbfounded with a piece of pure cynicism; he subjects himself to punishing labor for his people but shows a great scorn for people; he invokes God but enjoys uttering heresies. Notwithstanding all this, he is a great man, to whom one is happy to offer the best of oneself."[37]

Many other testimonies could be cited to show how powerful the effect of the Mussolini myth was on the very men who controlled and manipulated the totalitarian machine, men who were far from ignorant about the artifices of propaganda and the instruments of manipulation with which the cult of the Duce was disseminated among the people. They knew the man from close up, and for many years. They were not unaware of his weaknesses, his pettiness, his cynicism, the bigoted and vulgar way in which he used people to advance his own power. But until that myth became operative at the highest levels, suffused with a sacred awe, the defects of the man were obscured by the reverberations of the greatness that had been ascribed to him. He seemed somehow a man beyond measure, possessed of an intuition about history that made him a major protagonist in his times; he was invested with a mission that was to mark the fate of all Italians and the whole of humanity.

This image derived from a state of mind common to Mussolini's closest collaborators, those most directly involved with him and with Fascism from the earliest days. In the Giolittian period, most of them had lived through anxious times as they searched for a "new faith"; they had gone to war impelled by the myth of the "Italian revolution." Thus, a triumphant Mussolini seemed to them the "representative hero" of their times, of their aspirations for a new life and greatness, the interpreter and executor of their will for power—to mold the masses and reform the Italian character.

Precisely because of the cultural and emotional intensity with which it was perceived, the myth of Mussolini the "leader" aroused in the minds of his closest collaborators feelings of dedication to and identification with the Duce. These came, as Bottai noted in his diary, from their feeling that he had given them a "reason for living."[38] This very glorification of the Duce's figure was also the cause of the greatest problem that Fascism had to face as it pursued its totalitarian project and transformed the Fascist religion into a collective faith, one in which the cult of the Duce as living myth performed a vital pedagogical function. However necessary this mythologizing was to a totalitarian politics, how was Fascism to prevent that myth from rendering the future of the totalitarian state dependent on the fate of its founder?

Carlo Costamagna, though prudently hiding behind a quotation from Machiavelli, noted the problem in 1940: "The well-being of a republic or a monarchy depends not on having a prince who governs prudently while he lives, but one who so fashions it that when he dies it survives."[39] The problem arose many times in the minds of the more thoughtful Fascists. But even those who, in time and when faced with the successes of the Duce—successes that seemed to confirm his "genius," his "mission"— came to see the phagocytic element between Mussolinism and Fascism, stopped short, before being dragged, along with him, to catastrophe: "We have believed. We have believed in you, Duce, and your faith has been our faith, once again consecrated in blood. We won because at every moment you were present in our minds, because we have always followed you with an absolutely knowing trust, as we shall follow you in whatever bright new path you will now show us."[40] This declaration of blind devotion from Starace to Mussolini after the proclamation of the Empire will serve to show the charismatic dedication of the hierarchs; it sums up the *raison d'être* of the cult of the Duce as it was conceived and practiced by his followers—that is, in a fideistic world that matched the cult of the

Duce among the masses by its emotional charge, not by the motives and ends that Fascist culture attributed to the Mussolini myth.

The Faith of the Common People

When it took power, the Mussolini myth found a favorable atmosphere in which, outside the party and sometimes even against it, the myth could assert itself and spread. Conditions propitious to the birth of a popular cult of the "Providential Man" were offered by Italy's postwar crisis. As the old liberal Senator Giustino Fortunato noted, "Everyone can see that Italy is heading towards a civil war . . . but everyone invokes, as in any time of extreme danger, the providential intervention of a Man with a capital 'M' who will know how to impose order on the nation."[41] Not unnaturally, when Mussolini came to power, many saw him as that Providential Man, the one who would restore peace and order after a decade of unprecedented social and political upheaval.

Seen through bourgeois eyes, Mussolini saved the country and restored the state; among the people who had not suffered from Fascist violence, he was a true son of the people who had come to power without changing his spots or concealing his origins—on the contrary, boasting of them—and therefore was immediately surrounded with a guileless admiration, mingled with faith and hope in his goodwill.

Mussolini himself nurtured this image among the common people: he was the first prime minister to tour the length and breadth of Italy, visiting cities and whole regions where no predecessor had set foot, showing himself to the people, speaking to the masses. From May to October 1923 he visited the Veneto, Sardinia, Lombardy, Tuscany, Sicily, Campania, Abruzzo, Piedmont, Emilia, and Umbria, a feat that he repeated the following year. He established direct contact with the people, making them feel physically closer to power and allowing them to believe that they might now be heard and their needs attended to.

Then, too, the Fascist press contributed greatly to the myth, comparing Mussolini's tours to rituals reconsecrating the soil of Italy to the fatherland. *Il popolo d'Italia* announced that Turin was eagerly awaiting the Mussolini's visit, which would reconsecrate the "red city" to the fatherland.[42] In this way the sacralization of the myth advanced step by step. Mussolini was saluted as "the priest of the Fatherland" who, "after raising the chalice of our Italian bitterness and breaking the bread of our body and bloodless yet nonetheless tragic sacrifices, pledged to the crowd, with outstretched arms, that if it was necessary to start over again from the beginning, start they would."[43]

Mussolini used symbolic gestures that reinforced this image. In Perugia, for instance, before lighting the votive lamp in front of the altar consecrated to those who had fallen in the war, a priestly gesture, he received the oil from the hand of the mother of a dead son.[44] "Is there such a thing as a 'Fascist messianism'?" a French journalist asked him in 1924. The journalist noted that with Mussolini's rise to power, a legend had grown up around a living man:

> The personal prestige of the dictator has been on a rising curve; it has brought him to the heights of popular idolatry. Both spontaneously and artificially, there has grown up about him an atmosphere of silent and blind obedience, of dedication, veneration, and fear. The fact that this popularity survives the corrosion of time is a continuing miracle. But there is no doubt that it exists. You cannot call it mere curiosity that in tiny out-of-the-way stations, by the tracks, at crossings, in the middle of the night, thousands of peasants and workers, unknown, ignored, whose gestures have remained without acknowledgment, have stood perhaps for hours, waiting to salute the mysterious train that, as they were told, bore the fortunes of Italy.[45]

Mussolini, wrote Ferruccio Parri the day after the Matteotti murder, had stood on "a pedestal of unconscious trust and innocent and almost physical confidence, of ecstatic wonderment, on which the Italian people saw its dynamic Duce wave his arms and make speeches."[46] After the murder, the myth was seriously shaken, as Mussolini himself recognized: "If there ever was a myth, it went into sharp decline. Why then didn't it collapse altogether? The answer is very simple: because it was powerfully supported by the great mass of the Italian people."[47] Once the crisis was past and his power consolidated, the popular myth picked up where it had left off, now abetted by ample and more skillful use of propaganda and boosted by the successes, real or apparent, that Mussolini's policies achieved at home and abroad.

Mussolini's direct contact with crowds during the régime's anniversaries and during his tours nourished the cult of the Duce. Thanks to careful preparation and up-to-date staging, the ideal conditions were created for bringing about a state of collective emotional high tension, as a prelude to the ritual "mystical" union of the Leader with his people and the symbolic dramatization of national unity through its Duce. The workshop of the "consensus factory" and spontaneous enthusiasm worked hand in hand to create a state of collective exaltation. This was especially obvious in the rhythm of these ceremonies, partly preordained and partly spontaneous, whose different degrees and different rhythms—invocation, expectation, and apparition—were such as to transform these meetings into ritual events.

From an account of the thirteenth anniversary of the founding of Fascism, here is a typical description of this ritual in Piazza Venezia:

Squadrons of airplanes fly in ever-tighter circles overhead, as if to crown this splendid assembly.

The crowd never tires of following their maneuvers, and the thunder of their engines mixes with the peals of the fanfares and the songs of the Fascists. Meanwhile, Piazza Venezia has reached its flood point. The clamor of the music and the constant *alalà* deafens all. The people are carried away by the huge roar calling for the Duce.

It is nearly six. The north wind blows down ever harder, but who even notices it?

The planes have now disappeared. The great white mass of the monument to Vittorio Emanuele grows pale in the dusk. Palazzo Venezia emerges, red and majestic, from a shimmering sea of pennants and Black Shirts and gleaming brass instruments.

The crowd continues to swell. The square is thronged. Fifty thousand people are there waiting for Mussolini, fifty thousand shout his name. The first strike of the bell on the Campidoglio sounds. Not an eye but is fixed on the balcony where the Duce will appear.

The veterans of the Great War, the veterans of the Fascist Revolution, workers, young *squadristi,* students, people of all sorts and every age: although it has a thousand faces, the crowd is one person and has but a single heart. The impatience of the youngest, the "Mussolini kids," adds a picturesque note to the imposing spectacle. Every squad wants its pennant closest to the Duce and from ever closer they salute and acclaim him.

Here and there human pyramids take shape as in a race to see who is quickest and most agile; thus on high the flaming colors of Rome float over the blackening crowd.

It is twenty past six. The balcony doors open. H.E. Starace appears, waving the flag on its staff. The long wait is about to be rewarded, and indeed a huge cry breaks out in the square: "Long live the Duce!"

The bands break into "Giovinezza." The flags are raised high. Mussolini! In the great embrasure of the window his profile appears, giving the Roman salute. He wears the uniform of an honorary corporal of the Militia and his head is bare. His eyes dwell on the crowd; the crowd quivers with excitement.

"Duce! Duce!" The cry is infinitely multiplied over the clanging of the music.

The event takes on the dimension of a huge, ritual declaration of faith. A whole people is exalted by One Man; it sees itself in Him. Then there are shouts of "Attention!" and what seemed a clamor that would never end suddenly turns into absolute silence. And this discipline that a new way of thinking has created among Italians is no less a miracle.

It is now twenty-five past. Mussolini speaks to the people of Rome, to Italy.

The Duce concludes his speech with the question: "To whom does Italy belong?" The crowd gives the ritual answer: "To us!"

> The Duce's words are now locked away in the hearts of this huge crowd. That fantastic "To us!" is a proud renewal of absolute faith: faith in Fascism and in the future of the Fatherland. Mussolini's injunction, "Endure," has been absorbed and repeated like an oath. To the voice of a multitude, a multitude has responded.
> The ritual is over.
> Mussolini has left the balcony, but still the people want to see him, want to demonstrate their devotion. The Duce faces them, twice, three times, and salutes them.
> Then the great windows are shut.
> The square echoes with shouts, but Mussolini's words remain. It is as if the crowd can still hear them. The Fascist formations regroup; slowly the square empties, and a fantastic torchlight procession winds through the city.[48]

Marking time played an important role in creating the right mystical atmosphere for a ritual of this nature during Mussolini's visits to various parts of Italy, where he was greeted like a benevolent deity. Such visits were in general preceded by a request submitted by the prefect or the local Fascist secretary in the name of the local population. Mussolini would then announce his visit. But between his announcement and the actual visit, some years might pass, as happened, for instance, with his visit to Genoa. On July 9, 1934, Mussolini finally answered the request of the Genoese to "see him after an eight-year absence." He said he would visit them in 1936, but the visit did not actually take place until May 1937, which only made the expectation and the eventual welcome even greater.[49] The same thing happened in the case of his visit to the Veneto in 1938. A Ministry of Popular Culture informer wrote emphatically, but not entirely inaccurately, about the frenzy of expectation in Trieste once it had been announced that the Duce would visit the city after more than ten years of pleading:

> Trieste is working feverishly and breathlessly to be ready: in less than twenty-four hours the Duce will be here. This certainty takes the breath of all Triestines away. It fills them with emotion, it stuns them; on the one hand, it doubles and redoubles their energies; on the other, it renders them helpless in an ecstatic inner contemplation of the idea of having their beloved Duce among them . . . In Trieste the Duce may not find the sumptuousness and magnificence of decoration that other cities have afforded him, but he can certainly expect a fiery passion, an unbridled enthusiasm, and the same fanatical devotion to which the crowds' clamor for His presence has accustomed Him.

The next day the same informant orgiastically described—and the crowd probably felt much as he did—the city's reaction to Mussolini's triumphal arrival by sea and the ensuing grandiose ceremonial. In his speech, Mussolini described the current international crisis and foreshadowed the upcoming anti-Semitic legislation.

> Finally we have seen and heard Him! . . . These first reactions, expressed with indescribable joy, eyes moved to tears and an ineffable, agonizing joy . . .
>
> It is not easy to describe the expression on most faces, on those of the little people as on those of the educated, of the mass as a whole. Expressions of wonderful contentment and pride among those who saw Him pass close by—especially among the dockworkers He visited yesterday—and those whose eyes He met, those who caught His eye. "Never seen such eyes! The way he looks at you is irresistible! He smiled at me . . . I was close, I could almost touch him . . . When I saw him, my legs trembled" . . . and a thousand other similar statements show and confirm the enormous fascination exercised by his person.
>
> Women can't make sense or connect their thoughts, but they are even more eloquent in their naive and confused statements. They make long, apologetic speeches. One woman, who had been near the Duce for some time where his yacht was docked, sums up all their reactions: "He seemed godlike! I wanted to kiss His hands but I lacked the courage to do so. Tonight I will kiss his photograph."[50]

The Protecting Divinity

A visit by the Duce was seen as the arrival of a messiah bearing gifts, and he should be correspondingly thanked: "We have waited many years for You, nourishing a hope in our hearts that grew with the waiting," a group of peasant ex-combatants wrote him, asking that a "DUX Canal" should be built, "which has been held off for a decade while waiting for You."[51] Similar is the invocation of a widow of Catania on the eve of Mussolini's visit to Sicily in 1937:

> Duce
>
> The people of Catania have been awaiting you with great trepidation! My own heart beats unstoppably. *We await our father, the Messiah.* He is coming to visit his flock, to instill faith, and with words that bring about undreamed of heroism and the shedding of much blood.
>
> Duce! The word makes the heart beat as though an electric current has passed through it. As if by enchantment we, your little people, forget our woes and run to admire You. Your fatherly smile shines in the eagle-lightning of your look, the look of a man destined by fate to dominate human hearts, to form a thousand wills into one will, Yours! . . . I am poor and ill, and I

place great hopes in Your magnificent heart, the greatest heart we Italians have known from the Roman Empire to the present day.

My son is a rifleman, my daughter a member of Young Italian Women. Although I remain in the shadows, like the miserable crone who in a dark corner of the temple venerates the jewel-encrusted sacred icons, I admire You![52]

Such public meetings throughout Italy became a central and dominant part of Fascist liturgy. Seeing in flesh and blood what they saw everywhere glorified in images, they propagated the cult of the Duce among the masses. As an informant of the Ministry of Popular Culture wrote during the Duce's visit to Piedmont in 1939: "It is fascinating to hear ordinary people marveling at having taken part in the personification of a myth. To see in flesh and blood that chiseled face which they have seen countless times in the newspapers, on billboards, and on street corners is a surprise and an unforgettable joy."[53]

He made many such trips in the 1930s. He would stop in the provincial capitals and show himself to the crowds; his speeches were presented as announcements of decisions taken for which the Duce asked the plebiscitary consent of the people, thus making it seem as though the masses had a role to play in the decisions of their leader.

His speeches, and these direct encounters with the crowd, were always the high point of a Mussolini visit—not so much for the dialogue form that they sometimes assumed as for their character of revelation, in which the Duce's will was made known to the faithful and became an oracular statement of the will of the nation.

On other occasions, as on his frequent visits—in the guise of city founder or simple mower or thresher—to the Pontine Marshes after their reclamation, he seemed some benevolent deity descended from his altar on high to speak amicably with his people, ever ready to listen, comfort, and respond to their wishes. Such visits lacked the solemnity of major assemblies, but perhaps for that very reason they were even more successful in fostering the cult of the Duce. Corrado Alvaro gave a lively description of one of these meetings:

One of the great secrets of public fascination with the Leader is that each person feels in direct communication with him. It is as though he knows everything, and sooner or later he will come, he will know, he will provide. There are wrongs and injuries in every society; but the people think that if only he knew, their tears would be stanched, their hearts lifted up, and the wrong put right. In Mussolini, the Italian people saw incarnated an old ideal of justice, an ideal that throughout its history it had superimposed on many quite different figures. The crowd about me, seeing him stand on the table, did not miss a single gesture: not that he smiled; that his jacket of rough

Sardinian wool was spattered with mud; that a rose from a bouquet offered him at the inauguration of Borgo Sabotino was tucked into his belt, and that from time to time he grasped it delicately in his hand and sniffed its perfume; not the decisive gesture with which he handed over the prize money to each of the five hundred winners in Littoria, and each time with the same vigor, the same abrupt gesture. None of this was lost. In the eyes of those present these were the doings of imaginary, faraway beings who somehow were just one step away, and actually spoke. It was an extraordinary rape of the soul.[54]

Mussolini also fancied sudden, private, impromptu visits. These gave people the impression that he was everywhere and might appear anywhere and at any time, almost miraculously. One new colonist in the Pontine development remembers how Mussolini suddenly appeared at his father's farm: "He came by and we only just realized who he was . . . because . . . he was dressed sort of . . . as if he didn't want to be recognized. He asked my father a few questions, he being the head of the family, right? . . . and then . . . he suddenly disappeared. He was on a motorcycle."[55]

The Mussolini cult grew steadily among ordinary people. It remained a constant phenomenon throughout the régime, or at least until the war, although it was neither uniform nor equally extensive in all classes of society. To analyze the motives for this consensus, to break them down by social class, tracing their frequency and intensity over a twenty-year period, is not a task within the scope of this book. It would require much study and research; one would have to use the appropriate means to discriminate between the spontaneous and the propaganda-induced.

There were certainly certain classes and milieus in which the myth had little if any effect—for instance, among groups that had been powerfully secularized, or among those, especially peasants and workers, who had suffered violence at the hands of the *squadristi* or were more solidly attached to a socialist, republican, or Communist tradition. The myth irrupted in such groups only later, and largely among the younger generation.

But in the middle and petty-bourgeois classes, among the humblest, especially in rural areas, those without any lay or political tradition, those who had not suffered from the *squadristi,* the cult of Mussolini spread very rapidly. It put its roots down in a tradition that, anthropologically speaking, was already deeply dominated by religion, if not by superstition and magic, among those who projected onto the Mussolini myth forms of devotion and worship typical of Christian piety, even comparing him to Christ. "He seemed to me a Christ come back to earth," said one colonist in the Pontine development, "so that when he came along, there was a moment . . . let's say it was raining here in April on holidays, I don't know, there was some bad weather, all right, he arrived and Madonna! the clouds went away, the sun shone . . . well, he seemed like a god, finishing, you know, all his . . . his speech, you know, everything was fine, and then when he stopped suddenly the water fell out of the sky . . . by Saint Anthony, what a fellow this Duce is!"[56] Requests for photographs of the Duce, as a talisman bringing luck, were incessant; a widow with eleven children, presented with a portrait of Mussolini by the prefect, the party secretary, and the mayor, "thought the grace of God had come upon her house."[57]

To sum up the constituent elements of the Mussolini myth among the common folk, one might describe a great statesman meditating on the future of the world and in charge of Italy's destiny; a man who while seeking greatness and power was also like a loving father to all his children; a "man of providence" who was a channel of divine grace, a promise and a guarantee of peace for his people; a man with extraordinary magical and beneficent powers, who was physically close to the masses and in constant contact with them; a man close to them in spirit and able to interpret their aspirations.

The popular cult of Mussolini was without doubt the most important part of the Fascist liturgy, but it came about largely for reasons that referred back to traditions of faith rather than to belief in the values and dogmas of the Fascist religion. This fact needs emphasizing not only in order to distinguish the popular cult from the strictly Fascist cult, but also to appraise the effects of Fascist preaching on the masses, to bring out one of the reasons for its ultimate weakness.

For most ordinary people, the Mussolini myth outweighed their belief in Fascism. How typical this attitude was can be seen in this observation of the Viterbo Carabinieri in July 1930: "The Régime has ever-increasing support from the overwhelming majority of citizens, on whom Mussolini exercises a fascination that partakes of the supernatural, a fascination that is shared even by those who are not Fascist, and not just they, but also by many who have repeatedly stated their reservations about the philosophy and practice of the Fascist government."[58] The Rome Carabinieri made frequent reference to the "unlimited trust in Mussolini, which overcomes the opinion even of those who have reservations about Fascism and about other representative leaders of the Régime." They contrasted "the touching, improvisatory reactions of the people" to Mussolini's visits to that city to the accounts that appeared in newspapers, "with the usual flattery" that was perceived as "an overstated, base flattery . . . such as to affect adversely the usefulness and seriousness of the Duce's gesture."[59] The same feeling was expressed by a party informer during Mussolini's visit to Naples in October 1931. His judgment is all the more significant for being expressed in a party internal document:

The Duce has spoken. But He was particularly dramatic and expressive in what he could not say, but which this delirious crowd, in a moment of grace, "felt" and "intuited" through the spasms and contractions on that Roman mask of His: that something great and tremendous was about to take place for Italy and the world, and that Benito Mussolini was the invincible and undefeated man who would bring that something about.

For this hungry, undisciplined, anarchoid crowd, which has never "felt" or "intuited" the Fascism thrust upon them by the factious and wretched little men who have alternated in the past decade, "feels" and "understands" the Duce, through that divine gift they, above all the hundred other cities of Italy, have for exuberant fantasy and sensibility. Yesterday they offered him an apotheosis: to the consternation and panic of H.E. Castelli [high commissioner for the Province of Naples] and Natale Schiassi [federal secretary for Naples].[60]

Comments of this sort became more frequent as the years went by, confirming an attitude widespread in public opinion. As a Florence police informer wrote in June 1939:

The party of Mussolini has a genuine majority in Italy, and one might well say that so far as the Duce himself persists in talking about Fascism, the average Italian continues to see, in that word, only Mussolini. For the overwhelming majority, Fascism without Mussolini is incomprehensible, although a Mussolini without Fascism would be perfectly possible. In any case, it is the fate of genius to take such close control over an idea that he replaces it with his own personality.[61]

The same attitude is evident in the Rome of August 1940: "The refrain is ever the same: the Genius of the Duce prevails, but no one lets an opportunity go by to vituperate about the abuses and imposition of the Hierarchs, whoever they are and whatever position they hold." A Milanese informer echoed his Roman colleague: "The idea that Mussolini is isolated, that 99 percent of his close collaborators are unworthy of the jobs they have, that many in government indulge in speculation, is widespread . . . The people would gladly rally around Mussolini, with greater affection and loyalty, if the same energy that the Duce displays in foreign affairs were used to save his own people from these bloodsuckers."[62]

These observations are confirmed in the answers given in 1933 by an anonymous anti-Fascist to a questionnaire issued by *Giustizia e Libertà* (Justice and Liberty): "The 'cult of the Duce' (with the exception of cases in which the homage to the leader conceals a critical attitude toward the régime that might be considered too bold) still has a remarkable influence on people's minds. Even against evidence to the contrary, they retain their faith in the infallibility of the man, and the idea of his genius is accepted without argument."[63]

In fact, the more widespread among the masses was impatience with the totalitarian encroachment of the Fascist party and criticisms of the hierarchy, the greater by contrast seemed the myth of the Duce. Because he existed in an aura of trust, because he was the last hope, the one who might put right all the wrongs, including those inflicted by Fascism through its hierarchs, Mussolini was spared these criticisms. This came about because of the way ordinary people, beyond the orchestrated displays of Fascist propaganda and the liturgy of the régime, perceived the myth of Mussolini. Mussolini was seen as the protector god. On the basis of this innocent but tenacious belief in the goodness of the Duce, the myth generated spontaneous and superstitious forms of worship, accompanied by a miraculistic expectation that was widespread among the common people. This was both the strength and the weakness of the cult of Mussolini.

A god who proved himself fallible, who would have brought down on his believers the destructive fury of the Horsemen of the Apocalypse, in the form of bombardments, famine, and death, was destined to be dethroned and desecrated by his faithful with the same passion with which he had been adored. There is no way of knowing whether Mussolini ever read or pondered over what Roberto Michels, inspired by his political figure, wrote in 1927 about great men and the relationship between the duce and the masses:

> In placing too great a faith in these [great men], the masses put the leader and themselves in great peril. The collective faith that surrounds the leader can take on a mystical aspect. Then it happens that where his people thought the leader all-powerful, that collective faith collapses in the face of any natural event that shows that omnipotence to be false. Ancient peoples more than once overthrew an idolized leader when his authority, in the eyes of his followers, was overthrown by the eruption of a volcano or the flooding of a river that he had proved himself incapable of averting.[64]

Conclusion

We must become religious all over again. Politics should be our religion. This can be accomplished if there is in our vision of the world something supreme that will change our politics into religion.
—Ludwig Feuerbach

The sickness of our times, the sickness we must cure, is this: that we are unable to fall in love with pure ideas the way other times fell in love with the Christian religion, with Reason, or with Liberty; hence (and I am not alone in saying this) the health-giving crisis in our society will have to be, sooner or later, of a deeply religious nature.
—Benedetto Croce

W as Fascism a new religion? The definition may appear extravagant or extreme. But it will seem more plausible if we insert Fascism historically into the broader phenomenon of the sacralization of politics in modern society. In fact, even in this way Fascism has hardly been a strange or isolated phenomenon within the modern political world. Fascism belongs to the luxuriant and alarming modern phenomenon of secular religions. For more than two centuries now, these religions have inhabited the world of politics, arousing enthusiasm and fear, stirring up the masses to the arrogance of pride or the desperation of persecution, raising monuments to the eternal glory of demigods and sewing violence and death over whole continents.

Contrary to what secular rationalism foresaw and hoped for, the decline in the supremacy of traditional religions and the secularization of society and the state have not brought about a progressive withering away of the "sacred" in collective life. On the contrary, as innumerable historical examples throughout the world show, the frequent transfusion of the "sacred" from traditional religions into political mass movements of both right and left has given rise to new millennial religions. From the time of the American Revolution, but especially since the French Revolution and the birth of mass politics, the boundary between politics and religion, which was never properly established, has often been blurred; and now it is politics that has assumed its own autonomous religious dimension, and become one of the main areas in which the sacred has been metamorphosed in the contemporary world.

The process by which politics has become sacred has gone hand in hand with the growing autonomy and secularization of political power.[1] From the end of the eighteenth century, but especially in the twentieth, politics has tended to construct its own religiously charged symbolic universes; often these have assimilated liturgies, languages, and organizational models from the Christian tradition, adapting them to their own secular ends and conferring on these values a sacred aura. "Liberalism makes a mistake," wrote Thomas Mann during the Great War in his *Thoughts of an Unpolitical Man*, "in thinking that religion can be separated from politics. In the long run, politics—that is to say, inner politics, the politics of society—can make no headway without religion. For man is so made that, having lost all metaphysical religion, he transposes the religious into the social, he puts his social life on the altar."[2]

All modern revolutions have been either the creations or new extensions of symbols, myths, and rituals that, with varying intensities, have conferred a numinous power on politics. The various components of modern mass politics—nation, race, class, the state, party, the leader—have sought and brought forth acts of total devotion typical of traditional religious devotion. Even in those societies in which the process of secularization or deliberate de-Christianization has been most radical, these new forms of secular religiosity and political mysticism have shown up.

Among the various forms that this sacralization of politics has assumed in the modern world, nationalism has certainly been the most vital and universal. Nationalism has proved to be a powerfully seductive religion, one with an extraordinary syncretic capacity for assimilation and metamorphosis, and a similarly formidable ability to build and to destroy.[3]

The tendency of modern political movements to take on aspects of religion—in their ideology, the ways in which they socialize and integrate their affiliates, by the formulation of a body of beliefs, with a fideistic cult of their leaders, and the adoption of ritual and symbolism—was already noted at the end of the last century among the nascent mass parties, which were seen as institutions imitative of religious movements and modeled on the church. In a chapter of his *Elements of Political Science*, Gaetano Mosca analyzed in unitary fashion the associative phenomenon of "churches, parties, and sects." He interpreted the religious manifestations of politics according to a positivist model and took them to be the product of the masses' need for faith and of the shrewd demagoguery of politicians:

> Advantage has always been taken of the same human weaknesses. All religions, including those that deny the supernatural, have their own special, declamatory style used for preaching, in speech and sermon; they all stamp their fantasies with their own rituals and public pomp. Some walk in procession with candles and recite litanies; others walk with flags and sing the "Marseillaise" or the workers' hymn.[4]

For Gustave Le Bon, Vilfredo Pareto, and Georges Sorel, writing at roughly the same time, the definition of the "new religion" was the key to a realistic interpretation of socialism along the lines of the unstoppable power of the irrational in history and politics.[5] In 1920, on his return from Bolshevik Russia, Bertrand Russell asserted that in some respects Bolshevism was a religion similar to Islam.[6] And a few years later, John Maynard Keynes further developed this definition:

> Like other new religions, Leninism derives its power not from the multitudes but from a small number of enthusiastic converts whose zeal and intolerance make each one the equal in strength of a hundred indifferentists. Like other new religions, it is led by those who can combine the new spirit, perhaps sincerely, with seeing a good deal more than their followers, politicians with at least an average dose of political cynicism, who can smile as well as frown, volatile experimentalists, released by religion from truth and mercy, but not blind to facts and expedience, and open therefore to the charge (superficial and useless though it is where politicians, lay or ecclesiastical, are concerned) of hypocrisy. Like other new religions, it seems to take the color and gaiety and freedom out of everyday life and offer a drab substitute in the square wooden faces of its devotees. Like other new religions, it persecutes without justice or pity those who actively resist it. Like other new religions, it is unscrupulous. Like other new religions it is filled with missionary ardor and ecumenical ambitions. But to say that Leninism is the faith of a persecuting and propagating minority of fanatics led by hypocrites is, after all, to say no more or less than that it *is* a religion, and not merely a party, and Lenin a Mahomet, not a Bismarck.[7]

The twentieth century could be defined as the period in which politics was made sacred. In fact, this phenomenon reached its apogee and affirmation in the totalitarian movements of the first half of the century. As Gaetano Salvemini noted in 1932:

> Dictators need myths, symbols, and ceremonies with which to regiment, arouse, and terrify the multitudes and suppress their every attempt to think for themselves. The Catholic church's fantastic and pompous ceremonies and

mysterious rites in an alien tongue are masterworks of this sort. It is the church's model that Fascists and Communists followed when, with their mass meetings, they appealed to the irrational instincts of the mob.[8]

As has been remarked elsewhere, the difference between totalitarianism and tyranny lies in the former's "sacralization of politics."[9] It is certainly true that Communism, Fascism, and Nazism all gave a marked impetus to this sacralization, but this does not mean that we should overlook the contribution made by democratic movements to these new secular cults. In this respect, the cases of the United States and republican France are vitally important to the study of secular religions.

Though nourished by and developed through the assimilation of the traditions of the classic religions, the sacralization of politics is a modern phenomenon. Some say its origins can be attributed to the conflicts inherent in modernism itself: that is, to the structural tensions proper to modern society, with "growing secularization on the one hand, and on the other the need to maintain a prescriptive central nucleus sufficient for integration." This tension is "the consequence of a contradiction between the expansive nature of secularization and the need to maintain a universally accepted control mechanism without which society itself would cease to be."[10]

In secularized societies, such lay religions may provide one of the answers that modern society gives to the demand for integration through a movement, a party, the state, or other possible forms of organizations and institutions that may perform an integrative function by acting as a system of religious beliefs. In moments of crisis or extreme tension, the collectivity feels a need to grasp a total sense of life, which in turn is the basis for a new stability, achieved by adhering to political movements that offer a promise of overcoming chaos in a higher, communitarian form of order. In this sense, lay religions should be seen not as mere demagogic expedients, but as the social expression of a collective need.

This interpretation is certainly useful in explaining the origins and the workings of certain phenomena in secular religiosity, but it is far from being the only explanation valid for a historical interpretation. This is especially true because the sacralization of politics may, in different periods and the varying historical, social, and cultural situations in which they arise, have very different, and even opposing, origins, forms, and consequences. In a democratic society in a state of crisis, the function of guaranteeing a "prescriptive, central nucleus" may develop in a lay religion in a way that is totally different, as regards its consequences, according to whether this religion is based on the discrete and noncoercive forms of a *civil* religion of the sort typical to "open societies," or whether it adopts the integrative form of a *political* religion, typical of "closed societies" such as Fascism.

If democracy is always vulnerable because of the tension inherent in modern society, the threat to its survival—when there is a need to ensure a prescriptive, central nucleus—derives from the presence of a political rather than a civil religion, even though the latter may, in turn, take on authoritarian and integralist aspects and become a political religion. Furthermore, crises in modern society may indeed favor the birth and establishment of civil religions; at the same time they may also be, for civil religions that antedate those crises, a factor enabling such religions to fray themselves a path and emerge with success.

From a historical point of view, as George L. Mosse has shown in his classic studies on the "new politics" and the nationalization of the masses, the origins of civic religions precede the crises that favor their establishment. One could in fact venture the hypothesis that from the sacralization of politics emerge, like so many mountain streams, ancient and not-yet-dried-up currents of messianic passions and enthusiasms. This is why the analysis of civic religions cannot be limited just to their functional aspects but must also take in their true cultural and historical contexts.

Beyond their origins in the tensions of a society in crisis, the new secular religions may well have sprung from deep cultural motives, not the least of which would be a vocation for faith and a will for power. These may coexist in anyone who believes himself to possess the truth and for whom it is an imperative mission to change the world in which he lives, to change the nature of men and women, to create, in a new era of salvation, a "new order" and a "new man."

These prophets and leaders of new religions, unceasingly generated in the fertile womb of intellectuals and politicians anxious to mold human nature according to their prescriptions, readily find converts—not only because there are clever demagogues versed in the arts of seducing and manipulating the masses, but because their faith corresponds to the needs of a society thirsting for faith and security in a time of crisis, or because they represent deep and lasting currents within particular cultures, or simply because, as Dostoevsky's Grand Inquisitor held, because they satisfy a human need:

> This is what Thou hast rejected for the sake of that freedom that Thou hast exalted above everything. Yet in this question lies the greatest secret in the world. Choosing "bread," Thou wouldst have satisfied the universal and everlasting craving of humanity—to find someone to worship. So long as man remains free he strives for nothing so incessantly and so painfully as to find someone to worship. But man seeks to worship what is established

beyond dispute, so that all men would agree at once to worship it. For these pitiful creatures are concerned not only to find what one or the other can worship, but to find something that all can believe in and worship; what is essential is that all may be *together* in it. This craving for *community* of worship is the chief misery of every man individually and of all humanity from the beginning of time. For the sake of common worship they've slain each other with the sword. They have set up gods and challenged one another, "Put away your gods and come and worship ours, or we will kill you and your gods!" And so it will be to the end of the world, even when gods disappear from the earth; they will fall down before idols just the same.[11]

Movements such as Bolshevism, Fascism, and Nazism have affirmed themselves as *political* religions and intensified the aura of the sacred that always surrounds power. They have attributed to themselves those functions, proper to religions, of defining the meaning of life and the purpose of being. Political religions reproduce the typical structure of traditional religions as articulated in faith, myth, ritual, and communion. Through the state or a party they propose to realize a "metanoia" in human nature, whence a "new man" should emerge, regenerated and totally integrated into the community. To use a definition proposed by Raffaele Pettazzoni, such religions are "state" religions, and aim to supplant "human" religions in the collective mind.[12] Modern society has supplied, and may continue to supply, political religions with powerful means with which to organize collective life as though it were some vast human laboratory in which party and state perform experiments on the body social in order to create the "new man."

The use of political religion in Bolshevism and Nazism have already been studied, but this aspect of Italian Fascism has not really been considered, or at best only marginally. In his sketch of a history of "religious Italy," for instance, Pettazzoni leaps straight from the lay religiosity of the Risorgimento to that of the Resistance. He totally ignores Fascism, which, however, was, as we have seen, the only secular religion institutionalized by the state.[13] Even recent comparative studies of secular religions have also passed over the analysis of the political religion of Fascism. Yet the fact that Fascism was a form of civil religion is neither a recent discovery, nor does it derive solely from the view of it provided by Fascists themselves. It is a historical fact, and worthy of attention—if it is true that the "man who believes differently (I do not say the knowing man, but the believing man) also acts differently."[14]

After all, there is no concealing the fact that Fascism was the first European experiment since the French Revolution seeking to institutionalize a new civic religion. Until the advent of Nazism, analogy could only be made to the Bolshevik experiment. But Bolshevism differed from Fascism in that it preached and professed atheistic materialism, an antireligious scientism, and the myth of internationalism; and although it could show, especially in the early years after the Russian Revolution, a flowering of festivals and mass rituals, it was far less systematically concerned with the institutionalization of a collective cult.[15] Despite the development of a Lenin cult after his death, it was not until the end of the 1920s—and probably on the basis of an Italian model—that a personality cult devoted to a living leader was imposed.[16]

The importance of the religious aspect of Fascism did not escape some contemporary observers. Although at first they thought of it as no more than the expression of a generic and traditional "religion of the Fatherland," though one celebrated in a more emotive and exalted style, they did point to it as one of the most original aspects of the new movement. Some even perceived that Fascism contained the seeds of a new religion aware of its nature and objectives, and opportunely brought to the world's attention the myths, rituals, and symbols of what came to be known as the "Fascist religion."[17] Two American scholars had already noticed in 1929 that "Fascism . . . has the rudiments of a new religion. Whether or not these will grow remains to be seen, but there can be no doubt that already this new cult has taken some hold of the Italian heart and imagination."[18] In the 1930s a sympathetic French observer considered the mass political liturgy conducted by the régime to be proof that Fascism had given Italy a new life and a new civil religion.[19]

My research for this study has led me to conclusions that support the intuitive feeling of these observers. Once in power, Fascism instituted a lay religion by sacralizing the state and spreading a political cult of the masses that aimed at creating a virile and virtuous citizenry, dedicated body and soul to the nation. In the enterprise of spreading its doctrine and arousing the masses to faith in its dogmas, obedience to its commandments, and the assimilation of its ethics and its life-style, Fascism spent a considerable capital of energy, diverting those energies from other fields that might perhaps have been more important for the interests both of the régime and of the people. A commitment to the organization of mass rituals that persisted with obsessive determination for two decades, even when the foundations of the régime were crumbling as a result of defeat in war, is already and of itself a subject worthy of reflection.

The theme of Fascist religion is not to be summed up merely by its liturgical displays. These, though the most spectacular, are but one component. To take its symbols and rituals only in their aesthetic and propagandistic aspects, disregarding the system of beliefs and values, the theological politics that inspired them and that these represented, would give a partial and distorted view of the rituals themselves and would lead to a misrepresentation of their historical significance. All political movements have their rituals and symbols. It is no great task, making use of sociology and anthropology, to establish analogies between the different civil and political religions, or to demonstrate, beyond the diversity of the beliefs these embody, comparative points in their common natures and functions.[20]

As I have sought to show in these pages, the Fascist cult should not be reduced exclusively to matters of propaganda, of the aesthetics of its celebrations, of spectacles designed to entertain and deceive the masses; nor can it be seen solely in terms of sincerity or as a simulacrum of faith. The issue is more serious and more dramatic. Fascist rituals and celebrations wished to educate in order to convert; they were concerned with fundamental values and the meaning of life. Mass liturgy went far beyond its ludic or demagogic aspects, although these were certainly present; it was intended to conquer and mold the moral consciousness, the mentality, and the mores of the people, right down to its most intimate feelings about life and death. Reading history backward, in the light of later events, is not the best way to study history; it is even less satisfactory as a way of restoring the drama to a political experience in which millions of men and women were involved, the rulers and the ruled, without any of them being given the gift of knowing how the history in which they were actors would turn out.

There is another unavoidable problem in the study of secular religions, and it has probably dogged the reader from the beginning. Were the theology and liturgy of Fascism the expression of a genuine faith? the result of sincere convictions? Or do we face yet another form of demagoguery, complete with its sophisticated panoply of crafty and persuasive arts set in motion to deceive and manipulate the masses? Might not the cults of secular religions be no more than an extravagant ceremonial behind which hides, brutal in its nakedness, a will to power by the governors and the impartial art of hidden or visible persuaders?

It is hard to give a single answer to this question. No political cult exists without its orchestrated rituals and symbols. All liturgies set out, with all the artifice of the ruler, whatever they consider useful to arouse strong feelings among participants and spectators. Even the most austere cults entrust to the artifice of ritual and symbol the expression of their own devotion to the sacred. Alongside that artifice, however, and mixed with it, are the spontaneity and enthusiasm of the true believer who believes himself possessed of the truth. A public cult bears witness to a faith practiced even if through the artifice of propaganda. For the believer, propaganda is not only not subject to reprobation, to be undertaken undercover and exercised with dissimulation; it is raised to the level of theory and sublimated in the full light of day, as an activity perfectly apt to a profession of faith. The propagation of the faith is a duty for the believer; he aims not merely at contingent adherences, but at true conversion.

These are generalizations on the sincerity or simulation of faith in secular religions, but is the case different in other kinds of religion? The latter often base their pretensions to the truth more on prejudices as to the true nature of man than on verifiable and reliable facts. The failure of secular religions to date shows that they are fragile, but this is no evidence that they have arisen or been founded on bad faith, on lies, on political calculation, or on demagoguery; nor would it be wise to think that the sources from which they derive have dried up forever. Recent symptoms would lead one to the contrary conclusion, and several researchers have pointed to a process of resacralization currently under way, to a new politicization of the traditional religions and a new "religionizing" of politics.[21]

The problem of the sincerity of a given faith nonetheless remains open to adequate and thorough verification. After our experience of the political religions of the twentieth century, which, despite their spectacular recent collapse, are far from dead, we should perhaps resign ourselves to recognizing that even the absurd and the inhuman may arouse enthusiastic faith and religious belief. Cynicism can survive alongside fanaticism.

Beyond the problem of the sincerity of a faith, the phenomenon of the sacralization of politics, which is only now finally being examined scientifically, is an undisputable historical fact. Much progress has been made in recent years in the analysis of the religious dimension of politics in modern society, especially in sociology, but we remain at the very beginnings of the study of secular religions. As Clifford Geertz observed a few years ago, "the political theology of the twentieth century . . . has not yet been written, though there have been glancing efforts here and there. But it exists—or, more exactly, various forms of it exist—and until it is understood at least as well as that of the Tudors, the Majapahits, or the Alawites, a great deal of the public life of our times is going to remain obscure. The extraordinary has not gone out of the public life of modern politics, however much of the banal may have entered; power not only still intoxicates, it still exalts."[22] It is as a contribution to that history of the political theology of the twentieth century that this research was intended.

Abbreviations

Unless specified otherwise, depositories are in Rome.

CD	Chamber of Deputies
CP	Cabinet Papers
CPA	Communist Party Archives, Istituto Gramsci
CSA	Central State Archives (Archivio centrale della Stato)
DGPS	Directorate General of Public Safety (Direzione generale della Pubblica sicurezza)
DPS	Directorate of Public Safety
EFR	Exhibition of the Fascist Revolution, CSA
EUR	Esposizione universale romana
MFA	Ministry of Foreign Affairs (Ministero degli Affari esteri), Archivio storico
MI	Ministry of the Interior (Ministero dell'Interno)
MPC	Ministry of Popular Culture (Ministero della Cultura popolare), CSA
MRF	*Mostra della rivoluzione fascista*, ed. G. Fioravanti (Rome, 1990)
ND	National Directorate
NFP	National Fascist Party (Partito nazionale fascisto, Direttorio nazionale)
OO	B. Mussolini, *Opera omnia,* 44 vols. (Florence: Le Fenice, 1951–1980)
PI	*Il popolo d'Italia*
PMA	Prime Ministerial Archive, CSA
PMP	Prime Ministerial Papers, CSA
RD	Royal Decree
RDL	Royal Decree, Legislative

Notes

Introduction

1. *Religione della patria* is the term used here and often elsewhere in the text, as are *religione laica, civica,* or *secolare,* meaning respectively "lay," "civic," or "secular," in contradistinction to traditional theisms. In references to nineteenth-century Italy, "patriotic" or "national" has seemed the right word. The other three are used indifferently by the author and are so translated. For simplicity's sake, they are in the main rendered as the "religion of the fatherland." The word *patria* survives in English only in "patriot" or "patriotism." Although *patria* is feminine, like *la patrie* in French, and although most Italians think of their *patria* as a woman, most political thinking from the middle of the last century onward, led by the Germanic tradition, casts it as "the land of our fathers" or "fatherland," and it is so translated. *Trans.*

2. Abbé Coyer, *Dissertations pour être lues: La première sur le vieux mot de patrie; la seconde sur la nature du peuple* (The Hague, 1755), pp. 20–21.

3. J.-J. Rousseau, *Ecrits politiques,* ed. B. Gagnebin and M. Raymond (Paris: Pléiade, 1966).

4. J.-J. Rousseau, *Considérations sur le Gouvernement de Pologne et sur sa Réformation projettée* (1770), in *Rousseau* (Paris: Pléiade, 1964), vol. 3, p. 966. See also G. L. Mosse, *The Nationalization of the Masses* (New York, 1975). On the origins of the sacralization of politics in Enlightenment culture and the French Revolution, see J. L. Talmon, *The Origins of Totalitarian Democracy* (London, 1952); Mona Ozouf, *Festivals and the French Revolution,* trans. A. Sheridan (Cambridge, Mass.: Harvard University Press, 1988); idem, *L'homme régénéré: Essais sur la Révolution française* (Paris: Gallimard, 1989), pp. 116–182; Lynn Avery Hunt, *Politics, Culture, and Class in the French Revolution* (Berkeley, 1984).

5. Renzo De Felice, *Il triennio giacobino in Italia (1796–1799)* (Rome, 1990), pp. 92–93.

6. D. Cantimori, *Utopisti e riformatori italiani* (Florence, 1943), p. 175.

7. D. Cantimori, *Studi di storia* (Turin, 1959), p. 637.

8. A. Anzilotti, *Gioberti* (Florence, 1922), esp. chap. 4, "La religione civile." Extracts from Gioberti's texts, principally of his *Del primato morale e civile*

degli italiani (1843), are to be found in Denis Mack Smith, *Italy: A Modern History* (Ann Arbor: University of Michigan Press, 1969); and in Derek Beales, *The Risorgimento and the Unification of Italy* (London, 1971), Document 9, pp. 145–149. *Trans.*

9. Giuseppe Mazzini, *Fede e avvenire* (1835), in *Scritti politici,* ed. T. Grandi and E. Comba (Turin, 1972), p. 452. Numerous translations of Mazzini's works, though none of them complete, are available in English. Passages from Mazzini quoted in the text have been translated directly from the original. *Trans.*

10. Luigi Settembrini, *Ricordanza della mia vita,* ed. M. Themelly (Milan, 1961), p. 96.

11. Francesco De Sanctis, *La scuola liberale e la scuola democratica,* ed. F. Catalano (Bari, 1953), p. 421.

12. Mazzini to Giuseppe Ferretti, August 25, 1871, in *Scritti editi ed inediti di Giuseppe Mazzini,* vol. 91 (Imola, 1941), p. 162.

13. E. Gentile, *Il mito della Stato nuovo dall'antigiolittismo al fascismo* (Rome and Bari, 1982), pp. 3–28.

14. G. Mazzini, *D'alcune cause che impedirono finora lo sviluppo della libertà in Italia* (1832), in *Scritti politici,* p. 253.

15. De Sanctis, *La scuola liberale,* p. 391.

16. F. De Sanctis, "L'uomo del Guicciardini" (1869), in *Saggi critici,* ed. L. Russo (Bari, 1957), vol. 3, p. 23. *Vivit . . . venit:* "He lives on; he even comes to the Senate." *Trans.*

17. De Sanctis, *La scuola liberale,* pp. 424–425.

18. Ibid., p. 449. The "D'Azeglio" mentioned in the quotation is Massimo Taparelli, marchese d'Azeglio, a leader in the Risorgimento. *Trans.*

19. F. De Sanctis, "Giuseppe Parini" (1871), in *Saggi critici,* vol. 3, p. 117.

20. L. Russo, *Francesco De Sanctis e la cultura napoletana* (Venice, 1928), p. 311.

21. F. De Sanctis, "La scienzia e la vita," speech, October 16, 1872, in *Saggi critici,* vol. 3, p. 161.

22. De Sanctis, *La scuola liberale,* p. 423.

23. L. Borghi, *Educazione e autorità nell'Italia moderna* (Florence, 1974), pp. 13–15. For an overview of these questions, F. Chabod, *Storia della politica estera italiana dal 1870 al 1896* (Bari, 1951), pp. 179ff., remains unchallenged. See also G. Verucci, *L'Italia laica prima e dopo l'Unità* (Rome and Bari, 1981), pp. 66ff.

24. T. Tomasi, *L'idea laica nell'Italia contemporanea* (Florence 1971), pp. 28–29.

25. D. Bertoni Jovine, *Storia dell'educazione popolare in Italia* (Bari 1965), p. 183.

26. Quoted in A. A. Mola, *Michele Coppino, Scritti e discorsi* (Alba, 1978), pp. 555–558.

27. *Atti parlamentari, Camera dei deputati, Documenti, Legislatura XIII,* 1878 session, no. 48a, p. 2, quoted in G. Bonetta, *Corpo e nazione* (Milan, 1990), pp. 82–83.

28. Senator Alvisi, speech, July 6, 1888, quoted in M. Bartoli, *Ginnastica, pedagogia, educazione fisica e sport nella scuola italiana 1860–1892* (Naples, 1964), vol. 2, p. 335. For an overview of the role of physical education as a teaching instrument in liberal Italy, recent works include S. Giuntini, *Sport, scuola e caserma* (Padua, 1988); Bonetta, *Corpo e nazione*; and P. Ferrara, *L'Italia in palestra* (Rome, 1992).

29. Ferrara, *L'Italia in palestra*, esp. chap. 3.

30. *Programma della Società ginnastica fiorentina* (1877), quoted in Ferrara, *L'Italia in palestra*, p. 75.

31. On the army's role as a place of training for the nation and as the principal expression of the "national religion," as well as for the various ideas concerning the "nation in arms," see G. Conti, "Il mito della 'nazione armata,' " *Storia contemporanea*, December 1990, pp. 1149–95. In the framework of national military education, a special role was played by the Society for Target-Shooting, considered a popular institution that could support the educational work of the army. See S. Giuntini, "Al servizio della patria. Il tiro a segna dall'Unità alla 'Grande guerra,' " *Lancilotto e Nausicaa*, December 1987; Virgilio Ilari, *Storia del servizio militare in Italia*, vol. 2: *La nazione armata (1871–1918)* (1990), pp. 257–274.

32. E. Fanchiotti, *Il libro della lettura pel soldato italiano*, in *Rivista militare*, 1 (1886), 187–213.

33. Jovine, *Storia dell'educazione*, p. 184.

34. Ferrara, *L'Italia in palestra*, pp. 188–191.

35. A few brief notes on national education in the army are to be found in A. Visintin, "Esercito e società nella pubblicistica militare dell'ultimo Ottocento," *Rivista di storia contemporanea*, no. 1 (1987); and N. Labanca, "I programmi dell'educazione morale per soldato. Per un studio di pedagogia militare nell'Italia liberale," in *Esercito e città dall'unità agli anni Trenta* (Rome, 1989), vol. 1, pp. 521–536.

36. The terms of the competition are set out in the *Giornale militare ufficiale*, Part 1, 1885. One of the best texts, though it did not win the prize, was later published at the expense of the author, an artillery major: F. Mariani, *Perché e come si fa il soldato. Libro pel soldato italiano* (Pavia, 1889).

37. Some important aspects of the symbolic universe and the rites of patriotic instruction in Italy from 1870 to 1900 have been accurately reconstructed in B. Tobia, *Una patria per gli italiani* (Rome and Bari, 1991). Still useful is M. Venturoli, *La patria di marmo* (Pisa, 1957).

38. For a sketch of the September 20 celebrations, see "Le commemorazioni nel passato," *L'idea nazionale*, September 20, 1923.

39. Tobia, *Una patria*, pp. 100ff.

40. *Il 29 luglio 1901. Ricordi ed atti ufficiali del Comitato centrale per la commemorazione ed il pellegrinaggio alla tomba di S. M. Umberto I* (Rome, 1902), pp. 48, 108.

41. *I monumenti a ricordo delle battaglie per l'Indipendenza e l'Unità d'Italia*, comp. V. Cicala (Voghera, 1908). On patriotic monuments in the liberal period, see *Italia moderna. Immagini di un'identità nazionale. Dall'unità al*

nuovo secolo (Milan, 1982), pp. 26–38; M. Corgnati, G. Mellini, and F. Poli, eds., *Il lauro e il bronzo. La scultura celebrativa in Italia, 1800–1900* (Turin, 1990).

42. A general outline of the historical development of such groups can be found in G. Isola, "Un luogo d'incontro fra esercito e paese. Le associazioni dei veterani del Risorgimento (1861–1911)," in *Esercito e città*, pp. 499–519.

43. Tobia, *Una patria*, pp. 181ff.

44. *La festa popolare di S. Martino e i concorsi ai premi di patria storia* (Rome, 1880), pp. 20, 8.

45. *Il monumento al re Vittorio Emanuele in San Martino e le tabelle commemorative. Relazione ai soci della società di Solferino e San Martino del presidente Luigi Torelli* (Turin, 1887), p. 17.

46. *Il 29 luglio 1901,* p. 5.

47. On the concept of a "new politics," see Mosse, *Nationalization,* pp. 7–26. On fear of crowds, see Chabod, *Storia,* pp. 352ff.; Tobia, *Una patria,* pp. 114–129. On liberal Italy's failure to develop a political liturgy, see also S. Lanaro, *L'Italia nuova* (Turin, 1988), pp. 143–155.

48. On the monument, see *Il Vittoriano. Materiali per una storia* (Rome, 1986).

49. W. L. Adamson, "Fascism and Culture: Avant-Garde and Secular Religion in the Italian Case," *Journal of Contemporary History,* no. 3 (1989), 411–435; idem, "Modernism and Fascism: The politics of Culture in Italy, 1903–1922," *American Historical Review,* April 1990, pp. 359–390, which casts a new light on secular religion in the pre-Fascist period.

50. Lombardo Radice to Prezzolini, Catania, May 27, 1913, in I. Picco, ed., *Militanti dell'ideale. Giuseppe Lombardo Radice and Giuseppe Prezzolini. Lettere 1908–1930* (Locarno, 1991), p. 146.

51. Giuseppe Prezzolini, "Il problema dell'educazione religiosa," *La Voce,* July 28, 1914.

52. "Impazienze moderne," *La Voce,* June 13, 1914.

53. Benedetto Croce, *Storia del Regno di Napoli* (Bari, 1966), p. 143. An abridged version in English is *History of the Kingdom of Naples* (Chicago, 1970).

54. Benito Mussolini, "Da Guicciardini a . . . Sorel," *Avanti!* July 18, 1912.

55. On Mussolini's ideology at the time, see E. Gentile, *Le origini dell'ideologia fascista* (Rome and Bari, 1975), pp. 3–38.

56. Enrico Corradini, "Una nazione," *Il Regno,* June 19, 1904.

57. E. Corradini, *Scritti e discorsi,* ed. L. Strappini (Turin, 1980), pp. 140–141.

58. "La nazione gli eroi," *Il Tricolore,* June 1, 1909.

59. "La nostra azione," *Il Tricolore,* June 16, 1909. Corradini receives more detailed treatment in Zvi Sternhell with M. Sznaider and M. Asheri, *The Birth of Fascist Ideology* (Princeton, 1994), an expanded version of Sternhell's original work. Corradini, whose ideology was largely based on Maurice Barrès, was the first, in 1910, to use the term "National Socialism." His originality lies in his notion of a "proletarian nation" as a defining element of unity: "A régime of producers, a régime of class collaboration"; ibid., p. 12. *Trans.*

60. In this connection, see René Girard, *Violence and the Sacred*, trans. P. Gregory (Baltimore, 1977).
61. Vito Fanzio-Allmayer, "Disperazione religiosa contemporanea e le basi della morale," *La Voce*, August 13, 1914, pp. 2–3.
62. Guido De Ruggiero, "Il pensiero italiano e la guerra," *Revue de métaphysique et de morale*, September 1916, quoted in idem, *Scritti politici, 1912–1926*, ed. R. De Felice, pp. 141–142.
63. Carlo Rosselli, *Socialismo liberale* (Turin, 1979), p. 47. See also Robert Wohl, *The Generation of 1914* (Cambridge, Mass.: Harvard University Press, 1979); D. Settembrini, *Storia dell'idea antiborghese in Italia, 1860–1989* (Rome and Bari, 1991), chap. 4.
64. E. Durkheim, *The Elementary Forms of the Religious Life*, trans. Karen E. Fields (1947; reprint, Glencoe, Ill.: Free Press, 1995), p. 218.
65. Quoted in G. Prezzolini, *Tutta la guerra* (Milan, 1968), p. 271. On the sacred feeling inspired by the war, see also Pierre Teilhard de Chardin, *Writing in Time of War*, trans. R. Hague (New York, 1968). On the relationship between war and the sacred, see Georges Bouthoul, *War*, trans. Sylvie Lesson and George Lesson (New York: Walker, 1962).
66. Among the early promoters of a patriotic liturgy tied to the war, the Action Committee of Disabled Veterans was among the most prominent. Especially after Caporetto, it became the active organizer of rituals and manifestations to memorialize the fallen and recall the myth of the nation at war. See R. Fasani, *Il Comitato d'azione fra mutilati, invalidi e feriti di guerra* (Milan, 1938).
67. Agostino Lanzillo, *Le rivoluzioni del dopoguerra* (Città di Castello, 1922), p. xviii.
68. Filippo T. Marinetti, *Taccuini 1915–1921*, ed. A. Bertoni (Bologna, 1987), p. 488.
69. Sergio Panunzio, "La gravità della crisi attuale," *Polemica*, August 1922.
70. See G. L. Mosse, *Fallen Soldiers: Reshaping the Memory of the World Wars* (New York, 1990), esp. chaps. 3 and 5.
71. Gabriele D'Annunzio, "Orazione per la sagra dei Mille, V maggio, MDCCCLX, maggio MCMXV," reprinted in idem, *Per la più grande Italia* (Rome, 1943), p. 19. For this aspect of D'Annunzian politics, the fundamental work remains G. L. Mosse's essay "The Poet and the Exercise of Political Power: Gabriele D'Annunzio," *Yearbook of Comparative and General Literature*, no. 22 (1973). On the D'Annunzian rites in the capital during the interventionist period, especially important is A. Staderini, "L'interventismo romano 1914–1915," *Storia contemporanea*, April 1991, pp. 257–304. The Campidoglio, on the Capitoline Hill, was the home of one of the city's major temples and has always figured as one of the city's "sacred spaces"; hence D'Annunzio's inflammatory choice. *Trans.*
72. G. D'Annunzio, "Parole dette in una cena di compagni, all'alba del XXV maggio MCMXV," in *Per la più grande*, p. 108.
73. Fiume (modern Rijeka) was Adriatic territory disputed by Italy and the newly formed Yugoslavia. In September 1919 D'Annunzio led a volunteer

expedition that seized the city. He was not backed by the central government, and his short-lived "Republic" capitulated. The Treaty of Rapallo made Fiume a free port, and in 1924 it was absorbed into Mussolini's Italy. *Trans.*

74. On the mythical-liturgical aspects of the Fiume experience, see N. Valeri, *Da Giolitti a Mussolini* (Milan, 1967), pp. 32–72; R. De Felice, introduction to G. D'Annunzio, *La penultima ventura. Scritti e discorsi fiumani,* ed. De Felice (Milan, 1974), pp. vii–lxxviii; E. Gentile, *Le origini,* pp. 166–186; M. A. Ledeen, *D'Annunzio in Fiume* (Baltimore, 1977).

75. Mosse, *Fallen Soldiers,* chap. 9; *Monuments de mémoire. Les monuments aux morts de la première guerre mondiale* (Paris, 1991); A. Becker, *Les monuments aux morts. Mémoire de la Grande Guerre* (Paris, n.d.); A. Borg, *War Memorials* (London, 1991), pp. 69ff.; R. Shipley, *To Mark Our Place: A History of Canadian War Memorials* (Toronto, 1987), pp. 49ff.; W. Lloyd Warner, *The Living and the Dead* (New Haven, 1959), pp. 248ff.

76. The subject of Italian war memorials has not yet been studied in systematic fashion. For a preliminary overview, see C. Canal, "La retorica della morte. I monumenti ai caduti della Grande Guerra," *Rivista di storia contemporanea,* no. 4 (1982), 659–669; R. Monteleone and P. Sarasini, "I monumenti italiani ai caduti della grande guerra," in *La grande guerra,* ed. D. Leoni and C. Zadra (Bologna, 1986), pp. 631–670; C. Cresti, in *Il Mondo,* November 14, 1922.

77. Otello Cavara, *Il milite ignoto* (Milan, 1923).

78. "No patriotic celebration, from the Statute to the September 20 celebration, was ever as popular in Italy. It took the funeral cortège of the Unknown Soldier to show us a patriotic rite become an expression of religion by the people"; G. Prezzolini, "Vecchia e nuova democrazia: Rifarsi da capo," *Il Mondo,* November 6, 1921.

79. Nobiluomo Vidal, "Il soldato ignoto," *L'illustrazione italiana,* November 6, 1921.

1. The Holy Militia

1. For a more substantial, analytical treatment of the theme of this chapter, see E. Gentile, *Storia del partito fascista, 1919–1922* (Rome and Bari, 1989), chap. 7.

2. A. Mathiez made reference to E. Durkheim, "De la définition des phénomènes religieux," *Année sociologique,* 2 (1899); see also E. Durkheim, *The Elementary Forms of the Religious Life,* trans. Karen E. Fields (1947; reprint, Glencoe, Ill.: Free Press, 1995).

3. *Combattentismo* was the movement of the ex-combatants or veterans of the Great War; the *Arditi,* literally the "inflamed" or the "brave," were specially selected elite troops used in the war for hazardous, spectacular operations and wore black shirts and special insignia; futurism, an artistic and literary

movement defined by Filippo Marinetti, had a powerful political effect; *fiumanesimo* was the movement of those who had participated in D'Annunzio's abortive Republic of Fiume. *Trans.*

4. Giuseppe Bottai, "L'incontro di due generazione," *Critica fascista,* December 15, 1932.

5. S. W. Ray to the secretary of the Veterans' Fasces, Salerno, February 17, 1920, file 38, EFR. The *pussisti* were members of the Socialist party, best known by its initials, PUS, or Party of United Socialists. *Trans.*

6. B. Mussolini, *PI,* December 8, 1920.

7. The *popolari* formed a minority party (the Pertito popolare italiano, founded by Don Luigi Sturzo), but one with considerable influence. *Trans.*

8. In the early days of Fascism, the *squadristi* were the armed units of the movement. *Trans.*

9. Notebook 21, 1921, Pellizzi Archives. The *carbonari* were members of liberal political secret societies in the early nineteenth century. *Trans.*

10. Giacinto De Michelis, "Le nostre idee," *Il Fascio,* May 14, 1921.

11. Giuseppe Leonardi, "Siamo i superatori," *Il Fascio,* April 2, 1921.

12. R. Forti and G. Ghedini, *L'avvento del fascismo. Cronache ferrarese* (Ferrara, 1923), p. 90.

13. Italo Balbo, *Diario, 1922* (Milan, 1923), p. 90. There are few analyses of the genesis and development of militia symbolism at the local level. The only exception worthy of note is the study, in some regards exemplary if not always persuasive in certain of its historiographical judgments, of M. Fincardi, "I riti della conquista," *Contributi,* nos. 21–22 (1987), 1–127.

14. Asvero Gravelli, *I canti della rivoluzione* (Rome, 1928), pp. 84–86.

15. Balbo, *Diario,* p. 109.

16. *Il Fascio,* April 16, 1921.

17. "La magnifica affermazione della Lomellina fascista a Mortara," *PI,* May 10, 1921.

18. "Regolamento di disciplina per la milizia fascista," *PI,* October 3, 1922.

19. Outgoing telegrams, November 10, 1922, CSA.

20. C. Pellizzi, *Problemi e realtà del fascismo* (Florence, 1924), p. 165.

21. P. Zama, *Fascismo e religione* (Milan, 1923), pp. 12–13.

22. B. Mussolini, "Battisti!" *PI,* July 12, 1917.

23. *L'Intrepido,* July 10, 1921.

24. Francesco Meriano, "Rimini in un tripudio di sole, commemora Luigi Platania," *PI,* June 4, 1922.

25. *Dizionario di politica,* vol. 1 (Rome, 1940), pp. 146–147: "This rite symbolically expresses the spiritual continuity, beyond their own lifetimes, of those whose activity contributed to the reconstruction of Italian life promoted by Fascism. The 'presence' of those who sacrificed their lives in the struggle, or who have contributed to it by their acts, lives on in the new reality conquered by the Revolution. The dead are not absent; they live on in the record of their highest achievements. The reply 'Present!' shouted as one by their comrades expresses not just recognition for their lasting con-

tribution to the historical reality of the nation but the way in which there endures, in every soul, the high ideals that moved the departed comrade to his act of sacrifice."

26. G. Bottai, "Disciplina," *Critica fascista*, July 15, 1923.
27. Meriano, "Rimini."
28. *PI*, April 22, 1921.
29. Luigi Freddi, "Le sagre della rinascita," *PI*, September 26, 1922.
30. Ibid.
31. Otello Cavara, "I monumenti per i caduti di guerra," *L'illustrazione italiana*, December 31, 1922.
32. Filippo Burzio, *Politica demiurgica* (Bari, 1923), p. 111.

2. The Fatherland Dons the Black Shirt

1. In early 1923 the Italian Nationalist Association merged with the National Fascist Party. *Trans.*
2. Regulation governing the uniform of the prime minister, ministers, and undersecretaries, December 28, 1923, Acts, 1923, vol. 78 *bis*, PMP.
3. *L'illustrazione italiana*, December 17, 1922.
4. Roberto Giuseppe Mandel, "Mitologia fascista," *L'Assalto*, November 25, 1922.
5. CD, 27th legislature, *La legislazione fascista 1922–1928*, 7 vols. (Rome, n.d.), vol. 1, pp. 22–23.
6. B. Mussolini, telegram to the prefect of Forlì, June 18, 1923, deploring the failure to display the Italian flag on the occasion of the anniversary of the Statute. The association in question had claimed its "apolitical" nature, but that excuse was unacceptable, said Mussolini, at a time when the anniversary of the Statute was to be considered "the anniversary of the army and the nation"; MFA, folder 312, MPC.
7. Dario Lupi, ed., *La riforma Gentile e la nuova anima della scuola* (Milan and Rome, 1924), pp. 285–317.
8. D. Lupi, *Il comandamento della patria* (Milan, 1925), p. 71.
9. Ibid., pp. 68–69.
10. Lupi, *La riforma*, pp. 292–293.
11. Ibid., p. 207.
12. Ibid., pp. 207–271; See also G. F. Marini, "La rimembranza," *PI*, December 29, 1922; D. Lupi, *Parchi e viali della rimembranza* (Florence, 1923). On the symbolism of the tree and the spread of "Woods of Remembrance" after the Great War, see G. L. Mosse, *Masses and Man: Nationalist and Fascist Perceptions of Reality* (New York, 1980), chap. 11.
13. Lupi, *La riforma*, pp. 317 and 271.
14. See RD, December 9, 1923, no. 2747; Lupi, *La riforma*, pp. 411–426.
15. *L'idea nazionale*, June 2, 1923; "Un libro di propaganda nazionale," ibid., December 12, 1923.

16. Lupi, *La riforma*, pp. 230–231.
17. There is no specific study devoted to the symbolism and practice of the patriotic-Fascist liturgy, but useful elements are to be found in T. M. Mazzatosta, *Il regime fascista tra educazione e propaganda* (Bologna, 1978); A. Fava, "Chiesa e propaganda nella stampa locale: Riti e modelli 'religiose' della propaganda fascista in Umbria," in *Cattolici e fascisti in Umbria (1922–1945),* ed. A. Monticone (Bologna, 1978), pp. 247–295; M. Isnenghi, *L'educazione dell'italiano* (Bologna, 1979); A. Fava, "La guerra a scuola. Propaganda, memoria, rito (1915–1940)," in *La grande guerra,* ed. D. Leoni and D. Zadra (Bologna, 1986), pp. 685–713.
18. "Sagra nazionale," *Il giornale di Roma,* June 25, 1923. See also G. Bottai, "Sagra italica," ibid., April 22, 24, 1923.
19. CP, 1924, fasc. 2.4.1, no. 996, PMA.
20. "Finalmente!" *L'idea nazionale,* June 2, 1923.
21. "L'Italia celebra nella festa dello Statuto la sua fede e la sua disciplina," *PI,* June 5, 1923.
22. CP, 1926, fasc. 4.1, no. 2074; ibid., 1927, fasc. 2.4.1., no. 2033, PMA.
23. On Statute Day in 1931, Mussolini's daily paper devoted two columns on p. 5 to the parade in Rome and briefly noted provincial celebrations: "Statute Day was celebrated yesterday throughout Italy. The flag was everywhere displayed on public buildings and private houses. In garrison towns there were parades of troops and the militia and other ceremonies of a military nature, attended by the authorities and senior officers, as well as huge crowds. The solemn day was marked by other patriotic and Fascist ceremonies in various other towns. Offices and the principal monuments were brightly lit at night. The greatest enthusiasm was shown everywhere and at all times"; *PI,* June 9, 1931.
24. A typical ceremony during the régime is contained in a report from the prefect of Ascoli Piceno on Statute Day in 1931: "A solemn and austere military review took place at nine this morning. Present, grouped around the infantry's regimental flag, with its gold medal, and flanking the march, were all the Fascist organizations and representatives. Imposing spectacle of Fascist strength and patriotism. Prefect present in the uniform of his office, followed by the authorities in ceremonial dress. City splendidly beflagged, especially on route of march and in main square. Flowers thrown from the balconies as the regiment and party organizations marched by. Huge crowd jammed the avenue and square, showing its patriotic spirit and high enthusiasm. No incidents"; DGPS, 1930–31, cat. C4, file 373, MI. Other symbolic acts, such as the presentation of a flag or a dagger, accompanied these ceremonies, to mark "the fusion of Army and Militia"; telegram from the prefect of Alessandria, June 7, 1931, ibid.
25. Telegram from the prefect of Lucca, June 8, 1931, ibid.
26. Telegram from the prefect of Messina, June 7, 1931, ibid.
27. "Al di sopra delle sette e dei partiti," *PI,* September 21, 1923. For a detailed account of the celebrations, see *L'idea nazionale,* September 21, 1923.

28. CP, 1928–1930, fasc. 3.3.3., no. 4137; fasc. 14.4, no. 6735, both PMA; Political Affairs, 1919–1930, Holy See, file 9, fasc. "Abrogazione della festività del 20 settembre," MFA.

29. For an overview of these steps, see CD, 27th legislature, *La legislazione fascista 1922–1928*, vol. 1, pp. 574–588.

30. From the report accompanying the draft decree, quoted in Giorgio Alberto Chiurco, *Storia della revoluzione fascista* (Florence, 1929), vol. 5, pt. 2, p. 266.

31. François Charles-Roux, *Souvenirs diplomatiques. Une grande ambassade à Rome (1919–1925)* (Paris, 1961), pp. 192–193. In his report to his government dated November 2, Charles-Roux, chargé d'affaires at the French embassy in Rome, observed of Mussolini and Fascism: "Patriotism is the yeast he has used to prepare and carry out his insurrection: a vague sort of religious feeling for his country, which he will underline in a ceremony planned on the fourth, the anniversary of the Armistice. He will continue to appeal to the public in this way, to maintain the sympathy he has gained, and which his success has consolidated. His patriotism is of an exalted nature; among the mass of Fascists, I would almost say immoderate. Only a sense of responsibility tempers it in M. Mussolini and among the non-Fascist elements who have lined up alongside him"; Europe 1918–1940, Italy, vol. 62, Archives of the Ministry of Foreign Affairs, Paris.

32. "Il sacro pellegrinaggio," *PI,* May 23, 1923.

33. "La commovente adunata di Redipuglia," *PI,* May 25, 1923.

34. "Celebrazioni," *PI,* May 24, 1923.

35. "Cinque anni dopo!" *PI,* November 6, 1923.

36. This is a period in which Fascist strategy for conquering the universe of patriotic symbolism may be seen not only as ensuring that events were seen through Fascist eyes, but also by putting into practice a preordained policy to capture the leadership of patriotic events for the Fascist party. For instance, on the occasion of the anniversary of the annexation of Flume, in 1924, Mussolini instructed his prefects to study the organization of such celebrations, promoting "wherever possible popular demonstrations (processions, meetings, etc.), whose leadership local Fascist administrations, or the party itself, should ensure, perhaps in conjunction with veterans' and combatants' organizations," and with participation by "local or present representatives of the armed forces (Army, Navy, Air Force, Volunteer Militia of National Security)." These last should also mount the Guard of Honor at monuments and tablets to the fallen; CP, 1924, fasc. 2.4.2., no. 396, PMA.

37. For the organization of these demonstrations, the government and the party took care to ensure the greatest possible Fascist presence. Mussolini also sought to ensure the presence of the King at these ceremonies. See CP, 1924, fasc. 2.4.1, no. 2709, PMA.

38. L. Zani, *Italia libera* (Rome and Bari, 1975), pp. 102–103; *PI,* November 5 and 6, 1924. The party paper characterized the organizers of the Roman counterdemonstrations, among whom were the brothers Peppino and Sante

Garibaldi, and who marched under the banner of Garibaldism, as "profaners of the myth."

39. Decree of the *questura* of Rome, November 2, 1925, DGPS, cat. C4, file 98, MI. Analogous measures were taken in successive years.
40. CP, 1927, fasc. 2.4.1., no. 2033, PMA.
41. Ibid.
42. *PI,* May 25, 1931.
43. *PI,* May 23, 1930. In 1932, on the seventeenth anniversary of intervention, *Il popolo d'Italia* stated that the celebrations were "not just a re-evocation of Italy's entry into war; from now on, in the minds of the people, May 24, a fateful day, also represents the origin of the Fascist Revolution, and the beginning of a fresh history for Italy." Intervention was in fact "the first revolutionary manifestation in which the Italian people affirmed its new will to power and its liberation from the old political system"; "Le cerimonie odierne," *PI,* May 24, 1932.)
44. "Il giorno sacro," *PI,* November 4, 1924.
45. Some instances of tension are reported in telegrams from the prefects of Potenza and Venice, November 4, 1925, DGPS, cat. C4, file 98, MI.
46. Circular of the National Veterans Association, no. 24219, October 23, 1930, DGPS, 1930–1931, cat. C4, file 372, MI.
47. Ibid.
48. Telegram from the prefect of Enna, November 4, 1932, DGPS, 1932, cat. C4, sec. 2a, file 58, MI.
49. Ibid.
50. CP, fasc. 9.8, no. 3143, CSA.
51. *PI,* December 27, 1922, and January 2, 1923.
52. "Il Fascio romano simbolo dello Stato sulle nuove monete," *PI,* January 13, 1923. See CP, 1923, fasc. 9.8., no. 1379, PMA.
53. Margherita Sarfatti, *Dux* (Milan, 1930), p. 314.
54. "Il simbolo del Fascio Romano ricostituto nella sua storica realtà dal Sen. Boni," *Il giornale di Roma,* April 3, 1923; Luigi Falchi, "Le origini del Fascio littorio," ibid., April 12, 1923.
55. "I colori di Roma," ibid., October 21, 1923.
56. "I nuovi francobolli col Fascio," ibid., May 3, 1923.
57. "La nuova serie di francobolli commemorativi dell'ascesa del governo nazionale," *PI,* May 3, 1923.
58. Pericle Ducati, *Origine e attributi del fascio littorio* (Bologna, 1927).
59. *L'illustrazione italiana,* April 1, 1923.
60. *Il giornale d'Italia,* April 4, 1923.
61. RD, December 12, 1926, no. 2061; CD, 27th legislature, session 1924–1927, *Atti parlamenti, Camera dei deputati,* Documents, Draft Laws and Reports, no. 1189-A. See CP, 1928–1930, fasc. 3.3.2, no. 1880; and CP, 1940–1943, fasc. 3.3.2. no. 552, both in PMA.
62. RDL, December 20, 1926, no. 2273. See MI, *Disposizioni per l'uso dell'emblema del Fascio littorio* (Rome, 1927).
63. NFP, *Foglio d'ordini,* no. 26, March 19, V (1927).

64. RD, June 14, 1928; see *PI*, September 16, 1928.
65. RDL, April 11, 1929, no. 504.
66. The ban affected primarily the First of May, which could not be celebrated even in private. See CP, 1924, fasc. 2.4.1, no. 1562, PMA.
67. *PI*, February 8, 1923.
68. *PI*, October 6, 1923. The medal, which could be worn by any party member who had participated in mobilization for the March, bore on one face the Winged Victory, whose "luminous flight soars above the prophetic vision of the creators of a Fascist revolution, ripened in harsh expectation and austere spiritual battles." On the reverse was inscribed "March on Rome, October 27 to November 1, 1922."
69. EFC, file 45, fasc. 114, subfasc. 141, CSA.
70. NFP, *Il gran consiglio nei primi dieci anni dell'era fascista* (Rome, 1933), p. 64.
71. The unpublished text of the "provisional plan" is in EFR, file 50, fasc. 121, subfasc. 3, CSA; the official program was published in *PI*, October 16, 19, 23, and 24. The party committee consisted of De Bono, Bianchi, Giunta, Bastianini, Marinelli, and Freddi, as well as Filippo Cremonesi, Royal Commissioner in Rome.
72. The Voluntary Militia for National Security, or MVSN (Milizia Voluntaria per la Sicurezza Nazionale), was the official name of the Fascist militia. *Trans.*
73. B. Mussolini, OO, vol. 20, pp. 61–65, 66–67.
74. Michele Bianchi, *I discorsi, gli scritti* (Rome, 1931), pp. 101–103.
75. An account of the parade was published in *PI*, October 31–November 1, 1923.
76. Giovanni Amendola, "Commemorazione," *Il Mondo*, October 11, 1923, reprinted in G. Amendola, *La democrazia italiana contro il fascismo 1922–1924* (Milan and Naples, 1960), pp. 182–185.
77. G. Amendola, "Un anno dopo," *Il Mondo*, November 2, 1923; idem, *La democrazia*, pp. 194–195.
78. NFP, *Il gran consiglio*, p. 153.
79. "La marcia su Roma e gli ex-combattenti," *PI*, October 16, 1924.
80. CP, fasc. 2.4.1, no. 2564, PMA.
81. "Spettacolo di forza," *PI*, October 29 and 30, 1924. The militiaman swore to be loyal to the King and his successors, "faithfully to observe the Statute and other laws, and to do my duty for the inseparable good of King and Country."
82. For an account of the demonstrations, see ibid.
83. B. Mussolini, OO, vol. 21, pp. 125–126.
84. "Per la terza celebrazione anniversaria della marcia su Roma," *PI*, October 22, 1925.
85. *PI*, October 28, 1925.
86. *PI*, October 22, 1925.
87. B. Mussolini, OO, vol. 21, p. 425.

88. RDL, October 21, 1926, no. 1779, introduced into law March 6, 1927, no. 267; see CP, fasc. 2.4.1, no. 3904, PMA.
89. *PI*, March 23 and 27, 1923.
90. "Per la celebrazione fascista a Roma," *PI*, March 21, 1923; B. Mussolini, *OO*, vol. 20, pp. 205–217.
91. "Anniversario," *PI*, March 26, 1924.
92. Communiqué from the Stefani Agency, March 20, 1925, CP, 1928–1930, fasc. 14.2, no. 1016, PMA.
93. Circular, March 26, 1927, ibid.; for the following years, see fasc. 14.2, no. 1016; fasc. 3.3.3, no. 10695.
94. Law of December 27, 1930, no. 1726.
95. Cesare Sobrero, "Un anno di passione italiana," *PI*, October 18, 1923; B. Mussolini, "Messaggio alla nuova direzione del giornale Epoca," October 19, 1923, in *OO*, vol. 20, p. 336.
96. Telegram from the prefect, December 18, 1925, DGPS, 1925, cat. G1, "Fasci di combattimento," file 126, PMA.
97. Pietro Fedele to Mussolini, November 9, 1926, CP, 1940–1943, fasc. 3.17, no. 4198, PMA.
98. Circular, December 25, 1926, ibid.
99. Note to the head of government, January 10, 1927, CP, 1940–1943, fasc. 1.7, no. 49269, PMA.
100. Telegram from Suardo, undersecretary of Prime Minister's Office, to all ministers, October 27, 1927, ibid., no. 8403.
101. B. Mussolini, speech, November 11, 1924, in *OO*, vol. 21, p. 140.
102. Note to the head of government, May 12, 1926, CP, 1928–1930, fasc. 3.3.2, no. 1962, PMA.
103. Mussolini to all prefects, August 23, 1926, ibid. All dispositions for public events were now controlled by RDL, August 6, 1926, no. 1486, enacted into law February 27, 1927, no. 244.
104. Report on the conversion into law of RDL, August 6, 1926, no. 1486, converted into law on February 27, 1927, no. 244, ibid.
105. CP, fasc. 3.3.9, no. 1962; cabinet meeting, October 17, 1927, fasc. 1.3.4, no. 1660; circular from the head of government, November 15, 1927; all PMA.
106. FNP, *Foglio d'ordini*, no. 15, November 22, V (1926).
107. Ibid., no. 19, January 8, V (1927).

3. The Archangel of This World

1. B. Mussolini, maiden speech to CD, June 21, 1921, in *OO*, vol. 16, p. 44.
2. Idem, speech to Third Fascist Congress, November 9, 1921, ibid., vol. 17, p. 221.
3. Idem, speech in Milan, October 9, 1923, on the first anniversary of the March on Rome, ibid., vol. 20, p. 62.

4. "Un rito fascista," *PI*, December 13, 1923.

5. B. Mussolini, speech in Cremona, June 17, 1923, in *OO*, vol. 19, p. 274.

6. "Santa milizia," *I fasci italiani all'estero*, May 2, 1925.

7. D. Lupi, speech in Perugia, February 18, 1923, in *Il commandamento della patria* (Milan, 1925), p. 24.

8. Pietro Misciattelli, "La mistica del fascismo," *Critica fascista*, July 15, 1923.

9. Ettore Lolini, "La conquista ideale dello Stato," *La conquista dello Stato*, February 15, 1925, in idem, *Per l'attuazione dello Stato fascista* (Florence, 1928), pp. 58–64.

10. G. Bottai, "Disciplina," *Critica fascista*, July 15, 1923.

11. Guido Gamberini, "Sistematizzare la fede," *PI*, April 4, 1928.

12. E. Gentile, *Il mito della Stato nuovo dall'antigiolittismo al fascismo* (Rome and Bari, 1982); G. Chiosso, *L'educazione nazionale da Giolitti al primo dopo-guerra* (Brescia, 1983).

13. Giorgio Masi to Mussolini, November 13, 1937, MI, Political Prisoners, file 638, fasc. "G. Masi," CSA. Masi was a teacher, a fervent follower of Gentile, and a true representative of those idealists who took up the Fascist religion. "[I had] a sure faith in the divinity of this world," he wrote in the organ of the Fascist University Federation, "in the divine nature of our lives, in the absolute worth of what we were doing, animated and exalted, beyond grief and suffering, in this heroic, warrior generation of ours whose greatness was forged in war, faith, and sacrifice"; "Propaganda fascista," *La rivolta ideale*, July 9, 1925. Fallen into disgrace because of his extremism, Masi was sentenced to be interned in 1937.

14. Romolo Murri, *Fede e fascismo* (Milan, 1924), pp. 23, 6–7. See P. G. Zunino, "Romolo Murri e il fascismo," *Fonti e documenti*, no. 14 (1985), 631–667.

15. Balbino Giuliano, *L'esperienza politica dell'Italia* (Florence, 1924), p. 311.

16. For an analysis of the contribution made by Gentile and his disciples to the elaboration of Fascist theology, see E. Gentile, *Le origini dell'ideologia fascista* (Rome and Bari, 1975), pp. 323–400; for its philosophical bases, see A. Del Noce, *Giovanni Gentile* (Bologna, 1990).

17. Giovanni Gentile, *Fascismo e cultura* (Milan, 1928), p. 58.

18. G. Gentile, *Che cos'è il fascismo* (Florence, 1925), p. 145.

19. Ibid., pp. 53, 170.

20. G. Gentile, *Origini e dottrina del fascismo* (Rome, 1934), reprinted in idem, *Politica e cultura*, ed. H. A. Cavallera (Florence, 1990) vol. 1, p. 395.

21. Ibid., p. 89.

22. B. Mussolini, *La dottrina del fascismo. I: Idee fondamentali*, reprinted in *OO*, vol. 26, pp. 120–121. (The philosophical part of the text is the work of Gentile.)

23. Piero Pedrazza, "Facciamo gli italiani," *PI*, June 5, 1924.

24. Mario Appelius, quoted in "La religione nazionale del fascismo," *La vita italiana*, 1925, pp. 316–317.

25. Salvatore Gatto, "Di fronte al passato," *Il Raduno*, April 1928, reprinted in idem, *1925. Polemiche del pensiero e dell'ozione fasciste* (Rome, 1934);

compare idem, "Fascismo e religione," *La rivolta ideale,* September 13, 1925.

26. B. Mussolini, *La dottrina del fascismo,* p. 118.
27. Mario Giampaoli, *1919* (Rome, 1929), p. 346.
28. Balbino Giuliano, "L'idea etica del fascismo," *Gerarchia,* November 1932.
29. B. Mussolini, OO, vol. 26, pp. 120, 129. The last sentence was introduced by Mussolini himself into Gentile's text, which spoke more generally of "Fascism calling itself totalitarian," and of the Fascist state as "penetrating the lives of the people." The original text, with Mussolini's corrections, is in the archives of the Gentile Foundation, fasc. "Mussolini."
30. *PI,* December 20, 1931.
31. On this subject, worthy of note is what Felice Battaglia wrote under the rubric "Rousseau" in the NFP's *Dizionario di politica* (Rome, 1940), vol. 4, p. 157: "The Social Contract is not at the historical origin of the State; it is rather an intrinsic criterion of reason, either because it understands the innermost essence of the State or because it acts according to an ideal of justice. The general will is no longer the will of all, but the immanent, universal will, that will that, as it legitimates authority, likewise establishes authority. In this sense, Rousseau is the founder of those deep views of the state that have come down to us through German idealism, who put the State on the level of an absolute, beyond any form of empiricism. The people, on which it so insists, is not a disaggregated mass, as democrats would have it, in which each individual is a single and equal unit, but the depository of a value that goes well beyond any single life, because it belongs to the spirit, because to that perennial value which is association, it is the bond, the unity. Absolutism, others have said, democratic absolutism; but it isn't that at all, but rather, to repeat, a sense of rationality inherent in the State, which makes of it a moral subject, a field of accomplished rationality unfolding in politics."
32. Camillo Pellizzi, "L'iniziativa individuale nella politica fascista," *Gerarchia,* December 1931; idem, "Religiosità dello Stato," *PI,* August 20, 1927.
33. Paolo Orano, *Il Fascismo* (Rome, 1939), vol. 2, pp. 140–146.
34. G. Bottai, "Stato corporativo e democrazia," *Lo Stato,* March–April 1930.
35. G. Bottai, "Filosofia e rivoluzione," *Primato,* November 1, 1940.
36. G. Bottai, *Esperienza corporativa (1929–1835)* (Florence, 1935), p. 586.
37. NFP, *Il cittadino soldato* (Rome, 1936), p. 13.
38. G. Bottai, *Le carte della scuola* (Milan, 1941), pp. 417–418.
39. *Il libro della terza classe elementare* (Rome, 1936), p. 65. The author was Nazareno Padellaro.
40. *Autobiografie di giovani del tempo fascista* (Brescia, 1947), pp. 18–21.
41. Maurizio Maraviglia, *Alle basi del regime* (Rome, 1929), p. 36.
42. "Santa milizia," *I fasci italiani all'estero,* May 2, 1925.
43. Alfredo Rocco, *Scritti e discorsi politici* (Milan, 1938), vol. 3, pp. 944–945.
44. "Dallo Stato alla Chiesa," *Critica fascista,* July 15, 1931.
45. Carlo Scorza, "Odiare i nemici," *Gioventù fascista,* April 12, 1931.
46. "Relazione al duce sui fascisti giovanili de combattimento," July 11, 1931,

Duce's Private Secretariat, Confidential Correspondence, file 31, fasc. 1, CSA.

47. *PI,* October 29, 1926.
48. *PI,* July 16, 1929.
49. *La dottrina fascista* (Rome, 1929), pp. 3, 13.
50. NFP, *Il primo libro del fascista* (Rome, 1938), p. 7.
51. "Dogana," *Critica fascista,* May 1, 1939.
52. "Dopo la marcia," *PI,* November 1, 1923.
53. See Oddone Fantini, ed., *Il partito fascista* (Rome, 1931), pp. 92, 138; P. Pombeni, *Demagogia e tirannide* (Bologna, 1984), chap. 3.
54. NFP Statute, 1929, art. 13. The formula was introduced into the swearing-in of the Fascist Militia in 1926. See NFP, *Foglio d'ordini,* no. 7, September 15, IV (1926).
55. NFP Statute, 1932, art. 14.
56. M. Martignetti, "Giuramento," in NFP, *Dizionario di politica,* vol. 2, p. 316.
57. See the collection of NFP statutes in M. Missori, *Gerarchie e Statuti del PNF* (Rome, 1986).
58. "Istruzione sul libro della prima classe," *Annali dell'istruzione elementare,* no. 3, Year XVI (1938), quoted in T. M. Mazzatosta, *Il regime fascista tra educazione e propaganda, 1935–1943* (Bologna, 1978), p. 144. A *Balilla* was a member of the youngest of the Fascist Youth organizations. *Trans.*
59. *Eja,* party orders for the Fascist Federation of Ascoli Piceno, August 22, 1936.
60. Pietro Maria Bardi, "Mostra della Rivoluzione Fascista," *Gioventù fascista,* July 10, 1932.
61. Guido Gamberini, "Fede e competenza," *Critica fascista,* August 1, 1930.
62. NFP, *La dottrina del fascismo* (Rome, 1936), p. 15.
63. NFP, *Foglio d'ordini,* no. 27, March 27, V (1927).
64. Ibid., no. 25, March 17, VI (1928).
65. "Adunate del fascismo," *L'ordine fascista,* March 1928.
66. *PI,* March 22, 1928.
67. NFP, *Il partito nazionale fascista* (Rome, 1936), p. 53; NFP, *Il cittadino soldato* (Rome, 1936), p. 19.
68. Arturo Marpicati, *Il partito fascista* (Milan, 1935), pp. 129–130. From 1925 onward the party had cultivated the memory of fallen Fascists with special care. See NFP, *Pagine eroiche della rivoluzione fascista* (Milan, 1925).
69. G. Pucci, "Santa Croce sacrario dei nostri martiri," *Gioventù fascista,* November 1, 1934.
70. *PI,* October 9 and 30, 1923.
71. *Il Telegrafo,* May 21, 1928, in Duce's Private Secretariat, Confidential Correspondence, file 88, fasc. "Carlo Scorza," CSA.
72. The party secretary prescribed as follows in 1926 (NFP, *Foglio d'ordini,* no. 14, November 12, V [1926]):

"Off with the hats." Exacting the doffing of hats as we march by is a thoroughly legitimate custom among Fascists, a salute to our flags, which are the living symbol of a passion fed by sacrifice, and of our new Italian and fascist faith.

The Secretary-General of the party, seeking to establish the norms on this custom, limited this form of salute exclusively to: the standards of the legions and squadron pennants. The former are the emblems of out revolutionary armed forces; the second recall out unforgettable dead.

The Party does not require a salute to each of the thousands upon thousands of pennants of the *Balilla, Avanguardisti,* Sports or Girls' organizations.

73. NFP Statute, 1929, art. 2. New statutes in 1932 and 1938 further articulated and solemnized the homage paid to party banners and standards.
74. *PI*, March 24, 1932.
75. Carlo De Leva, "La Torre littoria," *Gioventù fascista*, December 30, 1932.
76. Guido Bortolotto, *Lo Stato e la dottrina corporativa* (Bologna, 1930), p. 39.
77. G. Gentile, "Fuori dell'equivoco," *Corriere della Sera*, September 4, 1929, p. 40.
78. Armando Carlini, *Filosofia e religione nel pensiero di Mussolini* (Rome, 1934), p. 9.
79. B. Mussolini, speech to CD, May 13, 1929, in OO, vol. 24, p. 89.
80. EFR, file 42, fasc. "Venezia Euganea," subfasc. "Vicenza"; fasc. "Lombardia," subfasc. "Milano."
81. B. Mussolini, "Stato e Chiesa," *Le Figaro*, December 18, 1934, reprinted in OO, vol. 26, pp. 399–401.
82. Antonio Pagliaro, "Chiesa," in NFP, *Dizionario di politica*, vol. 4, pp. 39–40.
83. G. Bottai, "Chiesa e risorgimento," *Il popolo di Trieste*, January 27, 1922, reprinted in idem, *La politica delle arti. Scritti, 1918–1943*, ed. A. Masi (Rome, 1982), pp. 66–67.
84. G. Bottai, "Il pensiero e l'azione di Giuseppe Mazzini," speech in Genoa, May 4, 1930, reprinted in idem, *Incontri* (Milan, 1943), p. 124. The complex relationships between Bottai and Catholicism have been studied with expertise and sensibility by R. Moro in his introduction to the correspondence between G. Bottai and Don G. de Luca, *Carteggio 1940–1957*, ed. R. De Felice and R. Moro (Rome, 1989). Moro's analysis, however, although it points to certain ambiguities in Bottai's thinking, fails to give adequate prominence to the totalitarian aspects of his Fascism, even in matters of religion. The reader is referred to E. Gentile, *Il mito dello Stato*, pp. 205ff. On the relationship between Fascist totalitarianism and Catholicism, see R. De Felice, *Mussolini il duce. II: Lo Stato totalitario 1936–1940* (Turin, 1981), pp. 129ff. For Fascist attitudes to antidemocratic fascism, see P. G. Zunino, *Interpretazione e memoria del fascismo. Gli anni del regime* (Rome and Bari, 1991), chap. 5.
85. Igino Giordani, "Motivi di religione fascista," *Il Popolo*, May 10, 1924, reprinted in *La terza pagina de "Il Popolo,"* ed. L. Bedeschi (Rome, 1973), pp. 207–211. For some aspects of this position among Catholics, see R.

Moro, "Afascismo e antifascismo nei movimenti intellettuali di Azione Cattolica dopo il '31," *Storia contemporanea,* December 1975, pp. 733–799.

86. Don Luigi Sturzo, *Pensiero antifascista* (Turin, 1925), pp. 7–16. An anti-Fascist newspaper in Brazil carried a story from Nice that ran as follows: "Efforts are being made in Italy to make Fascism appear a true and proper religion. To that end, despite violent objections from Catholic clergy and the Vatican, children and young people forced into the *Balilla* and the *Avanguardisti* are taught a Credo. This creed is a parody of the Nicene Creed. We quote it textually. *Q:* What does it mean to be a Fascist? *A:* It means blind obedience to the commands, the principles, and the sacraments of Italy. *Q:* What is the Fascist creed? *A:* It is the creed given by the apostles of Italy and by fascism. *Q:* How many articles does it have? *A:* It has twelve articles, as follows: I believe in eternal Rome, the mother of my country—And in Italy, its firstborn—Born of its virgin womb by the grace of God—Which suffered under barbarian invaders, was crucified, dead and buried—And rose to Heaven in 1918 and 1922—Which sits at the right hand of Mother Rome—Whence it will judge the evil and the dead—I believe in the genius of Mussolini—In our Holy Father, Fascism, and in the communion of martyrs—In the conversion of Italy—and the resurrection of the Empire—Amen"; *La Difesa,* São Paulo, February 27, 1927. The years 1918 and 1922 are those of the founding of Fascism and the March on Rome.

87. *Non abbiamo bisogno,* June 20, 1931, in *Tutte le encicliche dei sommi pontefici,* ed. E. Momigliano (Milan, 1959), pp. 971–972:

> We have observed a form of religiosity in action in rebellion against the instructions of the superior Authority of religion, in fact imposing and encouraging the faithful not to observe these; a religiosity that has become persecution and seeks to destroy that which the Supreme Head of Religion most appreciates and has most at heart; a religiosity that stoops to, and allows others to stoop to, insults in word and deed against the Father of all the faithful, with shouts of "Down" and "To Death" at him: the crude beginnings of parricide. Such religiosity can in no way be reconciled with Catholic doctrine or practice; it is as contrary to these as is possible.
>
> This opposition is the graver of itself, and the more ruinous in its effects, when it is not just a matter of external acts perpetrated and consummated, but when it is a matter of principles and maxims announced as programmatic and fundamental.
>
> A concept of the State that ties to itself the whole younger generation, from childhood to adulthood, is not reconcilable with Catholic doctrine, nor can it be reconciled with the natural rights of families. For Catholics, it is not compatible with Catholic doctrine to claim that the Church, the Pope, should limit themselves to the external practices of Religion (Mass and the Sacraments), and that the remainder of education belongs to the State.

See also P. Scoppola, *La Chiesa e il fascismo* (Rome and Bari, 1976), pp. 255ff.

88. On Evola, see M. Rossi, "L'interventismo polito-culturale nelle riviste tradizionaliste negli anni venti: Atanòr (1924) e Ignis (1925)," *Storia contem-*

poranea, no. 3 (1987), 457–504; idem, "L'avanguardia che si fa tradizione: L'itinerario culturale di Julius Evola, dal primo dopoguerra alla metà degli anni trenta," ibid., no. 6 (1991), 1039–90.

89. B. Mussolini, speech to CD, December 1, 1921, in *OO,* vol. 17, p. 292.
90. G. Gentile, "Roma eterna," *Civiltà,* June 21, 1940.
91. E. Gentile, *Il mito dello stato,* pp. 240–241.
92. Pietro De Francisci, *Civiltà romana* (Rome, 1939), p. 48.
93. P. De Francisci, "Roma," in NFP, *Dizionario di politica,* vol. 4, p. 134.
94. Franco Ciarlantini, "Il Fascismo e la Romanità," *Augustea,* April 21, 1938.
95. E. Ciaceri, "Paganesimo," in *Dizionario di politica.*
96. On the various historiographic interpretations of the Romanity myth in Fascism, see R. Vesser, "Fascist Doctrine and the Cult of the *Romanità,*" *Journal of Contemporary History,* no. 1 (1992), 5–21.
97. B. Mussolini, "Passato e avvenire," *PI,* April 21, 1922.
98. See S. Kostof, "The Emperor and the Duce: The Planning of Piazzale Augusto Imperatore in Rome," in *Art and Architecture in the Service of Politics,* ed. H. A. Millon and L. Nochlin (Cambridge, Mass., 1980), pp. 270–325.
99. B. Mussolini, speech at the Campidoglio on the occasion of being made an honorary citizen of Rome, April 21, 1924, in *OO,* vol. 20, p. 335.
100. C. Q. Gilioli, *Mostra Augustea della Romanità* (Rome, 1937–38).
101. The text of the inaugural address, approved by Mussolini, is in CP, 1937–1939, fasc. 14, no. 918/1, PMP.
102. See L. Quilici, "Romanità e civiltà romana," in *Dalla mostra al museo. Roma capitale 1870–1911* (Venice, 1983); and Anna Maria Liberati Silverio, "La Mostra Augustea della Romanità," in ibid., pp. 77–90. On the number and nature of those visiting, see the report to the head of government, CP, 1937–1939, fasc. 14, no. 918/7, PMP.
103. G. Bottai, "Roma e Fascismo," *Roma,* October 1937.
104. B. Mussolini, address to Gold Medalists, January 8, 1923, in *OO,* vol. 19, p. 94.
105. In thinking of a "mythical era" I have taken into special account Mircea Eliade, *Patterns in Comparative Religion,* trans. Rosemary Sheed (Cleveland, 1958), a translation of *Traité d'histoire des religions* (1948; rev. ed. 1970), pp. 388–408.
106. Emil Ludwig, *Conversations with Mussolini* (New York, 1930), p. 198.
107. B. Mussolini, speech at the Campidoglio on the occasion of being made an honorary citizen of Rome, April 21, 1924, p. 234.
108. Ludwig, *Conversations,* p. 100.
109. B. Mussolini, speech in Milan, October 28, 1923, in *OO,* vol. 20, p. 65.
110. N. Padarello, *Fascismo educatore* (Rome, 1938), p. 18.
111. Massimo Scaligero, "Natale di Roma," *Gioventù fascista,* April 21, 1933.
112. B. Mussolini, *PI,* April 21, 1922.
113. Eliade, *Patterns in Comparative Religion,* p. 407.
114. B. Mussolini, address on the seventh anniversary of the founding of Fascism, March 26, 1926, in *OO,* vol. 22, p. 100.

115. On the crisis of 1931, see R. De Felice, *Mussolini il Duce. Gli anni del consenso 1929–1936.* (Turin, 1974), vol. 1, pp. 246ff.; on the 1938 crisis, ibid., vol. 2, pp. 133ff.

4. The Liturgy of Collective Harmony

1. Emil Ludwig, *Conversations with Mussolini* (New York, 1930), p. 120.
2. C. Costamagna, *Dottrina del Fascismo* (1982), p. 108.
3. G. Sorel, *Reflections on Violence.* For further study of the seminal importance of Sorel and other French thinkers on early fascism, see Zvi Sternhell with M. Sznaider and M. Asheri, *The Birth of Fascist Ideology* (Princeton, 1994), intro. and chap. 1. *Trans.*
4. B. Mussolini, speech in Naples, October 24, 1922, in OO, vol. 18, p. 457. See E. Gentile, *Il mito della Stato nuovo dall'antigiolittismo al fascismo* (Rome and Bari, 1982), pp. 163–170.
5. Giovanni Neri, "La tradizione mitica che ritorna," *Il popolo di Lombardia,* February 23, 1924.
6. Report of the prefect of Pesaro, February 23, 1924, Finzi Cabinet, file 2, fasc. 72, CSA.
7. G. Gentile, *Fascismo e cultura* (Milan, 1928), pp. 48–49.
8. Carlo Curcio, in NFP, *Dizionario di politica* (Rome, 1940), vol. 3, p. 186; See C. Curcio, *Miti della politica* (Rome, 1940).
9. Rodolfo De Mattei, "Miti politici e fatti economici," *Educazione fascista,* July 1928.
10. Carlo Costamagna, "Razza," in NFP, *Dizionario di politica,* vol. 4, pp. 23–29.
11. C. Costamagna, "Regime," ibid., pp. 31–35.
12. D. Marchesini, *La scuola dei gerarchi* (Milan, 1976), p. 105.
13. "I miti moderni," *Primato,* February 15, 1942.
14. Gustave Le Bon, *Aphorismes du temps présent* (Paris, 1919), p. 96.
15. C. Pellizzi, *Problemi e realtà del fascismo* (Florence, 1924), p. 116. Pellizzi returned to this question many years later and reflected on the sociology of myth, ritual, and symbolism. Some of his remarks anticipate the scientific analysis of political liturgy and remain worthy of attention. See C. Pellizzi, *Rito e linguaggio* (Rome, 1964), esp. chap. 8.
16. *PI,* March 19, 1927.
17. Roberto Michels, *Studi sulla democrazia e sull'autorità* (Florence, 1933), p. 75.
18. Guido Bortolotto, *Lo Stato e la dottrina corporativa* (Bologna, 1930), p. 35.
19. See J. L. Talmon, *The Origins of Totalitarian Democracy* (London, 1952).
20. N. Padellaro, *Fascismo educatore* (Rome, 1938), p. 165.
21. Gustave Le Bon, *La vie des vérités* (Paris, 1920), pp. 38–39.
22. Ludwig, *Conversations,* p. 121.
23. "Veterans Speak of the Diplomatic Service," *International Affairs,* no. 9

(1989), 132. See R. De Felice, *Mussolini l'alleato* (Turin, 1990), vol. 1, pt. 2, p. 1281, n. 1. A further confirmation of Mussolini's interest in Soviet ritual is the fact that in 1927 he asked the Ministry of Foreign Affairs to provide information on the use of the "Great Banner" in Soviet celebrations. See CP, fasc. 15.19, no. 2446, PMP.

24. Ludwig, *Conversations,* pp. 66–67.

25. See G. L. Mosse, "Fascism and the French Revolution," *Journal of Contemporary History,* 24 (1989), 5–26.

26. Volt, "Vilfredo Pareto e il fascismo," *Gerarchia,* October 1922.

27. Raul De Nolva, "Le mysticisme at l'ésprit revolutionnaire du fascisme," *Mercure de France,* November 1, 1924: "The Revolution had the Altar of the Nation, the red-white-and-blue cockade, the Tables of the Constitution, the Column of the Rights of Man, the Trees of Liberty, the Fasces of Unity, funeral rites, and commemorative celebrations in the shape of processions, ceremonies, symbolic games, and educational pastimes. Fascism has the Altar of the Nation, the Lictorial Fasces, the Table of Laws (the decisions of the Fascist Grand Council), Trees of Remembrance, its schoolboy and its women's battalions, a brutal and threatening language, civic marches, vulgar uniforms, a skull sewn onto its black shirts, a 'Holy Militia' instead of the 'Sacred Mountain.' "

28. H. W. Schneider, *Making the Fascist State* (New York, 1928), p. 222.

29. H. Finer, *Mussolini's Italy* (London, 1935), p. 404.

30. Measures taken by the Rome questura, October 23, 1929, MI, DGPS, 1930–1931, cat. C4, file 373, CSA.

31. NFP, *Foglio d'ordini,* no. 10, October 9, IV (1926).

32. Ibid., no. 11, October 15, IV (1926).

33. *PI,* October 27, 1926.

34. NFP, *Foglio d'ordini,* no. 11.

35. That is, those who had participated in the founding meeting of the Fascist party, held in the Piazza San Sepolcro in Milan. *Trans.*

36. Ottavio Dinale, *La rivoluzione che vive* (Foligno, 1934), pp. 57–69.

37. "Il rogo simbolico," *PI,* October 28, 1928.

38. *Befana,* or Epiphany, January 6, marks the traditional end of the twelve days of Christmas; it is the day on which most Italians exchange presents. *Trans.*

39. "Una circolare di S. E. Turati," *PI,* January 15, 1929.

40. *PI,* December 12, 1939.

41. Report from Rome, January 2, 1939, MI, Division of Political Police, 1927–1944, file 220, CSA.

42. "L'uva," *PI,* September 17, 1931.

43. MS [Student Movement], "Spirito rurale," *Gioventù fascista,* September 30, 1932.

44. "Il Duce alla festa dell'uva a Roma," *PI,* September 29, 1931.

45. "Rustico," "Vendemmia in città," *PI,* September 21, 1932.

46. G. L. Mosse, *The Crisis of German Ideology* (New York, 1964); also R. A.

Pois, *Nationalsocialism and the Religion of Nature* (London, 1986). On the Earth Myth in Fascism, see P. G. Zunnino, *L'ideologia del fascismo* (Bologna, 1985), pp. 300–309.

47. *PI*, September 29, 1931.
48. Alceo Toni, "Il Littoriale polisportivo," *PI*, August 28, 1926.
49. Commissione per lo studio di un progetto relativo all'ordinamento dell'educazione fisica e della preparazione militare del Paese, *Relatione e Proposte* (Rome, 1926), p. 8, quoted in P. Ferrara, *L'Italia in palestra* (Rome, 1992), p. 214.
50. Toni, "Il Littoriale polisportivo."
51. C. R. Maccaroni, "La 'colonna del Duce' verso il mare di Roma," *Carlino della sera,* January 16, 1929, quoted in S. Setta, *Renato Ricci* (Bologna, 1986), p. 159.
52. Setta, *Renato Ricci,* pp. 159–165.
53. Circular, May 16, 1932, in NFP, *Atti 1931–1931* (Rome, 1932).
54. "P. L.," "La coscienza della collettività e lo sport," *Bibliografia fascista,* February 1933.
55. Ranieri Nicolai, "Sport," in NFP, *Dizionario di politica,* vol. 4, p. 343.
56. "Lettere romane," *PI*, July 6, 1932.
57. "Le opinione delgi altri sul Fascismo," *PI*, May 5, 1922.
58. "Ritorno ideale," *PI*, October 23, 1931.
59. Arnaldo Mussolini, "La celebrazione," *PI*, April 23, 1925.
60. Massimo Scaligero, "La folla," *Gioventù fascista,* November 10, 1931.
61. B. Mussolini, speech in Milan, October 4, 1922, in *OO*, vol. 18, p. 428.
62. Ludwig, *Conversations,* p. 195.
63. Padellaro, *Fascismo educatore,* p. 154.
64. Ibid., pp. 156–157.
65. Toni, "Il Littoriale polisportivo."
66. G. Bottai, "Fine della guerra," *Mel,* November 28, 1918, reprinted in idem, *La politica delle arti. Scritti, 1918–1943,* ed. A. Masi (Rome, 1982), p. 59.
67. S. Gatto, "Di fronte al passato," *Il Raduno,* May 1928, reprinted in idem, *1925. Polemiche del pensiero dell'azione fascista* (Rome, 1934), pp. 61–62.
68. "Il divenire del Regime," *Il Legionario,* the organ of Fascists abroad, September 10, 1927. On Fascist views of the nation, see E. Gentile, *Le origini dell'ideologia fascista* (Rome and Bari, 1975), pp. 149–154; P. G. Zunino, *L'ideologia del fascismo* (Bologna, 1985), pp. 192–202.
69. S. Gatto, "Della cultura fascista," *Bibliografia fascista,* May 1926, reprinted in idem, *1925,* pp. 63–65.
70. CPA, 907/2.
71. "Entusiastica partecipazione di popolo ai raduni di propaganda," *PI*, May 24, 1932.
72. "Ritorno all'apostolato," *PI*, June 24, 1932.
73. Summary of a speech by the Hon. Mario Janneli at the Propaganda Meeting in Monti, May 29, 1932, MI, DGPS, cat. G1, file 60, CSA. The experiment

of such "Meetings" seems not to have produced the desired effect, to judge from the comments of party informers. "There is no doubt," wrote one such in Rome on July 6, 1932, "that in the 'meetings' held throughout Italy, huge crowds attended; but for the results obtained, were such meetings really necessary? Do our leaders really believe they can reach the people with these 'means'? Or are our party leaders satisfied simply by appearances, by the numbers attending?" NFP, Political and Economic Situation in the Provinces (PESP), file 19, fasc. "Roma," CSA. A similar comment was registered by the Fascist federation in Pistoia: "The propaganda meetings held this month, like those held last month, were marked by poor attendance, in part because of poor organization by local officials, and in part because conferences with high-level political argument arouse little interest in rural areas and are not really accessible to the average agricultural laborer's mind, they being primarily concerned with the problems of everyday life, increasingly as a result of the continued [economic] crisis"; report for June 1932, NFP, PESP, file 15, fasc. "Pistoia."

74. Decree no. 1010, June 20, 1935.

75. "R. N.," "Sabato fascista," *Gioventù fascista,* March 30, 1935.

76. MI, Division of Political Police, 1927–1944, file 220, CSA. On the negative effects of this continuous indoctrination, compare a party member who referred to a writer whom he characterized as an "intelligent observer." This writer considered that the time for speechmaking was passing. "One can smell it in the air: there is a weariness with these 'meetings' and 'groups.' there is something basically wrong with them that our party leaders have perhaps not noticed—that is, their coercive character, their improvisation, their threatening nature. The little provincial chiefs employ all these methods to draw their crowds, crowds ready to clap on a signal from the chief. We are abusing these assemblies, anniversaries, meetings, committees, and so on. Every occasion, every trifling event calls for a parade, and this begins to bore people; it tires them and leads to recriminations. Military parades may be fine for the young: but for grownups? For workers?" Report for July 6, 1932, NFP, PESP, file 19, fasc. "Roma," CSA.

77. 1028/3, CPA.

78. Letter from Alessandria, April 19, 1933, 1138/1, CPA.

79. Giaime Pintor, *Doppio diario,* ed. M. Serri (Turin, 1989), p. 38.

80. Mario Rivoire, *Vita e morte del fascismo* (Milan, 1947), p. 141.

81. "Il Duce assiste al saggio ginnico degli avanguardisti," *PI,* September 10, 1932.

82. Umberto Bernasconi, "Vita di masse," *Gioventù fascista,* May 1, 1934.

83. G. Bottai, "Commemorazione di Francesco Paolo Michetti," speech at Francavilla al Mare, July 31, 1938, in idem, *La politica delle arti. Scritti 1918–1943* (Rome, 1992), pp. 153–162.

84. "Popolo sano," *PI,* July 5, 1933.

85. Roberto Pavese, "Appunti di etica fascista," *Critica fascista,* June 15, 1933.

86. Giorgio Pini, "Valore della fede," *Critica fascista,* June 15, 1933.

5. The Temples of the faith

1. B. Mussolini, in *OO*, vol. 19, pp. 187–188.
2. Ibid., vol. 22, p. 230.
3. G. Bottai, "L'artista dello Stato," speech at the inauguration of the Third Quadrennial of Art, February 5, 1939, reprinted in idem, *La politica delle arti. Scritti 1918–1943* (Rome, 1992), pp. 179–184.
4. G. Bottai, "Modernità a tradizione dell'arte italiana di oggi," *Le arti*, February 1939, reprinted in idem, *La politica fascista,* pp. 89–90.
5. Ibid., p. 80.
6. G. Bottai, "L'arte moderna," *Critica fascista,* December 1, 1938, reprinted in idem, *La politica delle arti,* pp. 63–67.
7. Salvatore Gotta, *Mistica patria* (Milan, 1924), p. 79.
8. Valentino Piccoli, "I valori civili del Fascismo," *PI,* June 5, 1932.
9. O. Taddeini and L. Marcante, *Arte fascista arte per le masse* (Rome, 1935), p. 46.
10. DPS, Ordinary Correspondence, fasc. 515.115, CSA; see also Giuseppe Pagano, *Architettura e città durante il fascismo*, ed. C. De Seta (Rome and Bari, 1976).
11. A new perspective on the relationship between the modernist avant-garde and totalitarian cultural politics is afforded by Igor Golomshtok, *Totalitarian Art in Soviet Union, the Third Reich, Fascist Italy, and the People's Republic of China*, trans. Robert Chandler (New York, 1990).
12. Ardengo Soffici, "Fritto misto," *PI,* November 7 1922.
13. CP, 1928–30, fasc. 3.3.3, no. 10227, PMP. The project was presented to Mussolini on February 14, 1930, and proposed a Triennial Exhibition and a royal prize for drawings, entry to be limited to the children of Italians living abroad between the ages of six and twelve. "Discovering artistic temperament wherever it is to be found," ended Cascella, "we will automatically obtain a greater penetration of the Italian Idea. From there it will expand irresistibly, for Art is great, where love and passion are but small things that have always led the young to leave their homes. Where else, in what school or family, shall we so effortlessly find our little friend, our young spiritual fellow citizen, who will then become our loyal soldier? . . . Such a movement will naturally lead to a total renewal of the arts, which will now have a single guide, a new form of education that will bring them to serve faithfully as political propagandists and glorifiers of the FASCIST ERA." Mussolini approved the proposal, and it was considered by Balbino Giuliano, the minister of education, but apparently the project was never put into action.
14. Pier Luigi Maria Rosso di San Secondo, "Il teatro di domani," *PI,* February 12, 1932.
15. Anton Giulio Bragaglia, "Arte fascista," *Bibliografia fascista,* March 1933. See also A. C. Alberti, *Il teatro nel fascismo* (Rome, 1974).
16. Francesco Sapori, *Il fascismo e l'arte* (Milan, 1934). See also Victor De Grazia, *The Culture of Consent: Mass Organization of Leisure in Fascist Italy* (New York: Cambridge University Press, 1981).

17. RDL, December 28, 1936, no. 2470; RDL, December 15, 1938, no. 2207.
18. G. Bottai, "Popolo e teatro," radio broadcast, January 8, 1937, reprinted in idem, *La politica delle arti,* pp. 211–216.
19. Ascanio Zapponi, "Funzione politica del teatro," *Battaglie fasciste–Conquiste dell'Impero,* January–February 1936.
20. "K. C.," "Concezione Mussoliniana del teatro," *Bibliografia fascista,* November 1933.
21. See P. Cavallo, *Immaginario e rappresentazione. Il teatro fascista di propaganda* (Rome, 1990).
22. R. De Felice, *Mussolini il duce. II: Lo Stato totalitario 1936–1940* (Turin, 1981), vol. 1, pp. 31–32.
23. On Sironi and his relationship to aspects of his work treated here, especially recommended are E. Braun, "Die Gestaltung eines kollektiven Willens," in *Mario Sironi (1885–1961),* ed. J. Harten and J. Potter (Cologne, 1988), pp. 40–49; E. Braun, "Mario Sironi and a Fascist Art," in *Italian Art in the 20th Century,* ed. Braun (London, 1989), pp. 173–180; and essays by E. Ponteggia and F. Benzi in *Sironi: Il mito dell' achitettura* (Milan, 1990).
24. Sironi to Mussolini, DPS, Ordinary Correspondence, fasc. 545.895, CSA.
25. Note for the Duce, December 12, 1942, ibid.
26. Mario Sironi, "Pittura murale," *PI,* January 1, 1932, reprinted in idem, *Scritti editi ed inediti,* ed. E. Camesasca (Milan, 1980), pp. 113–115.
27. M. Sironi, "Pubblicazioni d'arte," *PI,* March 13, 1929, in idem, *Scritti,* pp. 42–44.
28. M. Sironi, "Basta!" *PI,* March 31, 1929, in idem, *Scritti,* pp. 143–148.
29. M. Sironi, "Antelami," *PI,* February 1936, in idem, *Scritti,* pp. 210–213.
30. Sironi, "Pittura murale."
31. Sironi, "Antelami," p. 211. The nonce word *insanzionabili,* "unsanctionable," presumably refers to League of Nations sanctions over Ethiopia. *Trans.*
32. M. Sironi, "Ragioni d'artista," in *Dodici tempere di Mario Sironi* (Milan, 1943), reprinted in idem, *Scritti,* pp. 248–251.
33. M. Sironi, "Il Maestro," *PI,* March 13, 1931 (dedicated to the sculptor Adolph Wildt).
34. Massimo Campigli, Carlo Carrà, Achille Funi, and Mario Sironi, "Manifesto della pittura murale," *La colonna,* December 1933, reprinted in Sironi, *Scritti,* pp. 155–157.
35. Ibid., p. 155 (emphasis added).
36. Ibid., p. 156. What Sironi had in mind was the long Italian tradition, particularly dominant from the late Middle Ages through the Renaissance, of the artist as *fabbro,* or "maker." As is pointed out in much of the literature on futurism and Italian art in the immediate postwar period, Marinetti and many other futurists derived their aesthetic both from this old, communal enterprise in art and from a parallel, and romantic, tradition of flamboyant individual gestures. *Trans.*
37. M. Sironi, "Il Quadriennale d'arte nazionale," *PI,* illustrated review, February 1935, reprinted in idem, *Scritti,* pp. 186–190.
38. "He not only gave of his austere, religious, and tragic mind to the rooms

that he personally constructed, but he permeated the whole exhibition with his example and the mark of his inventiveness and art, which in Italian painting, and not just painting, have long imposed themselves by their spontaneous and incontestable authority"; M. G. Sarfatti, "Architettura, arte e simbolo alla mostra del fascismo," *Architettura,* January 1933.

39. Ibid.

40. On the history of the Exhibition, see G. Fioraventi, introduction to *MRF.* Similarly useful are the catalogues of the Exhibition itself: *Guida alla mostra della rivoluzione fascista* (Florence, 1932), a historical guide edited by Dino Alfieri and D. Luigi Freddi (Bergamo, 1933). Also worthy of note is O. Dinale, *La rivoluzione che vince,* illustrated by Sironi (Foligno, 1934). This last represents, in luxuriant allegorical and metaphorical style, a sort of later and more epicene version of the Exhibition itself. On historical and artistic questions, from a critical standpoint, the best works are D. Y. Ghirardo, "Architects, Exhibitions, and the Politics of Culture in Fascist Italy," L. Andreotti, "The Aesthetics of War: The Exhibition of the Fascist Revolution," and J. T. Schnapp, "Fascism's Museum in Motion," all in *Journal of Architectural Education,* February 1992.

41. Antonio Monti to Dino Alfieri, February 24, 1928, Correspondence, Alfieri Letters, CSA.

42. "La mostra storica del fascismo," *PI,* March 31, 1928.

43. Fioravanti, introduction to *MRF,* pp. 16–18.

44. "Appunti sul programma della mostra del fascismo," NFP, ND, Miscellaneous Services, sec. 2, file 332, fasc. "D. Alfieri," CSA. See also "La mostra del fascismo," *Bibliografia fascista,* May 1932.

45. The exhibition devoted to achievements, as outlined by Alfieri and approved by Mussolini at a session of the Grand Council on July 14, 1931, was to have opened on October 27, 1933, and was meant to "express in visual form what had been achieved by fascism in its first ten years," demonstrating these achievements "in spectacular, lively and provocative form. It should be made up primarily of the confrontation and comparison of elements, with no fear of using the most modern forms of advertising and propaganda. The visitor should be able to grasp readily, without really being aware of it, the most important part of what we wish to demonstrate"; Alfieri report to Starace, Rome, June 28, 1933, in NFP, ND, Miscellaneous Services, sec. 2, file 332, fasc. "D. Alfieri," CSA.

46. "Il Duce impartisce le direttive per la Mostra della Rivoluzione fascista," *PI,* June 10, 1932.

47. Giacomo Marinelli to Dino Alfieri, September 13, 1932, NFP, ND, Miscellaneous Services, sec. 2, file 332, fasc. "D. Alfieri," CSA.

48. Circular from the head of government's press office and "Il contributo delle Camicie nere romane," *PI,* March 15, 1932; "Per la Mostra del Fascismo. I lavori delle sezioni," *PI,* May 12, 1932.

49. "Per la Mostra," ibid. There were printed 100,000 leaflets, 200,000 postcards, and 1,300,000 posters to be displayed in cities, at section headquarters of party organizations, hotels, in railway carriages and trolleys,

ships, etc.; NFP, ND, Miscellaneous Services, sec. 2, file 332, fasc. 3, CSA. A special commemorative book, to be prepared by Leo Longanesi, and a film, to be directed by Alessandro Blasetti, were also proposed. There was also a competition for the best article on the Exhibition.

50. C. Cresti, *Archittetura e fascismo* (Florence, 1986), p. 313.

51. Pietro Maria Bardi, "Mostra della Rivoluzione Fascista," *Gioventù fascista,* July 10, 1932.

52. *MRF,* p. 8.

53. Quoted in F. T. Marinetti, "La mostra della rivoluzione fascista segna in trionfo dell'arte futurista," *La gazzetta del popolo,* October 29, 1932. "Giolitti's frock coat" is a reference to a staple of antiparliamentary caricature (equally common in Germany and France). Although all prewar deputies wore formal dress, as did Mussolini, Giolitti was the longest-serving prime minister in pre-Fascist Italy and bore the brunt. *Trans.*

54. *MRF,* p. 65.

55. Ibid., pp. 65–66.

56. See Schnapp, "Fascism's Museum in Motion."

57. B. Mussolini, speech to CD on the Decennial, November 16, 1932, in *OO,* vol 25, p. 164.

58. *MRF,* pp. 8, 9. See also the report by the architect Adalberto Libera, probably to Alfieri, on the overall preparations, quoted in Fioravanti, introduction to *MRF.*

59. *MRF,* p. 46.

60. Ibid., p. 72.

61. M. Sironi, "Arte e tecnica della mostra 'Schaffen Volk' a Düsseldorf," *PI,* illustrated review, November 1937, reprinted in Sironi, *Scritti,* pp. 222–226.

62. "What recently opened in Rome is not just an 'exhibition,' but rather the 'demonstration' of the Fascist Revolution. I use the word 'demonstration' in its literary and figurative sense as well as its mathematical and physical: the Exhibition makes the Revolution manifest, clear and intelligible, while at the same time being its proof, thanks to figures and calculations which conclusively confirm the experiment"; Sarfatti, "Architettura."

63. On cultural aspects of the Exhibition, see the observations of Andreotti, "Aesthetics of War," who was the first to note this important feature of the Exhibition, without, however, connecting it to the wider issue of Fascism as a political religion.

64. *MRF,* p. 78.

65. Ibid.

66. Ibid., pp. 72–83.

67. Ibid., pp. 93, 73.

68. Ibid., p. 93.

69. Ibid., p. 118.

70. Ibid., p. 188.

71. Ibid., pp. 204–205.

72. Ibid., p. 215.

73. Ibid., p. 221.
74. Ibid., p. 227.
75. See Antonio Monti, *Rapsodia Eroica: dall'Intervento all'Impero* (Milan, 1937); see also Andreotti, "Aesthetics of War," p. 86, n. 19. An early version of the sanctuary included a set of sculptured figures with a nude holding aloft in its arms a horizontal fasces, and at its feet the body of one of the fallen. On Mussolini's intervention a symbolic cross was substituted. The early project is reproduced in *L'illustrazione italiana*, October 29, 1933, p. 640.
76. *MRF*, pp. 227–229. At the very beginning, as is discernible in the designs of the painter Orazio Amate, a room for the party itself had been mooted. This exhibition room, "free of any drama," was inspired by the "glory of the OATH, which is the summing-up of our party." Its design synthesizes the whole symbolic apparatus of the Exhibition, with a backdrop in part quite like that of the actual Sanctuary:

   "Four solid pillars (which could, wherever possible, become four fasces-caryatids) support the entablature of the cupola. Within the vaulting, carved in large Roman letters, is the text of the Oath. At the head of each column appears one of the four words of the Oath: FAITH, COURAGE, WORK [*LABORIOSITÀ*], HONESTY, according to the Statutes, the fundamental words of Fascism.

   "The Duce's effigy is absent, but his spirit illuminates and pervades the whole. A polygon (greater than life-size) rises between the columns; it is made of opalescent glass from which emerges a sheaf of light (a parabolic mirror) rising to the dome, which in return reflects the light back on the floor, creating in light the mythical dimension of the spirit of Benito Mussolini, all brought together in the word DUX written in luminous form at the peak of the polyhedron." The text of the plan is in High Commission for Sanctions against Fascism, Title 17, no. 10, vol. 3, fasc. "O. Amato," CSA.
77. Circular no. 95 from Starace to the federal party secretaries, Rome, March 31, 1933, PMA; CP, 1931–1933, fasc. 14.1, no. 800, CSA.
78. "Suggestiva potenza evocatrice della Mostra della Rivoluzione fascista," *Il telegrafo*, December 5, 1933.
79. "S. F." to Achille Starace, Cagliari, Sardinia, October 11, 1933, NFP, ND, Administrative Services, sec. 2, file 331, fasc. 27, "Richieste agevolazioni," CSA.
80. Sarfatti, "Architettura," p. 10.
81. Francesco Gargano, *Italiani e stranieri alla Mostra della Rivoluzione fascista* (Turin, 1935), p. 716. This is a chronological reconstruction, in hyperbolic style, of the day-to-day visits to the Exhibition, together with a list of both individual and group visits, as well as an account of the many events linked to the Exhibition, from its inauguration to its closing.
82. Letter to G. Marinelli, December 2, 1932, NFP, ND, Miscellaneous Services, sec. 2, file 332, fasc. "Richieste agevolazioni varie," CSA.
83. "E. S." to Marinelli, Venice, April 30, 1933, ibid.

84. See the documentation on visitors in NFP, ND, Miscellaneous Services, sec. 2, file 332, fasc. "Richieste agevolazioni," CSA; and Gargano, *Italiani e stranieri.*

85. Gargano, *Italiani e stranieri,* p. 605.

86. "La cerimonia inaugurale," *PI,* October 30, 1932. Andreotti draws a parallel between the various stages of the ceremony and a mass. See "Aesthetics of War," pp. 76–77.

87. Gargano, *Italiani e stranieri,* pp. 266, 673.

88. Ibid., pp. 715–723.

89. Gianfilippo Usellini, "La Mostra della Rivoluzione Fascista," *Emporium,* April 1932, pp. 199–249.

90. Roberto Pacini, "Il valore educativo e patriottico della mostra," ibid., April 1933, pp. 251–256.

91. O. Dinale, *Tempo di Mussolini* (Rome, 1934), p. 204.

92. G. Bottai, "Vedere il fascismo," *Critica fascista,* November 1, 1932.

93. "S. F." to Achille Starace, NFP, ND, Miscellaneous Services, file 331, fasc. 27, CSA. "Rather than closing an Exhibition, as Your Excellency has disposed," a Florentine Fascist wrote to Mussolini, "an Exhibition that has raised so many ineffable feelings, brought back so many unforgettable memories, and lit up the spirits of so many visitors, might not Your Excellency respectfully consider that the Exhibition of the Fascist Revolution remain permanently open? . . . That it become instead the Sanctuary of Fascism, slowly acquiring all that is and will be the result, the scope, the aim of the Fascist Revolution? . . . Eternal Rome would thus harbor the documentary history of that holy Revolution which You willed, guided, and inspirited with Your fervent passion, which came about because of Your love of the fatherland, which has produced and will produce tangible results which already make it, and will continue to make this beloved fatherland of ours ever more appreciated, feared and respected: as You, Duce, willed it, and as it shall be! . . . Thus present and future generations would have forever available all phases, even the sanguinary ones, of the Fascist Revolution: a perpetual example, warning and inspiration!" Letter from "R. M.," Florence, 9 October, 1933, ibid.

94. Alessandro Melchiori, "Una grande opera di fede," *L'illustrazione italiana,* October 29, 1922.

95. *MRF,* p. 66. A new version of the Exhibition was inaugurated on September 3, 1937, and a third on October 28, 1942, but both were now museums and lacked the dynamism and mysticism of the first.

96. See Albert Speer, *Inside the Third Reich: Memoirs,* trans. R. Winston and C. Winston (London, 1973); on the cult of ruins, see also N. Zapponi, "Futurismo e fascismo," in *Futurismo, cultura e politica,* ed. R. De Felice (Turin, 1988), pp. 172–173.

97. Alessandro Chiapelli, "Il fascismo e la suggestione delle rovine monumentali," *Educazione fascista,* April 20, 1931.

98. Quoted in Dinale, *Tempo di Mussolini,* p. 225.

99. Franco Ciarlantini, "E '42," *Augustea,* August 15, 1938.

100. M. Sironi, "Monumentalità fascista," *PI,* illustrated review, November 1934, reprinted in idem, *Scritti,* pp. 181–185.

101. M. Sironi, "Templi," *PI,* illustrated review, December 1935, reprinted in idem, *Scritti,* pp. 206–209.

102. Emil Ludwig, *Conversations with Mussolini* (New York, 1930), p. 211.

103. "Petizione a Mussolini per l'architettura," *L'Ambrosiano,* February 13, 1931, quoted in M. Estermann-Juchler, *Faschistische Staatbaukunst* (Cologne, 1982), p. 102. On the relationship between Fascism and architecture, see D. Y. Ghirardo, "Italian Architects and Fascist Politics: An Evaluation of the Rationalist's Role in Regime Building," *Journal of the Society of Architectural History,* no. 39 (1980), 109–127; Cresti, *Architettura e fascismo;* G. Ernesti, ed., *La costruzione dell'utopia. Architetti e urbanisti nell'Italia fascista* (Rome, 1988); G. Ciucci, *Gli architetti e il fascismo* (Turin, 1989); T. L. Schumacher, *Surface and Symbol: Giuseppe Terragni and the Architecture of Italian Rationalism* (New York, 1991); R. A. Etlin, *Modernism in Italian Architecture, 1890–1940* (Cambridge, Mass., 1991).

104. Antonio Pagliaro, "Archittetura," in NFP, *Dizionario di politica* (Rome, 1940), vol. 1, p. 159.

105. Gio Ponti, "Architettura," *PI,* July 13, 1932.

106. Request for authorization of an Exhibition of Rational Architecture, CP, 1931–1933, fasc. 14.1, no. 128, PMP, quoted in Estermann-Juchler, *Fascistische Stadtbaukunst,* p. 97. On the myth of "construction" in Fascist art, see E. Pontiggia, "Mario Sironi: Il mito dell'architettura," in *Sironi: Il mito,* 19–21.

107. Mario Palantini, *L'Eternale Mole Littoria* (Milan, 1926), pp. 33–35. A *mole* is any giant structure, e.g., Hadrian's Mole in Rome, or the famous tower in Turin. *Trans.*

108. Ibid., pp. 24–25.

109. Sapori, *Il fascismo e l'arte,* p. 55.

110. NFP, *Foglio d'ordini,* no. 21, February 1, V (1927).

111. "Le nuova sede della Federazione fascista," *PI,* May 18, 1930.

112. Report of Federal Secretary Bianchi Mina to Mussolini, January 15, 1930, EFR, file 52, fasc. "Piemonte," subfasc. "Torino," CSA.

113. Giuseppe Terragni, "La costruzione della Casa del Fascio di Como," *Quadrante,* October 1936. See also D. Y. Ghirardo, "Politics of a Masterpiece: The Vicenda of the Decoration of the Façade of the Casa del Fascio, Como, 1936–1939," *Art Bulletin,* 57 (1980), 466–478; Etlin, *Modernism,* pp. 439–479; Schumacher, *Surface and Symbol,* pp. 139–170.

114. Kenneth Frampton, *Modern Architecture: 1851–1945* (New York, 1983).

115. Starace to Duke Marcello Visconti di Modrone, Rome, February 13, 1935, NFP, ND, Miscellaneous Services, sec. 2, file 332, fasc. "Corrispondenza generale," CSA. The Exhibition materials were moved to the Gallery of Modern Art while awaiting a new exhibition, which was in fact mounted in 1937, in conjunction with the bimillennial of Augustus Caesar. See Fioravanti, introduction to *MRF,* pp. 37–42.

116. "Professori e studenti per la Casa del Littorio sulla Via dell'Impero," *Gioventù fascista,* March 15, 1934. With RDL, March 8, 1934, no. 550, the

construction of the Casa Littoria was declared to be of "public utility," and successive decrees authorized the minister of public works to supervise its construction (RDL, March 7, 1938, no. 322) and the NFP to issue a loan for building it (RDL, March 24, 1938, no. 279).

117. The text of the competition is given in *Il nuovo stile Littorio* (Rome, 1936), pp. xv–xviii, which gives illustrations of the projects approved and parts of those rejected.

118. See Ciucci, *Gli architetti*, pp. 139–151; Cresti, *Architettura e fascismo*, pp. 178–188; Etlin, *Modernism*, pp. 426–434.

119. *Il nuovo stile Littorio*, pp. 371–372.

120. Ibid., p. 241.

121. Ibid., pp. 41, 105, 59.

122. Ibid., p. 321.

123. Ibid., pp. 183–184. The reference is to Dante and to the *veltro,* or greyhound, as symbol of the Holy Roman Empire. *Trans.*

124. Report accompanying Project A, quoted in F. Benzi, "Sironi," in *Sironi: Il mito,* p. 120.

125. Carminati, Lingeri, Saliva, Terragni, Vietti, Sironi project, reprinted in *Il nuovo stile Littorio,* pp. 1–4.

126. The committee included Giovanni Marinelli, administrative secretary of the party; Prince Francesco Boncompagni Ludovisi, governor of Rome; the architects Armando Brasini, Cesare Bazzani, and Marcello Piacentini; Senator Corrado Ricci; the national secretary of the Fascist Syndicate of Architects; the national secretary of the Fascist Syndicate of Engineers; the inspector-general of technical services for the governor; and the director of the Institute of Fine Arts.

127. "La 'Casa Littoria' a Roma," *Annali dei Lavori Pubblici,* no. 11 (1937).

128. It currently houses the Ministry of Foreign Affairs.

129. *E42: Utopia e scenario del regime,* vol. 1, ed. T. Gregory and A. Tartaro; vol. 2, ed. M. Calvesi, E. Guidoni, and S. Lux (Venice, 1987).

130. "Primo abozzo della Mostra della Civiltà Italiana per la Quinta Sezione, dal Settecento all'anno MCMXXIII (1923)," EUR, SOM, fasc. OA D/21–19, CSA, quoted in E. Garin, "La civiltà italiana nell'esposizione del 1942," in *E42,* vol. 1, p. 15.

131. "Revisione del programma di massima del 1937," CP, 1937–1939, fasc, 14, no. 200.6.3, PMP, quoted in P. Ferrara, "L'EUR: un ente per l'E42," in *E42,* vol. 1, p. 81.

132. Gian Luigi Banfi and Ludovico Barbiano di Belgoijoso, "Urbanistica anno XII (1935). La Città Corporativa," *Quadrante,* no. 13 (May 1934), quoted in E. Guidoni, "L'E 42, Città della rappresentazione," in *E42,* vol. 2, p. 30.

133. V. Cini, "Significato e aspetti dell'esposizione universale di Roma," *Civiltà,* no. 1 (April 1940), 11.

134. *Mostra della Civiltà Italiana. Lineamenti programmattici,* p. 28, quoted in S. Lux, "Oppo: La committenza," in *E42,* vol. 2, p. 211.

135. Report of the architects Banfi, Belgiojoso, Peressutti, and Rogers, in *E42,* vol. 2, p. 74.

136. Guidoni, "L'E 42," p. 23.

137. G. Ponti, "Olimpiade della civiltà. L'E42 città fabulosa," *Corriere della sera,* May 4, 1938, quoted in Guidoni, "L'E 42," p. 62.
138. "Revisione," quoted in Ferrara, "L'EUR," p. 169.
139. Cini project, approved by Mussolini January 4, 1941, quoted in *E42,* vol. 2, p. 65.
140. See *E42,* vol. 2, pp. 467–470.
141. Guidoni, "L'E 42," p. 35.
142. E. Cecchi, "Il palazzo della civiltà italiana," *Civiltà,* no. 3 (October 1940).
143. G. L. Banfi, L. B. Belgiojoso, G. Ciocca, E. Peressutti, and E. E. N. Rogers, "Relazione sul progetto architettonico per il Palazzo della Civiltà italiana," quoted in A. Mantoni, "E42, i concorsi," in *E42,* vol. 2, p. 91.
144. Report by Guerrini, La Padula, and Romano, in *E42,* vol. 2, p. 354.
145. *Mostra della Civiltà Italiana. Criteri fondamentali per la presentazione della Mostra* (Rome, 1939), p. 32.

6. Italy's New God

1. There are no systematic studies of the myth of Mussolini. For preliminary information on some aspects of this myth, see D. Biondi, *La fabbrica del Duce* (Florence, 1967); P. Melograni, "The Cult of the Duce in Mussolini's Italy," *Journal of Contemporary History,* 1976, pp. 221–237; A. B. Hasler, "Das Duce-Bild in der Faschistischen Literatur," *Quellen und Forschungen,* 60 (1980), 421–506; J. Peterson, "Mussolini: Wirklichkeit und Mythos eines Diktators," in *Mythos und Moderne* (Frankfurt am Main, 1983), pp. 242–260; E. Gentile, "Il mito di Mussolini," *Mondo operaio,* nos. 7–8 (1983), 113–128; A. M. Imbriani, "Il mito di Mussolini tra propaganda a culto di massa: Le origini (1923–1926)," *Prospettive settanta,* nos. 2–4 (1988), 492–512. The best critical introduction to the Mussolini myth, rich with contemporary documents and photographs showing the immediate impact of the myth as projected through the régime's propaganda, remains R. De Felice and L. Goglia, *Mussolini. Il mito* (Rome and Bari, 1983). The apologetic literature of the fascist publicity machine is, on the other hand, enormous; it is useful insofar as it permits the reader to follow the development of the Mussolini myth through the years of fascist power. In this regard, in addition to Hasler, see L. Passerini, *Mussolini immaginario* (Rome and Bari, 1991).
2. As prime minister repeatedly, as symbol of the parliamentary régime, and as ambiguous statesman prior to intervention, Giolitti was forced into resignation in 1915, marking the collapse of the so-called liberal Italy and paving the way for the rise of a Mussolini newly converted to intervention. *Trans.*
3. *La Voce,* December 4, 1913. See E. Gentile, *Mussolini e "La Voce"* (Florence, 1976).
4. *L'Unità,* September 26 and October 24, 1912; June 9, 1914.
5. Carlo Carrà to G. Prezzolini, quoted in E. Gentile, "Il mito," p. 122.

6. *PI*, November 29, 1914.

7. See M. Gradi, *Il sindacato nel fascismo* (Rome, 1987), p. 45.

8. See R. De Felice, *Mussolini il fascista. I. La conquista del potere 1921–1925* (Turin, 1966), pp. 149–193; E. Gentile, *Storia del partito fascista, 1919– 1922. Movimento e milizia 1919–1922* (Rome and Bari, 1989), chap. 4. On Hitler's position in the National Socialist party, see D. Orlow, *The History of the Nazi Party* (Newton Abbot, U.K., 1969), vol. 1, pp. 23–36; W. Horn, *Führerideologie und Parteiorganisation in der NSDAP (1919–1933)* (Düsseldorf, 1972), pp. 45–74. On the complex and controversial issue of Max Weber's "charismatic leader," see especially L. Cavalli, *Il capo carismatico* (Bologna, 1981); A. Schweitzer, *The Age of Charisma* (Chicago, 1984).

9. C. Pellizzi, *Fascismo-aristocrazia* (Milan, 1925), p. 8.

10. See M. Rivoire, *Vita e morte del fascismo* (Milan, 1947), p. 107.

11. *La dottrina fascista* (Rome, 1928), p. 62.

12. *Il primo libro del fascista* (Rome, 1938).

13. *La legislazione fascista nella XXIX Legislatura 1934–1939* –(Rome, n.d.), vol. 1, p. 13.

14. See E. Gentile, "Partito, Stato e Duce nella mitologia a nella organizzazione del fascismo," in *Fascismo e nazionalsocialismo,* ed. K. D. Bracher and L. Valiani (Bologna, 1986), pp. 265–294.

15. De Felice and Goglia, *Mussolini,* p. 11.

16. A. Turati, *Una rivoluzione e un capo* (Rome and Milan, [1927]), p. 143.

17. A. Turati, *Ragioni ideali di vita fascista* (Rome, [1926]), pp. 58, 79.

18. A. Turati, *Il partito e i suoi compiti* (Rome, [1928]) p. xxv.

19. See P. Pombeni, *Demagogia e tirannide* (Bologna, 1984), pp. 245–247. With the founding of the empire, Starace altered the form of this salute to "Black-Shirts, salute the Duce, founder of the Empire." The new formula displeased Mussolini, who asked for it to be revoked, saying, "It sounds like a litany. One wants to add an 'amen' . . . It's too long. If no one else says 'amen,' I will." See telegram from Mussolini to O. Sebastiani, Forlì, May 27 and 28, 1937, PS, RC, file 46, CSA, quoted in S. Setta, "Achille Starace," in *Uomini e volti del fascismo,* ed. F. Cordova (Rome, 1980), p. 468.

20. See P. V. Cannistraro, *La fabbrica del consenso. Fascismo e mass media* (Rome and Bari, 1975).

21. Quoted in Hasler, "Das Duce-Bild," p. 485.

22. NFP, *Situazione politica ad economica delle provincie,* file 7, Milan, Feb. 5, 1931, CSA.

23. O. Dinale, "La Mostra della Rivoluzione. Lui: Mussolini," *Gioventù fascista,* March 1, 1934.

24. *Il breviario dell'Avanguardista* (Rome, 1928), p. 631. See M. Ostenc, "La mystique du chef et la jeunesse fasciste de 1919 à 1926," *Mélanges de l'Ecole française de Rome,* 1 (1978), 275–290. The reader sensitive to Fascist transformations of liturgical language will note in this formulation *Antequam que Abraham fuerit, Ego sum,* "Before Abraham was, I am." *Trans.*

25. Quoted in D. Marchesini, *La scuola degli gerarchi* (Milan, 1976), p. 121;

see also M. L. Betri, "Tra politica e cultura. La scuola di mistica fascista," *Storia in Lombardia,* nos. 1–2 (1989), 377–398.

26. NFP, ND, file 202, fasc. "Scuola di Mistica Fascista," CSA.
27. Angelo Cammarata, *Pedagogia di Mussolini* (Palermo, 1932).
28. Roberto Cantalupo, *La classe dirigente* (Milan, 1928), pp. 74–75.
29. Francesco Ercole, foreword to F. Ciarlantini, *Il Capo e la folla* (Milan, 1935).
30. Paolo Orano, *Mussolini da vicino* (Rome, 1928), pp. 21–24.
31. G. Pini, "Divagazioni," *Critica fascista,* December 1, 1927.
32. G. Gentile, *Fascismo e cultura* [Fascism and Culture] (Milan, 1928), p. 47, Inaugural address at the National Fascist Institute of Culture, December 19, 1925.
33. Quoted in E. Gentile, introduction to Giovanni Giuriati, *La parabola di Mussolini nelle memorie di un gerarca* (Rome and Bari, 1981), p. xxviii.
34. DPS, Restricted Correspondence, file 65, fasc. "Bottai," CSA.
35. Giurati, *La parabola,* p. 39.
36. G. Bottai, *Diario 1935–1944,* ed. G. B. Guerri (Milan, 1982), p. 256.
37. Tullio Cianetti, *Memorie dal carcere di Verona,*ed. R. De Felice (Milan, 1983), p. 373.
38. Bottai, *Diario,* p. 247.
39. Niccolò Machiavelli, *Discorsi sopra la prima deca di Tito Livio,* vol. 1, p. 11, quoted in C. Costamagna, *Dottrina del fascismo* (1982), p. 575.
40. *Il messaggero,* May 9, 1936.
41. Giustino Fortunato, *Dopo la guerra sovvertitrice* (Bari, 1922), reprinted in *Il mezzogiorno e lo Stato italiano* (Florence, 1973), vol. 2, p. 702.
42. PI, October 24, 1923.
43. "Il sacerdote della Patria," *L'Idea nazionale,* August 23, 1923.
44. PI, October 31, 1923.
45. R. De Nolva, "Le mysticisme et l'esprit révolutionnaire du fascisme," *Mercure de France,* November 1, 1924.
46. Ferruccio Parri, "Il nostro posto," *Il caffè,* July 1, 1924, reprinted in *Il Caffè 1924–25* (Milan, 1961), p. 81. In 1924 the thirty-nine-year-old reformist socialist deputy Giacomo Matteotti had rashly claimed Fascist violence in recent elections. His killing, whether with (as some claim) or without Mussolini's consent, caused a major crisis, even within Fascism: Mussolini could not do without his *squadristi,* and he could not admit that Fascism was not a legitimate government but a criminal conspiracy. He overcame the crisis by his notable speech on January 3, 1925, in which he defied parliament to indict him. Parliament's failure to do so is seen by many as the beginning of the end of the old parliamentary system and the installation of the dictatorship. *Trans.*
47. Taken from the text of a speech given by Mussolini to the National Fascist Council on August 7, 1924 (reproduced in its entirety in De Felice, *Mussolini il fascista,* pp. 775–785). This extract was omitted in the published text.
48. *PI,* March 24, 1932.

49. CP, 1937–1939, fasc. 20.2, no. 946, PMP.
50. Report, September 17, 1938, Trieste, CP, file 32, fasc. "Viaggio nel Veneto," MPC.
51. Letter from the Combatants of Faedis, August 8, 1938, CP, fasc. 20.2, no. 5597/4–2, PMP.
52. Quoted in T. M. Mazzatosta and C. Volpi, *L'Italietta fascista (1936–1943)* (Bologna, 1980), pp. 55–56.
53. Report, "Viaggio del duce in Pemonte," Alessandria, May 17, 1939, CP, file 168, MPC. On Mussolini's visits to Piedmont, see L. Passerini, *Torino operaia e fascismo* (Rome and Bari, 1984), pp. 225ff.
54. Corrado Alvaro, *Terra nuova* (Rome, 1934), quoted in R. De Felice, *Autobiografia del fascismo* (Rome, 1978), pp. 426–427.
55. Interview recorded by O. Gaspari, "Il mito di Mussolini nei coloni venete dall'Agro pontino," *Sociologia*, May–August 1983, p. 171.
56. Ibid., p. 172. Significant examples of this sort of popular understanding of the cult of Mussolini, which continued right up to the spring of 1943, were collected in Mazzatosta and Volpi, *L'Italietta fascista;* A. Lepre, *Le illusioni, la paura, la rabbia* (Naples, 1990) and *L'Occhio del Duce. Gli italiani e la censura di guerra 1940–1943* (Milan, 1992). On public opinion toward Mussolini in general, see S. Colarizi, *L'opinione degli italiani sotto il regime* (Rome and Bari, 1991).
57. Letter from A. C. Petrosino, August 5, 1936, quoted in Mazzatosta and Volpi, *L'Italietta fascista*, p. 49.
58. Archives of the General Headquarters of the Carabinieri, Situation Office, 1930, fasc. "Viterbo."
59. Ibid., Rome, February and December 27, 1930.
60. NFP, "Situazione politica per provincie," file 9, fasc. "Napoli," CSA.
61. MI, DGPS, Division of Political Police, 1927–1944, file 220, CSA.
62. Ibid., file 223.
63. *Quaderni di Giustizia e libertà*, no. 6 (March 1933), 103.
64. Roberto Michels, *Corso di sociologia politica* (Milan, 1927), pp. 98—99.

Conclusion

1. For a complete study of these problems from a sociological point of view, the fundamental text is J. P. Sironneau, *Sécularization et réligions politiques* (The Hague, 1982). On the relationship between "the metamorphosis of the sacred" and modernity, see G. Filoramo, *I nuovi movimenti religiosi* (Rome and Bari, 1986), pp. 3–29. On the relationships between religion and politics, as discussed here, see especially Raymond Aron, *The Opium of the Intellectuals* (Westport, Conn., 1977) (Aron was probably the first, in an article dating back to 1943, to use the term "a secular religion"); E. B. Koenker, *Secular Salvations* (Philadelphia, 1964); D. E. Apter, "Political Religion in the New Nations," in *Old Societies and New States*, ed, C. Geertz (London, 1963), pp. 57–104; W. Stark, *The Sociology of Religion* (London,

1966), vol. 1; R. E. Richey and D. G. Jones, eds., *American Civil Religion* (New York, 1974); G. L. Mosse, *The Nationalization of the Masses* (New York, 1975); L. Pelicani, *I rivoluzionari di professione* (Florence, 1975); C. Lane, *The Rites of Rulers* (Cambridge, 1981), pp. 35–44; C. S. Liebman and E. Don-Yehiya, *Civil Religion in Israel* (Berkeley, 1983), pp. 125–127; P. M. Merkl and N. Smart, eds., *Religion and Politics in the Modern World* (New York, 1983); "Religion Ideology and Nationalism," in *Europe and America* (Jerusalem, 1986); C. Arvidsson and L. E. Blomqvist, eds., *Symbols of Power* (Stockholm, 1987); B. Kapferer, *Legends of People, Myths of State* (Washington, D.C., 1988); C. Rivière, *Les liturgies politiques* (Paris, 1988); W. Zelinsky, *Nation into State* (Chapel Hill, 1988).

2. Thomas Mann, *Reflections of an Nonpolitical Man,* trans. F. Unger (New York, 1983).

3. Carlton J. H. Hayes, *Essays on Nationalism* (New York, 1928); idem, *Nationalism: A Religion* (New York, 1960); G. L. Mosse, *Masses and Man: Nationalist and Fascist Perceptions of Reality* (New York, 1980).

4. Gaetano Mosca, *Elementi di scienza politica* (1st ed., 1895; Bari, 1953), vol. 1, p. 284. On "the broad interchangeability of religious and political models," see P. Pombeni, "Il problema del partito politico come soggetto teorico: sull'origine del 'Partito moderno.' Premesse ad una ricerca," in *Movimento operaio e società industriale in Europa, 1870–1970,* ed. F. Piro and P. Pombeni (Venice, 1981), pp. 65–67.

5. See Gustave Le Bon, *Psychologie du Socialisme* (Paris, 1898); Vilfredo Pareto, *I sistemi socialisti* (1st ed., 1902–03; Turin, 1974).

6. Bertrand Russell, *Bolshevism: Theory and Practice* (orig. pub. London, 1920, as *Theory and Practice of Bolshevism)* (New York, 1972), pp. 118–119: "What Mohammedanism did for the Arabs, Bolshevism may do for the Russians," etc.

7. John Maynard Keynes, *Essays in Persuasion* (New York, 1963), chaps. 1, 4.

8. Gaetano Salvemini, "Il mito dell'uomo-dio," *Giustizia e libertà,* March 1932.

9. J. Monnerot, *Sociologie du communisme* (Paris, 1949), p. 380: "Totalitarianism's originality with respect to tyranny lies in its sacralization of politics. Totalitarianism offers a secular, all-conquering religion of the 'Islamic' sort: that is, it makes no distinction between the religion of politics or the religion of economics; it exercises a centralized power that is above all inchoate."

10. G. Germani, "Democrazia e autoritarismo nella società moderna," *Storia contemporanea,* April 1980, pp. 177–216.

11. F. M. Dostoevsky, *The Brothers Karamazov,* trans. Constance Garnett (New York: Modern Library, 1943), p. 301.

12. R. Pettazzoni, *Italia religiosa* (Bari, 1952), pp. 7–8.

13. Ibid., pp. 67–81.

14. Giacomo Leopardi, *Zibaldone,* in *Tutte le opere,* ed. W. Binni (Florence, 1969), vol. 2, p. 151.

15. See Lane, *Rites of Rulers.*

16. On the cult of Lenin, see L. Tumarkin, *Lenin Lives!* (Cambridge, 1983); for that of Stalin, see J. L. Weizer, "The Cult of Stalin, 1929–1939" (Ph.D. diss., University of Kentucky, 1977).

17. In this regard see G. Prezzolini, *Le Fascisme* (Paris, 1925), pp. 72–73; H. W. Schneider, *Making the Fascist State* (New York, 1928); H. W. Schneider and S. B. Clough, *Making the Fascists* (Chicago, 1929), p. 73.

18. Schneider and Clough, *Making the Fascists,* p. 73. The whole of chap. 4, "Fascism and Catholicism," is remarkably prescient. *Trans.*

19. P. Gentizon, *Souvenirs sur Mussolini* (Rome, 1958), p. 225.

20. For a theoretical analysis of the question of political symbolism and liturgy, see, most recently, J. M. Edelman, *Politics as Symbolic Action* (New York, 1971). and, for a critique of Edelman's theories and, more generally, of political symbolism, G. Fedel, *Simboli e politica* (Naples, 1991); D. I. Kertzer, *Ritual, Politics, and Power* (New Haven, 1988); Rivière, *Liturgies politiques.*

21. See J. A. Beckford and T. Luckmann, eds., *The Changing Face of Religion* (London, 1991), pp. 13–14.

22. Clifford Geertz, *Local Knowledge: Further Essays in Interpretative Anthropology* (New York, 1983).

Index